Robert Neilson Stephens

A Gentleman Player

His Adventures on a Secret Mission for Queen Elizabeth

Robert Neilson Stephens

A Gentleman Player
His Adventures on a Secret Mission for Queen Elizabeth

ISBN/EAN: 9783337176334

Printed in Europe, USA, Canada, Australia, Japan

Cover: Foto ©ninafisch / pixelio.de

More available books at **www.hansebooks.com**

A GENTLEMAN PLAYER

QUEEN ELIZABETH AND HARRY MARRYOTT.

(*See page 57.*)

A
GENTLEMAN PLAYER

His Adventures on a Secret Mission for Queen Elizabeth

BY

ROBERT NEILSON STEPHENS

AUTHOR OF
"AN ENEMY TO THE KING," "THE
CONTINENTAL DRAGOON," "THE
ROAD TO PARIS," ETC.

"And each man in his time plays many parts."
— *As You Like It.*

BOSTON
L. C. PAGE AND COMPANY
(INCORPORATED)
1899

CONTENTS.

CHAPTER		PAGE
I.	THE FIRST PERFORMANCE OF "HAMLET"	11
II.	AT THE TAVERNS	36
III.	QUEEN AND WOMAN	69
IV.	THE UNEXPECTED	93
V.	THE PLAYER PROVES HIMSELF A GENTLEMAN	104
VI.	AND THE GENTLEMAN PROVES HIMSELF A PLAYER	116
VII.	MISTRESS ANNE HAZLEHURST	129
VIII.	"A DEVIL OF A WOMAN"	137
IX.	THE FIRST DAY OF THE FLIGHT	152
X.	THE LOCKED DOOR	174
XI.	WINE AND SONG	184
XII.	THE CONSTABLE OF CLOWN	199
XIII.	THE PRISONER IN THE COACH	220
XIV.	HOW THE PAGE WALKED IN HIS SLEEP	233
XV.	TREACHERY	251
XVI.	FOXBY HALL	276
XVII.	A WOMAN'S VICTORY	295
XVIII.	THE HORSEMEN ARRIVE	309
XIX.	THE HORSEMEN DEPART	320
XX.	ROGER BARNET SITS DOWN TO SMOKE SOME TOBACCO	332

CHAPTER		PAGE
XXI.	ROGER BARNET CONTINUES TO SMOKE TOBACCO	342
XXII.	SPEECH WITHOUT WORDS	360
XXIII.	THE LONDON ROAD	368
XXIV.	HOW A NEW INCIDENT WAS ADDED TO AN OLD PLAY	375
XXV.	SIR HARRY AND LADY MARRYOTT	398
	NOTES	409

LIST OF ILLUSTRATIONS.

	PAGE
QUEEN ELIZABETH AND HARRY MARRYOTT	*Frontispiece*
"SHE GAVE NO OUTWARD SIGN OF ANGER" .	190
"THE BRAZEN NOTES CLOVE THE AIR" . . .	267
"RUMNEY . . . BACKED QUICKLY TO THE WINDOW, AND MOUNTED THE LEDGE"	327

A GENTLEMAN PLAYER.

CHAPTER I.

THE FIRST PERFORMANCE OF "HAMLET."

"Who ever loved that loved not at first sight?" — *Quoted in "As You Like It," from Marlowe's "Hero and Leander."*

AT three o'clock in the afternoon of the cold first Monday in March, 1601, a red flag rose, and a trumpet sounded thrice, from a little gabled turret protruding up out of a large wooden building in a field in that part of Southwark known as the Bankside and bordering on the Thames west of London Bridge. This rude edifice, or enclosure, was round (not like its successor, hexagonal) in shape; was in great part roofless; was built on a brick and stone foundation, and was encircled by a ditch for drainage. It was, in fact, the Globe Theatre; and the flag and trumpet meant that the "Lord Chamberlain's servants" were about to begin their performance, which, as the bill outside the door told in rough letters, was to be that of a new "Tragicall Historie of Hamlet Prince of Denmark," written by William Shakespeare. London folk knew this Master Shakespeare well as one of the aforesaid "servants," as the maker of most of the plays enacted now by those servants, and, which was deemed far more to his honor, as the poet of "Venus and Adonis" and "The Rape of Lucrece." Many who read the playbill guessed rightly that the new "tragicall historie" was based in part upon another author's old play, which they had seen performed many times in the past.[1]

The audience, in all colours and qualities of doublet and hose, ruff and cloak, feathered hat and plain cap and scholar's coif, had awaited noisily the parting of the worsted curtains of the stage projecting from one side of the circular interior of the barnlike playhouse. Around the other sides were wooden galleries, and under these was a raised platform divided into boxes called "rooms," whose fronts were hung with painted cloth. The stage and the actors' tiring-room behind it were under a roof of thatch. The boxes had the galleries for cover. But the great central O-shaped space, known as the "yard," where self-esteeming citizens, and assertive scholars, and black-robed lawyers, and burly soldiers, and people of countless occupations, and people of no occupation at all, stood and crowded and surged and talked and chaffed, and bought fruit and wine and beer from the clamorous venders, had no ceiling but the sky. It had no floor but the bare ground, and no seats whatever.

The crowd in this so-called "yard" was expectant. The silk and velvet gentry sitting in the boxes, some of whom smoked pipes and ogled the few citizenesses in the better gallery, were for the most part prepared to be, or to seem, bored. The solid citizens in gallery and yard were manifestly there to get the worth of their eightpence or sixpence apiece, in solid entertainment. The apple-chewing, nut-cracking, fighting apprentices and riff-raff in the topmost gallery were turbulently ready for fun and tumult, whether in the play or of their own making. In the yard a few self-reliant women, not of the better order, and some of them smoking like men, struggled to hold their own amidst the hustling throng. Two or three ladies, disdaining custom and opinion, or careless or ignorant thereof, were present, sitting in boxes; but they wore masks.

Now and then, before the performance began, some young foppish nobleman, scented, feathered, bejewelled, armed with gilt-hilted rapier in velvet sheath, and sporting huge rosettes on his shoes, would haughtily, or disdainfully, or flippantly, make his way to the lords' room, which was the box immediately overlooking the stage; or would pass to a place on the rush-covered stage itself, he or his page bearing thither a three-legged stool, hired of a theatre boy for sixpence. There, on similar stools at the sides of the stage, he would find others of his kind, some idly chatting, some playing cards; and could hear, through the rear curtains of arras screening the partition behind the stage, the talk and movements of the players in their tiring-room, hurrying the final preparations for the performance.

One of these gallants, having lighted his pipe, said, lispingly, to another, and with a kind of snigger in the expression of his mouth:

"'Twill be a long time ere my lord of Southampton shall again sit here seeing his friend Will's plays."

Southampton, indeed, was in the Tower for complicity in the insurrection of his friend, the Earl of Essex, who had died on the block in February, and whose lesser fellow conspirators were now having their trials.

"A long time ere any of us may see Will's plays here, after this week," answered the other lord, dropping the rush with which he had been tickling a third lord's ear. "Don't you know, the chamberlain's actors are ordered to travel, for having played 'Richard the Second' for the Essex men when the conspiracy was hatching?"[a]

"Why, I've been buried in love, — a pox on the sweet passion! — dallying at the feet of a gentlewoman in Blackfriars, the past month; and a murrain take me if I know what's afoot of late!"

"What I've told you; and that is why we've had so many different plays all in a fortnight, and two new ones of Will Shakespeare's. The players must needs have new pieces ready for the country towns, especially for the universities. These chamberlain's actors were parlously thick with the Essex plotters; 'tis well they have friends at court, of other leanings, like Wat Raleigh, — else they might find themselves ordered to a tower instead of to a tour!"

Ignoring the pun, and glancing up at the black drapery with which the stage was partly hung, the first exquisite remarked:

"Will Shakespeare must be in right mood for tragedy nowadays, — his friend Southampton in prison, and Essex a head shorter, and himself ordered to the country. Burn me if I know how a high-hearted knave like Shakespeare, that gentlemen admit to their company, and that has had the court talking of his poems, can endure to be a dog of an actor, and to scribble plays for that stinking rabble out yonder to gape at!"

Whatever were Will Shakespeare's own views on that subject, he had at that moment other matters in mind. In the bare tiring-room beyond the curtained partition at the rear of the stage, he moved calmly about among the actors, some of whom were not yet wholly dressed in the armor or robes or other costume required, some of whom were already disguised in false beard or hair, some already painted as to the face, some walking to and fro, repeating their lines in undertones, with preoccupied and anxious air; and so well did Master Shakespeare overcome the agitations of an author who was to receive five pounds for his new play, and of a stage-manager on whom its success largely depended, that he seemed the least excited person in the room. He had put on the armor for the part of the ghost, but his flowing hair — auburn, like his small pointed beard — was not yet confined by the helmet he should soon don. His soft light brown eyes moved in swift but careful survey of the whole company; and then, seeing that the actors for the opening scene were ready, and that the others were in sufficient preparation for their proper entrances, he gave the signal for the flag and trumpet aloft.

At sight of the flag, late comers who had not yet reached the playhouse mended their speed, — whether they were noblemen conveyed by boat from the great riverside mansions of the Strand; gentlemen riding horseback, or in coaches, or borne in wherries from city water-gates; or citizens, law scholars, soldiers, sailors, rascals, and plain people, arriving by ferry or afoot by London Bridge or from the immediate neighborhood. At sound of the trumpet, the crowd in the theatre uttered the grateful "Ah!" and other exclamations natural to the moment. From the tiring-room the subordinate actor who played the first sentinel had already passed to his post on the stage, by way of the door in the partition and of an interstice in the rear curtains; other actors stood ready to follow speedily; the front curtains were drawn apart, and the first performance of Mr. William Shakespeare's earliest stage version of "Hamlet" — a version something between the garbled form now seen in the "first quarto" and the slightly altered form extant in the "second quarto" — was begun.

In the tiring-room, — where the actors awaiting their entrance cues could presently hear their fellows spouting on the stage without, and the "groundlings" in the yard making loud comments or suggestions, and the lords laughing lightly at their own affected chaff, — the pale yellow light of the chill March afternoon fell from high-placed narrow windows. It touched the face of one tall, slender young player, whose mustaches required a close inspection to detect that they were false, — for at that time, when the use of dye was general, it was common for natural beards to look artificial. The hair of this youth's head also was brown, but it was his own. His blue eyes and rather sharp features had a look half conciliating, half defiant, and he was manifestly trying to conceal, by standing perfectly still instead of fidgeting or pacing the floor, a severe case of that perturbation which to this day afflicts the chief persons concerned in a first performance of a play.

He was approached by a graceful young person in woman's clothes, — with stomacher, puffed sleeves, farthingale, high-heeled shoes, — who had been gliding about, now with every step and attitude of the gentle damsel he seemed to be, now lapsing into the gait and manner of the pert boy he was, and who said to the inwardly excited but motionless player:[3]

"Marry, Hal, take it not as 'twere thy funeral! Faith, thou'rt ten times shakier o' the knees than Master Shakespeare himself, and he writ the play. See how he claps his head-piece on, to go and play the ghost, as if he were but putting on his hat to go to the tavern for a cup of claret."

Hal looked as if he would deny the imputed shakiness; but seeing that the clever boy "Ophelia" was not to be fooled, he gave a quick sigh, and replied:

"'Tis my first time in so prominent a part. I feel as if I were the sign in front of the theatre, — a fellow with the world on his back. May I be racked if I don't half wish they'd given this 'Laertes' to Gil Crowe to play, after all!"

"Tut, Master Marryott! An thou pluck'st up

no more courage, thou shalt ever be a mere journeyman. God knows thou art bold enough in a tavern or a brawl! Look at Mr. Burbage, — he has forgot himself and us and all the world, and thinks he is really Hamlet the Dane."

Hal Marryott, knowing already what he should see, glanced at Burbage, who paced, not excitedly but as in deep meditation, near the entrance to the stage. A short, stout, handsome man, with a thoughtful face, a fine brow, a princely port; like Shakespeare, he was calm, but while Shakespeare had an eye for everything but apparently the part himself was to play, Burbage was absorbed entirely in his own part and unconscious of all else, as if in the tiring-room he was already Hamlet from the moment of putting on that prince's clothes.[4]

"What a plague are you looking at, Gil Crowe?" suddenly demanded Hal Marryott of another actor, who was gazing at him with a malicious smile evidently caused by Hal's ill-concealed disquietude. "An it be my shoes, I'll own you could have made as good if you'd stuck to your proper trade!"

"Certes," replied Crowe, who wore the dress of Rosencrantz, and whose coarse face bore marks of dissipation, "I'm less like to deny having been a shoemaker, which is true, than some are to boast of having been gentlemen, which may be doubtful."

Young Marryott's eyes flashed hot indignation.

Before he could control himself to retort, an actor in a rich robe and a false white beard,[5] who had overheard Master Crowe's innuendo, strode up and said:

"Faith, Crowe, you wrong the lad there. Who hath ever heard him flaunt his birth before us? Well you know it, if he doth at times assert his gentle blood, 'tis when forced to it; and then 'tis by act and manner, not by speech. Go your ways, Crowe; thou'st been overfree with the pottle-pot again, I'm afeard!"

"Nay," put in the impudent Ophelia, his elbows thrust out, his hands upon his hips, "Master Crowe had picked out the part of Laertes for himself; and because Master Shakespeare chose Hal to play it, Hal is a boaster and not truly gentle born."

"You squeaking brat," said Crowe, "but for spoiling thy face for the play, I'd put thee in thy place. I might have played Laertes, but that—"

Here he paused, whereupon the white-bearded Corambis (such was the name of Polonius in the first version) finished for him:

"But that y'are not to be trusted with important parts, lest the play be essentially spoiled an you be too drunk to act."

"Why, as for that," replied Crowe, "beshrew me but our gentleman here will stay as late at the tavern, and be roaring as loud for more sack when daylight comes, as any one."

For this home thrust Marryott had no reply. Crowe thereupon walked away, the Corambis joined another group, and the Ophelia sauntered across the room to view the costly raiment that a tiring man was helping Mr. William Sly to put on for the part of the foppish courtier, later christened Osric. Left to his thoughts, the Laertes, nervously twirling his false mustaches, followed the ex-shoemaker with his eyes, and meditated on the latter's insolence. The more he reviewed it, and his own failure to rebuke it properly, the more wrathful he inwardly became. His anger served as a relief from the agitation he had formerly undergone. So deeply buried was he in his new feelings, that he heeded not the progress of affairs on the stage; and thus he was startled when he felt his arm caught by Shakespeare, who was pointing to the entrance, and saying:

"What ails thee, Harry? They wait for thee on the stage."

Roused as from sleep, and seeing that Burbage and the others had indeed gone forth from the tiring-room, Hal ran to the entrance and out upon the stage, his mind in a whirl, taking his place before King Claudius with such abruptness that Burbage, surprised from his mood of melancholy self-absorption, sent him a sharp glance of reproof. This but increased his abashment, and he stared up at the placard that proclaimed the stage to be a room in the palace at Elsinore, in a kind of panic. The audience moved and murmured, restlessly, during the king's long speech, and Hal, imagining that his own embarrassment was perceptible to all, made an involuntary step backward toward the side of the stage. He thus trod on the toe of one of the noble spectators, who was making a note in his tables, and who retaliated with an ejaculation and a kick. Feeling that some means must be taken to attain composure, the more as his heart seemed to beat faster and his stomach to grow weaker, Hal remembered that he had previously found distraction in his wrath toward Gilbert Crowe. He therefore brought back to mind the brief passage in the tiring-room. So deeply did he lose himself in this recollection, gazing the while at the juniper burning on the stage to sweeten the air, that it was like a blow in the face when he suddenly became aware of a prolonged silence, and of the united gaze of all the actors upon himself.

"What wouldst thou have, Laertes?" the king was repeating for the third time.

Hal, aware now that his cue had been given more than once, opened his lips to reply, but his first line had fled completely from his mind. In his blank confusion he flashed a look of dismay toward the entrance. His eyes caught those of Shakespeare, who had parted the arras curtains sufficiently to be visible to the players. Rather in astonishment than in reproach, the poet, serving on occasion as prompter, uttered half audibly the forgotten words, and Hal, caught back as from the brink of a bottomless pit, spoke out with new-found vigor:

> "Dread my lord,
> Your leave and favor to return to France,"

and the ensuing lines. But his delivery did not quiet down the audience, — which, indeed, though it had hushed for a moment at the play's opening, and again at the appearance of the ghost, was not completely stilled, until at last, upon the king's turning to Hamlet, the "wondrous tongue" of Burbage spoke.

When Hal presently made exit to the tiring-room, after the king and courtiers, he craved the pardon of Master Shakespeare, but the latter merely said:

"Tut, Hal, it hath happened to all of us in our time."

The derisive smile of Crowe did not sweeten Harry's musings while he waited for his next going on. Indeed, he continued to brood bitterly on the exhibition he had made of himself, and the stay he had caused in the play. His chagrin was none the less for that it was his friend and benefactor Shakespeare that had nominated him for the part of Laertes, and whose play he had brought to a momentary halt.

In deep dejection, when the time came, he returned to the stage with the boy-Ophelia for his scene with her and Corambis.

This passed so smoothly as to give Hal new heart, until it was near its very end; and then, having replied to Corambis's excellent advice with the words, "Most humbly do I take my leave, my lord," Hal happened to let his glance wander past the old man, and across a surging mass of heads in a part of the yard, to a certain face in one of the boxes; and that face had in it something to make his gaze remain delightedly upon it and his lips part in admiration.

Yes, the face was a lady's. Hal had never seen it before; of that he was instantly sure, for had he seen it he could not have forgotten it. He would not have seen it now but that its youthful possessor had removed her mask, which had become irksome to her skin. She seemed above all concern as to what might be thought of her for showing her face in a Bankside theatre. A proud and wilful face was hers, as if with the finest feminine beauty she had something of the uncurbed spirit and rashness of a fiery young gentleman. Her hair and eyes were dark, her skin fair and clear and smooth, her forehead not too high, her chin masterful but most exquisitely shaped, her cheeks rich with natural color. In fine, she was of pronounced beauty, else

Master Marryott had not forgot himself to look at her. Upon her head was a small gray velvet hat, peaked, but not very high, and with narrow brim turned up at the sides. Her chin was elevated a little from contact with a white cambric ruff. Her gown was of murrey cloth with velvet stripes, and it tightly encased her figure, which was of a well-made and graceful litheness. The slashed sleeves, although puffed out, did not make too deep a secret of her shapely, muscular arms. She might have been in her twenty-second year.

With this fine young creature, and farther back in the box, sat a richly dressed old gentleman, comfortably asleep, and a masked lady, who shrank as far as possible into the shadow of the box corner. Standing in the yard, but close to the front of the box, was a slim, dark-faced youth in the green attire then worn by the menservants of ladies.

Not all these details, but only the lady, held the ravished Laertes's attention while he recited:

> "Farewell, Ophelia; and remember well
> What I have said to you."

So heedless and mechanical was his utterance of these lines, in contrast with his previous lifelike manner, that the nearest auditors laughed. The Corambis and Ophelia, seeking the cause of his sudden lapse, followed his gaze with wondering side-glances, while Ophelia replied, in the boy's musical soprano:

> "'Tis in my memory lock'd
> And you yourself shall keep the key of it."

"Farewell," said Laertes, this time with due expression, but rather to the lady in the distant box than to Ophelia and Corambis. Reluctantly he backed toward the rear curtains, and was so slow in making his exit, that Corambis, whose next line required to be spoken in Laertes's absence, gave him a look of ireful impatience and a muttered "Shog, for God's sake," which set the young lords at the stage-side tittering.

At sight of Shakespeare, who was whispering to the Horatio and the Marcellus, near the entrance, Master Marryott had another twinge of self-reproach, but this swiftly yielded to visions of the charming face. These drove away also all heed of the presence of Crowe. Hal would have liked to mount the steps to the balcony at the rear of the stage, in which the unemployed actors might sit when it was not in other use, and whence he might view the lady at leisure; but the balcony was soon to be in service as a platform of the castle, in the scene between Hamlet and the ghost.

His imagination crossing all barriers, and making him already the accepted wooer of the new beauty, Hal noted not how the play went on without, even when a breathless hush presently told of some unusual interest on the part of the audience; and he was then but distantly sensible of Shakespeare's grave, musical voice in the ghost's long recitals, and of the awestricken, though barely whispered, exclamations of Burbage.

In the second act Hal had to remove his mustaches, change his cloak, and go on as an attendant in the presence-chamber scene. His first glance was for the lady. Alas, the face was in eclipse, the black velvet mask had been replaced!

Returning to the tiring-room, he had now to don the beard of an elderly lord, in which part he was to help fill the stage in the play scene. As he marched on in the king's train, for this scene, to the blare of trumpet and the music of instruments in a box aloft, — violins, shawms, sackbuts, and dulcimers, — he saw that the lady was still masked. His presence on the stage this time gave him no opportunity to watch her; he had to direct his eyes, now at the king and queen on their chairs at one side of the stage, and now at the platform of the mimic players.

When he made his exit with the royal party, he saw on every face a kind of elation. "They are hit, and no question," said Master Taylor. "Ay," quoth Master Condell, "that shout of the groundlings, when the king fled, could have been heard as far as the bear-garden." "But the stillness of both lords and groundlings before that," said Master Heminge,—"never was such stillness when Tom Kyd's Hamlet was played." "We shall see how they take the rest of it," said Shakespeare, softly, —though he could not quite conceal a kind of serene satisfaction that had stolen upon his face.

Hal Marryott doffed his beard, and resumed his Laertes cloak, resolved to have some part in the general success. His next scene, that in which Laertes calls the king to account for his father's death, and beholds his sister's madness, held the opportunity of doing so,—of justifying Shakespeare's selection for the part, of winning the young lady's applause, of hastening his own advancement to that fortune which would put him in proper state to approach a wealthy gentlewoman. Perhaps she was one of those who were privileged to attend the Christmas court performances. Could he first win her admiration in some fine part at Whitehall, the next time the chamberlain's men should play there; then — by getting as much wealth as Mr. Alleyn and other players had acquired — leave the stage, and strut in the jewels and velvet suitable to his birth, to what woman might he not aspire? He had all planned in a minute, with the happy facility of youth in such matters.

So he stood in a remote corner of the tiring-room, getting into the feeling of his next scene, repeating the lines to himself, assuming a Burbage-like self-absorption to repel those of his fellow players who, otherwise, would now and then have engaged him in talk. Much conversation was going on in undertone among the groups standing about, or sitting on the tables, chairs, stools, and chests that awaited their time of service on the stage, — for, although scenery was merely suggested by word or symbol, furniture and properties, like costume and makeup, were then used in the theatres. In due time, Hal placed himself at the entrance, working up his mood to a fine heat for the occasion; heard the cue, "The doors are broke;" and rushed on, crying "Where is this king?" with a fury that made the groundlings gape, and even startled the lolling lords into attention.

Having ordered back his Danes, and turned again to the king, he cast one swift glance toward the lady's box, to see how she had taken his fiery entrance; and perceived — no one. The box was empty.

He felt as if something had given way beneath him. In a twinkling his manner toward the king fell into the most perfunctory monotone. So he played the scene out, looking again and again to ascertain if his eyes had not deceived him; but neither was she there, nor the other lady, nor the gentleman, nor the page in green who had stood before the box. The theatre was dark and dull without her; though as much light came in as ever, through the gallery windows and the open top of the playhouse.

With a most blank and insipid feeling did Hal finish this scene, and the longer and less interesting one that came almost immediately after. He carried this feeling back to the dressing-room, and dropped upon a stool in utter listlessness.

"Hath life then lost all taste and motive?" It was the voice of Shakespeare, who had read Hal's mood. The question came with an expression half amused, half sympathetic. At this, in place of which he had deserved a chiding, Hal was freshly stricken, and more deeply than before, with a sense of the injury he did his benefactor by his lifeless acting. So his answer was strangely wide from the question.

"Forgive me," he said. "I swear I'll make amends in the rest of the play."

And he rose, resolved to do so. Perhaps, after all, the lady and her companions had but gone to another box, or would return to the theatre before the play was over. And, moreover, what a fool should he be, to throw away this chance of advancement that might equip him for some possible future meeting with her! And what malicious triumph was glowing darkly on the countenance of Gilbert Crowe! There remained to Hal two opportunities to retrieve himself.

The first was the encounter with Hamlet in the graveyard. Choosing to believe that his enchantress was indeed looking on from some to-him-unknown part of the house, he put into this short scene so excellent a frenzy that, on coming off the stage, he was greeted with a quiet " Sir, that was well played," from Burbage himself, who had made exit a moment earlier. " Bravely ranted," said the Corambis; and the Ophelia, now out of his woman's clothes and half into a plain doublet, observed, with a jerk of his head toward Master Crowe :

" Thou'st turned Gil's face sour of a sudden."

But Master Marryott, disdaining to take gratification in Gil's discomfiture, found it instead in a single approbative look from Shakespeare; and then, choosing his foil, began making passes at the empty air, in practice for the fencing match.

It was partly for his skill with the foils that Hal had got Shakespeare's vote for the character of Laertes. Being a gentleman by birth, though now alone in the world and of fallen fortunes, he had early taken kindly to that gentleman among weapons, the rapier, that had come to drive those common swaggerers, the sword and buckler, out of general service. At home in Oxfordshire, in the lifetime of his parents, and before the memorable lawsuit with the Berkshire branch of the family had taken the ancestral roof from over his head, and driven him to

London to seek what he might find, he had practised daily with the blade, under whatever tuition came his way. In London he had picked up what was to be learned from exiled Frenchmen, soldiers who had fought in Flanders and Spain, and other students of the steel, who abounded in the taverns. With his favorite weapon he was as skilful as if he had taken at least a provost's degree in the art of fence. The bout in "Hamlet" was, of course, prearranged in every thrust and parry, but, even so, there was need of a trained fencer's grace and precision in it. Good fencing was in itself a show worth seeing, in a time when every man knew how to wield one weapon or another.[6]

The audience was wrought up to that pitch of interest which every fifth act ought to witness, when the final scene came on. Each man — especially among the apprentices, the soldiers, and the lords — constituted himself an umpire of the contest, and favored the fighters with comments and suggestions. The sympathy, of course, was with Hamlet, but no one could be blind to the facile play of the Laertes, who indeed had the skill to cover up his antagonist's deficiency with the weapon, and to make him appear really the victor. The courteous manner in which Hal confessed himself hit put the spectators into suitable mind for the better perceiving of his merit. There could be little doubt as to the outcome, had the fight been real, for Burbage was puffing in a way that made the queen's observation, "He's fat and scant of breath," most apt. During the swordwork, the lords and soldiers aired Italian fencing terms then current, in praising the good defence that "the mad girl's brother" made; and when he seemed to wound Hamlet, there burst out a burly voice from the midst of the yard, with:

"I knew that thrust was coming, Master Marryott! Tis I — Kit Bottle!"

When Laertes confessed his treachery and begged Hamlet's forgiveness, so well had Hal fenced and so well acted, he won such esteem of the audience as to die in the best odor. And when, at last, the rushes covering the stage boards were in turn covered with dead bodies, when the curtains closed, and the audience could be heard bustling noisily out of the theatre, Hal partook of the general jubilant relief, and hoped the beautiful young lady had indeed seen the last act from somewhere in the house. The actors arose from the dead, looked as if they had jointly and severally thrown off a great burden, and hastened to substitute their plainer clothes for their rich costumes.

"Come with us to the Falcon for a cup or two, and then to the Mermaid to supper," said Shakespeare to Hal, as the latter was emerging from the theatre a few minutes later, dressed now in somewhat worn brown silk and velvet. With the poet were Masters Heminge, Sly, Condell, and Laurence Fletcher, manager for the company of players. The six walked off together, across the trodden field and along the street or roadway, drawing their short cloaks tight around them for the wind. The Falcon tavern was at the western end of the Bankside, separated from the river by a little garden with an arbor of vines. As the players were about to enter, the door opened, and a group of gentlemen could be seen coming from within, to take boat for the city or Westminster.

"Stand close," said Fletcher, quickly, to the actors. "We may hear an opinion of the play. My lord Edgebury is the best judge of these matters in England."

The players moved aside, and pretended to be reading one of their own bills, as the nobles passed.

"It holdeth attention," my lord was saying to his companions, "but — fustian, fustian! Noise for the rabble in the yard. 'Twill last a week, perchance, for its allegory upon timely matters. But I give it no longer. 'Twill not live."

"Gramercy!" quoth Sly to the players, with a comical smile. "He is more liberal than Gil Crowe, who gives it but three afternoons. Come into the tavern, lads, and a plague on all such prophets!"

My lord Edgebury and Gil Crowe, ye are not dead

yet. At all first nights do ye abound; in many leather-covered study-chairs do ye sit, busy with wet blankets and cold water. On this occasion, though no one knew it at the time, you were a trifle out of your reckoning, — three hundred years, at least, as far as we may be sure now; not much, as planets and historians count, but quite a while as time goes with children.

CHAPTER II.

AT THE TAVERNS.

"We have heard the chimes at midnight, Master Shallow."—Henry IV., Part II.

THAT this narrative — which is to be an account of things done, not an antiquarian "picture" of a past age — need not at every step be learnedly arrested by some description of a costume, street, house, aspect of society, feature of the time, or other such matter, let the reader be reminded at the outset that the year 1601 was of Elizabeth's reign the forty-second; that England was still in the first thrill of the greatest rejuvenescence the world ever knew; that new comforts, and new luxuries, and new thoughts, and new possibilities, and new means of pleasure, had given Englishmen a mad and boisterous zest for life; that gentlemen strutted in curiously shaped beards, and brilliant doublets, and silken trunk-hose, and ruffs, and laced velvet cloaks, and feathered hats; that ladies wore stiff bodices and vast sleeves, and robes open in front to show their petticoats, and farthingales to make those petticoats stand out; that many of these ladies painted their faces and used false hair; that the attire of both sexes shone with jewels and gold and silver; that London folk were, in brief, the most richly dressed in the world; that most ordinary London houses were of wood and plaster, and gabled, and built so that the projecting upper stories darkened the narrow streets below; that the many-colored moving spectacle in those streets was diversified by curious and admiring foreigners from everywhere; that although coaches were yet of recent introduction, the stone paving sounded with them as well as with the carts and drays of traffic; that gray churches, and desolated convents, and episcopal palaces, and gentlemen's inns, and turreted mansions of nobility, abounded in city and suburbs; that the Catholics were still occasional sufferers from such persecution as they in their time had dealt to the Protestants; that there were still some very proud and masterful great lords, although they now came to court, and had fine mansions in the Strand or other suburbs, and no longer fostered civil or private war in their great stone castles in the country; that bully 'prentices, in woollen caps and leather or canvas doublets, were as quick to resent real or fancied offence, with their knives, as gentlemen were with silver-gilt-hilted rapiers; that the taverns resounded with the fanciful oaths of heavily bearded soldiers who had fought in Flanders and Spain; that there were eager ears for every amazing lie of seafaring adventurers who had served under Drake or Raleigh against the Spanish; that tobacco was still a novelty, much relished and much affected; that ghosts and witches were believed in by all classes but perhaps a few "atheists" like Kit Marlowe and Sir Walter Raleigh; that untamed England was still "merry" with its jousts, its public spectacles, its rustic festivals, its holiday feasts, and its brawls, although Puritanism had already begun to show its spoil-sport face; and, to come to this particular first Monday in March, that the common London talk, when it was not of the private affairs of the talkers, had gone, for its theme, from the recent trial and death of the brave but restless Earl of Essex, to the proceedings now pending against certain of his lesser satellites in the Drury House conspiracy.

Before entering the Falcon, Hal Marryott sent a last sweeping look in all directions, half daring to hope that the lady in gray and murrey had not yet left the vicinity of the theatre. But the audience had gone its countless ways; at the Falcon river-stairs the watermen's cries and the noise of much embarking had subsided; and the only women in sight were of the Bankside itself, and of a far different class from that of her whom he sought. He sighed and followed his companions into the tavern.

They were passing through the common hall, on their way to a room where they could be served privately, when they were greeted by a tall, burly, black-bearded, bold-featured, weather-browned, middle-aged fellow in a greasy leather jerkin, an old worn-out red velvet doublet, and patched brown silk trunk-hose, and with a sorry-feathered remnant of a big-brimmed felt hat, a long sword and a dagger, these weapons hanging at his girdle. His shoes barely deserved the name, and his brown cloth cloak was a rag. His face had been glum and uneasy, but at sight of the players he instantly threw on the air of a dashing, bold rascal with whom all went merrily.

"'The actors are come hither, my lord,'" he cried, with a flourish, quoting from the play of the afternoon. "A good piece of work, Master Shakespeare. Excellent! More than excellent!"

"Despite thyself, for doing thy best to spoil it,—bawling out in the fencing match, Kit Bottle," put in Will Sly.

"Captain Bottle, an it please you, Master Sly," said the other, instantly taking on dignity; "at least when I carried Sir Philip Sidney off the field at Zutphen, and led my company after my lord Essex into Cadiz."

"And how goes the world with thee, Captain Kit?" inquired Mr. Shakespeare, with something of a kindly sadness in his tone.

"Bravely, bravely as ever, Master Will," replied Kit. "Still marching to this music!" And he shook a pouch at his belt, causing a clinking sound to come forth.

As the players passed on to their room, Kit plucked the sleeve of Hal Marryott, who was the last. When the two were alone in a corner, the soldier, having dropped his buoyant manner, whispered:

"Hast a loose shilling or two about thy clothes, lad? Just till to-morrow, I swear on the cross of my sword. I have moneys coming; that is, with a few testers to start dicing withal, I shall have the coin flowing me-ward. Tut, boy, I can't lie to thee; I haven't tasted meat or malt since yesterday."

"But what a devil — why, the pieces thou wert jingling?" said Hal, astonished.

"Pox, Hal, think'st thou I would bare my poverty to a gang of players — nay, no offence to thee, lad!" The soldier took from the pouch two or three links of a worthless iron chain. "When thou hast no coin, lad, let thy purse jingle loudest. 'Twill serve many a purpose."

"But if you could not buy a dinner," said Hal, smiling, "how did you buy your way into the play-house?"

"Why, body of me," replied Bottle, struggling for a moment with a slight embarrassment, "the mind, look you, the mind calls for food, no less than the belly. Could I satisfy both with a sixpence? No. What should it be, then? Beef and beer for the belly? Or a sight of the new play, to feed the mind withal? Thou know'st Kit Bottle, lad. Though he hath followed the wars, and cut his scores of Spanish throats, and hath no disdain of beef and beer, neither, yet as the mind is the better part —"

Moved at thought of the hungry old soldier's last sixpence having gone for the play, to the slighting of his stomach, Hal instantly pulled out what remained of his salary for the previous week, about five shillings in amount, and handed over two shillings sixpence, saying:

"I can but halve with thee, Kit. The other half is owed."

"Nay, lad," said Kit, after a swift glance around to see if the transaction was observed by the host or the drawers, "I'll never rob thee, persuade me as thou wilt. Two shillings I'll take, not a farthing more. Thou'rt a heart of gold, lad. To-morrow I'll pay thee, an I have to pawn my sword! To-morrow, as I'm a soldier! Trust old Kit!"

And the captain, self-styled, in great haste now that he had got the coin, strode rapidly from the place. Hal Marryott proceeded to the room where his fellow actors were. His cup of canary was already waiting for him on the table around which the players sat.

"What, Hal," cried Sly, "is it some state affair that Bottle hath let thee into?"

"I like the old swaggerer," said Hal, evading the question. "He hath taught me the best of what swordsmanship I know. He is no counterfeit soldier, 'tis certain; and he hath a pride not found in common rogues."

"I think he is in hard ways," put in Laurence Fletcher, the manager, "for all his jingle of coin. I saw him to-day lurking about the door of the theatre, now and again casting a wishful glance within, and then scanning the people as they came up, as if to find some friend who would pay for him. So at last I bade him come in free for the nonce. You should have seen how he took it."

"I warrant his face turned from winter to summer, in a breath," said Mr. Shakespeare. "Would the transformation were as easily wrought in any man!"

A winter indeed seemed to have settled upon his own heart, for this was the time, not only when his friends of the Essex faction were suffering, but also when the affair of the "dark lady," in which both Southampton and the Earl of Pembroke were involved with himself, had reached its crisis.

Hal smiled inwardly to think how Bottle had seized the occasion to touch a player's feelings by appearing to have spent his last sixpence for the play; and forgave the lie, in admiration of the pride with which the ragged warrior had concealed his poverty from the others.

As Hal replaced his remaining three shillings in his pocket, his fingers met something hairy therein, which he had felt also in taking the coin out. He drew it forth to see what it was, and recognized the beard he had worn as the elderly lord. He then remembered to have picked it up from the stage, where it had accidentally fallen, and to have thrust it into his pocket in his haste to leave the theatre and see if the girl in murrey was still about. He now put it back into his pocket. After the wine had gone round three times, the players left the Falcon, to walk from the region of playhouses and bear-gardens to the city, preferring to use their legs rather than go by water from the Falcon stairs.

They went eastward past taverns, dwelling-houses, the town palace of the Bishop of Winchester, and the fine Church of St. Mary Overie, to the street then called Long Southwark; turned leftward to London Bridge, and crossed between the tall houses of rich merchants, mercers, and haberdashers, that of old were built thereon. The river's roar, through the arches beneath, required the players to shout when they talked, in crossing. Continuing northward and up-hill, past the taverns and fish-market of New Fish Street, their intention being to go at once to the Mermaid, they heeded Master Condell's suggestion that they tarry on the way for another drink or two; and so turned into Eastcheap, the street of butchers' shops, and thence into the Boar's Head Tavern, on the south side of the way.

On entering a public parlor, the first person they saw was Captain Bottle, sitting at a table. On the stool opposite him was a young man in a gay satin doublet and red velvet cloak, and with an affected air of self-importance and worldly experience. This person and the captain were engaged in throwing dice, in the intervals of eating.

"What, old rook — captain, I mean," called out Mr. Sly; "must ever be shaking thine elbow, e'en 'twixt the dishes at thy supper?"

"An innocent game, sir," said Kit, promptly, concealing his annoyance from his companion. "No money risked, worth speaking of. God's body, doth a sixpence or two signify?" And he continued throwing the dice, manifestly wishing the actors would go about their business.

"'Tis true, when Captain Bottle plays, it cannot be called gaming," said Master Condell.

"He means," explained Bottle to his companion, in a confidential tone, "that I am clumsy with the dice. A mere child, beshrew me else! A babe in swaddling clothes! 'Tis by the most marvellous chance I've been winning from you, these few minutes. 'Twill come your way soon, and you'll turn my pockets inside out. Pray wait for me a moment, while I speak to these gentlemen. We have business afoot together."

Kit thereupon rose, strode over to the players, drew them around him, and said, in a low tone:

"What, boys, will ye spoil old Kit's labor? Will ye scare that birdling away? Will ye keep money from the needy? This gull is clad in coin, he is lined with it, he spits it, he sweats it! He is some country beau, the dandy of some market town, the son of some rustical justice, the cock of some village. He comes up to London once a year, sees a little of the outside of our life here, thinks he plays the mad rascal in a tavern or two, and goes home to swagger it more than ever in his village, with stories of the wickedness he hath done in London. An I get not his money, others will, and worse men, — and, perchance, leave him in a worse condition."

"We shall leave him to thy mercy, and welcome, Kit," said Mr. Shakespeare. "He shall never know thy tricks from us. Come our ways, lads. These village coxcombs ought to pay something for their egregious vanity and ignorance. This fellow will have the less means of strutting it in the eyes of the louts, when Kit hath had his way." The poet was doubtless thinking of the original of his Justice Shallow.[7]

So the players went on to another room, Hal remaining to say in Kit's ear:

"I knew fellows like this ere I came from the country, and how they prated of London, and of their wildness here. Gull such, if thou must be a cheater."

"Cheater," echoed Kit. "Nay, speak not the word as if it smelt so bad. Should a man resign his faculties and fall back on chance? Do we leave things to chance in war? Do we not use our skill there, and every advantage God hath given us? Is not a game a kind of mimic war, and shall not a man use skill and stratagem in games? Go to, lad. Am I a common coney-catcher? Do I cheat with a gang? Do I consort with gull-gropers? An this rustic hath any trick worth two of mine, is he not welcome to play it?" [8]

Whereupon Kit, making no allusion to the borrowed two shillings, although he had already won several times two shillings from the country fopling, returned to the latter and the dice, while Hal joined his own party.

The sight of savory pastry and the smell of fish a-cooking had made some of the players willing to stay and sup at the Boar's Head; but Shakespeare reminded them that Mr. Burbage was to meet them at the Mermaid later. So they rose presently to set forth, all of them, and especially Hal Marryott, the warmer in head and heart for the wine they had taken. Hal had become animated and talkative. A fuller and keener sense of things possessed him, — of the day's success, of his own share therein, of the merits of his companions and himself, and of the charms of the lady in murrey and gray. So rich and vivid became his impression of the unknown beauty, that there began to be a seeming as if she were present in spirit. It was as if her immaterial presence pervaded the atmosphere, as if she overheard the talk that now rattled from him, as if her fine eyes were looking from Gothic church windows and the overhanging gables of merchants' houses, while he walked on with the players in the gathering dusk of evening. The party went westward, out of Eastcheap, past London stone in Candlewick Street, through Budge Row and Watling Street, and northward into Bread Street. The last was lined with inns and taverns, and into one of the latter, on the west side of the street, near "golden Cheapside," the actors finally strode. Its broad, plastered, pictured front was framed and intersected by heavy timbers curiously carved, and the great sign that hung before it was the figure of a mermaid in the waves. The tavern stood a little space back from the street, toward which its ground-floor casements projected far out; and, in addition to its porched front entrance, it had passageways at side and rear, respectively from Cheapside and Friday Street.⁹

The long room to which the players ascended had a blaze already in the fireplace (chimneys having become common during the later Tudor reigns), a great square oak table, a few armchairs, some benches, and several stools. The tapestry on the walls was new, for the defeat of the Spanish Armada, which it portrayed, had occurred but a dozen years before. Ere the actors were seated, lighted candles had been brought, and Master Heminge had stepped into the kitchen to order a supper little in accord with the season (it was now Lent) or with the statutes, but obtainable by the privileged, — ribs of beef, capon, sauces, gravies, custard, and other trifles, with a bit of fish for the scrupulous. For players are hungriest after a performance, and there have ever been stomachs least fishily inclined on fish-days, as there are always throats most thirsty for drink where none is allowed; and the hostess of the Mermaid was evidently of a mind with Dame Quickly, who argued, "What's a joint of mutton or two in a whole Lent?"¹⁰ After their walk in the raw air, and regardless of the customary order at meals, the players made a unanimous call for mulled sack. The drawer, who had come at their bidding without once crying "Anon," used good haste to serve it.

"Times have changed," said Mr. Shakespeare,

having hung up cloak, hat, and short rapier, and leaning back in his chair, with a relish of its comfort after a day of exertion and tension. "'Tis not so long since there were ever a dozen merry fellows to sup with us when we came from the play."

"'Tis strange we see nothing of Raleigh," said Sly, standing by the carved chimneypiece, and stretching his hands out over the fire.

"Nay, 'twould be stranger an he came to meet us now," said Laurence Fletcher, "after his show of joy at the earl's beheading."

The allusion was to Raleigh's having witnessed from a window in the Tower the death of his great rival, Essex.

"Nay," said Shakespeare, "though he was a foe to Essex, who was of our patrons, Sir Walter is no enemy to us. I dare swear he hath stood our advocate at court in our present disfavor. But while our friends of one side are now in prison or seclusion, those of the other side stand aloof from us. And for our player-fellowship, as rivalry among the great hath made bitter haters, so hath competition among actors and scribblers spoilt good comradeship."

"Thou'rt thinking how brawny Ben used to sit with us at this table," said Sly.

"And wishing he sat here again," said Shakespeare.

"Tut," said Condell, "he is happier at the Devil

tavern, where his heavy wisdom hath no fear of being put out of countenance by thy sharper wit, Will."

"A pox on Ben Jonson for a surly, envious dog!" exclaimed Laurence Fletcher. "I marvel to hear thee speak kindly of him, Will. After thy soliciting us to play his comedy, for him to make a mock of thee and our other writers, in the silly pedantic stuff those brats squeak out at the Blackfriars!" Master Fletcher was, evidently, easily heated on the subject of the satirical pieces written by Jonson for the Chapel Royal boys to play at the Blackfriars Theatre, in which the Globe plays were ridiculed. "A pox on him, I say, and his tedious 'humors!'" Whereupon Master Fletcher turned his attention to the beef, which had just arrived.

"Nay," said Shakespeare, "his merit hath had too slow a greeting, and too scant applause. So the wit in him hath soured a little, — as wine too long kept exposed, for want of being in request."

"Well," cried Hal Marryott, warmed by copious draughts of the hot sugared sack, "may I never drink again but of hell flame, nor eat but at the devil's own table, if aught ever sour *me* to such ingratitude for thy beneficence, Master Shakespeare!"

"Go to, Harry! I have not benefited thee, nor Ben Jonson neither."

"Never, indeed! God wot!" exclaimed Hal,

spearing with his knife-point a slice of beef, to convey it from his platter to his mouth (forks were not known in England till ten years later). "To open thy door to a gentleman just thrown out of an alehouse, to feed him when he hath not money to pay for a radish, to lodge him when he hath not right of tenure to a dung-hill, — these are no benefits, forsooth."

"Was that thy condition, then, when he took thee as coadjutor?" Fletcher asked, a little surprised.

"That and worse," answered Hal. "Hath Mr. Shakespeare never told you?"

"Never but thou wert a gentleman desirous of turning player. Let's hear it, an thou wilt."

"Ay, let us!" cried Heminge and Condell; and Sly added: "For a player to turn gentleman is nothing wonderful now, but that a gentleman should turn player hath puzzled me."[12]

"Why," quoth Harry, now vivacious with wine, and quite ready to do most of the talking, "you shall see how a gentleman might easily have turned far worse than player. 'Twas when I was newly come to London, in 1598, not three years ago. Ye've all heard me tell of the loss of mine estate in Oxfordshire, through the deviltry of the law and of my kinsman. When my cousin took possession, he would have got me provided for at one of the universities, to be rid of me; but I had no mind to be made a poor scholar of; for, look you, my bringing up in my father's house had been fit for a nobleman's son. I knew my Latin and my lute, could hunt and hawk with any, and if I had no practice at tilt and tourney, I made up for that lack by my skill with the rapier. Well, just when I should have gone to Italy, Germany, and France, for my education, my father died, and my mother; and I was turned out of house, wherefore I say, a curse on all bribe-taking judges and unnatural kin! I told my cousin what he might do with the dirty scholarship he offered me, and a pox on it! and swore I would hang for a thief ere I would take anything of his giving. All that I had in the world was a horse, the clothes on my body, — for I would not go back to his house for others, having once left it, — my rapier and dagger, and a little purse of crowns and angels. There was but one friend whom I thought it would avail me to seek, and to his house I rode, in Hertfordshire. He was a Catholic knight, whose father had sheltered my grandfather, a Protestant, in the days of Queen Mary, and now went I to him, to make myself yet more his debtor in gratitude. Though he had lived most time in France, since the Babington conspiracy, he now happened to be at home; yet he could do nothing for me, his estate being sadly diminished, and he about to sail again for the country where Catholics are safer. But he gave me a letter to my lord of Essex, by whom, as by my father, he was no less loved for being a Catholic. When I read the letter, I thought my fortune made. To London I rode, seeing myself already high in the great earl's service. At the Bell, in Carter Lane, I lodged, and so gleesome a thing it was to me to be in London, so many were the joys to be bought here, so gay the taverns, so irresistible the wenches, that ere ever I found time to present my letter to the earl I had spent my angels and crowns, besides the money I had got for my horse in Smithfield. But I was easy in mind. My lord would assuredly take me into his house forthwith, on reading my friend's letter. The next morning, as I started for Essex House, a gentleman I had met in the taverns asked me if I had heard the news. I had not; so he told me. My lord of Essex had yesterday turned his back on the queen, and clapped his hand upon his sword, — you remember the time, masters — "

"Ay," said Sly. "The queen boxed his ears for it. The dispute was over the governorship of Ireland."

"My lord was in disgrace," Hal went on, "and like to be charged with high treason. So little I knew of court matters, I thought this meant his downfall, and that the letter, if seen, might work only to my prejudice and my friend's. So I burned it at the tavern fire, and wondered what a murrain to do. I went to lodge in Honey Lane, pawned my weapons, then my cloak, and finally the rest of my clothes, having bought rags in Houndsditch in the meantime. Rather than go back to Oxfordshire I would have died in the street, and was like to do so, at last; for my host, having asked for his money one night when I was drunk and touchy, got such an answer that he and his drawer cudgelled me and threw me out. So bruised I was, that I could scarce move; but I got up, and walked to the Conduit in Cheapside. There I lay down, full of aches; and then was it that Mr. Shakespeare, returning late from the tavern, happened to step on me as I lay blocking the way. What it was that moved him to stop and examine me, I know not. But, having done so, he led me to his lodgings in St. Helen's; whence, for one in my condition, it was truly no downward step to the playhouse stage,—and thankful was I when he offered me that step!"

"I perceived from the manner of thy groan, when I trod on thee, 'twas no common vagabond under foot," said Shakespeare.

Later in the evening, Mr. Burbage came in, not to eat, for he had already supped at his house in Holywell Street, Shoreditch, but to join a little in the drinking. The room was now full of tobacco smoke, for most of the players had set their pipes a-going. Mr. Shakespeare did not smoke; but Hal

Marryott, as a youth who could let no material joy go by untasted, was as keen a judge of Trinidado or Nicotian as any sea-dog from "the Americas."

"'Tis how many hundred years, Will, since this Prince Hamlet lived?" said Heminge, the talk having led thereto; and he went on, not waiting for answer, "Yet to-day we players bring him back to life, and make him to be remembered."

"Ay," replied Shakespeare, "many a dead and rotten king oweth a resurrection and posthumous fame to some ragged scholar or some poor player."

"And we players," said Burbage, with a kind of sigh, "who make dead men remembered, are by the very nature of our craft doomed to be forgot. Who shall know our very names, three poor hundred years hence?"

"Why," said Condell, "our names might live by the printing of them in the books of the plays we act in; a printed book will last you a long time."

"Not such books as these thievish printers make of our plays," said Sly, himself a writer of plays.

"Marry, I should not wish long life to their blundering, distorted versions of any play I had a hand in making," said Shakespeare.

"But consider," said Condell; "were a decent printing made of all thy plays, Will, all in one book, from the true manuscripts we have at the theatre, and our names put in the book, Dick's name at the head, then might not our names live for our having acted in thy plays?"

Mr. Burbage smiled amusedly, but said nothing, and Shakespeare answered:

"'Twould be a dead kind of life for them, methinks; buried in dusty, unsold volumes in the booksellers' shops in Paul's Churchyard."

"Nay, I would venture something," said Master Heminge, thoughtfully, "that a book of *thy* plays were sure to be opened."

"Ay, that some shopman's 'prentice might tear out the leaves, to wrap fardels withal," said Shakespeare. "Three hundred years, Dick said. 'Tis true, books of the ancients have endured to this day; but if the world grows in learning as it hath in our own time, each age making its own books, and better and wiser ones, what readers shall there be, think you, in the year of our Lord 1900, for the rude stage-plays of Will Shakespeare, or even for his poems, that be writ with more care?"

"'Twould be strange, indeed," said Burbage, "that a player should be remembered after his death, merely for his having acted in some certain play or set of plays." He did not add, but did he think, that Will Shakespeare's plays were more like to be remembered, if at all, for Mr. Burbage's having acted in them?"

"Why art thou silent, lad," said Shakespeare to

Hal Marryott, by way of changing the subject, "and thy gaze lost in thy clouds of smoke, as if thou sawest visions there?"

"I' faith, I do see a vision there," said Harry, now in the enraptured stage of wine, and eager to unbosom himself. "Would I were a poet, like thee, that I might describe it. Ye gods, what a face! The eyes have burned into my heart. Cupid hath made swift work of me!"

"Why, this must be since yesterday," said Sly.

"Since four o' the clock to-day," cried Hal.

"Then thou canst no more than have seen her," remarked Fletcher.

"To see her was to worship her. Drink with me to her eyes, an ye love me, masters!"

"To her nose also, and mouth and cheeks and ears, an thou wilt," said Sly, suiting action to word.

"Don't think this is love in thee, lad," said Fletcher. "Love is of slower growth."

"Then all our plays are wrong," said Sly.

"Why, certes, it may be love," said Shakespeare. "Love is a flame of this fashion: the first sight of a face will kindle it in shape of a spark. An there be no further matter to fan and feed the spark withal, 'twill soon die, having never been aught but a spark, keen though its scorch for a time; a mere seedling of love, a babe smothered at birth. But an there be closer commerce, to give fuel and breeze to the spark, it shall grow into flame, a flame, look you, that with proper feeding shall endure forever, like sacred fires judiciously replenished and maintained; but too much fuel, or too little, or a change in the wind, will smother it, or starve it, or violently put it out. Harry hath the spark well lighted, as his raving showeth, and whether it shall soon burn out, or wax into a blaze, lies with future circumstance."

Harry declared that, if not otherwise fed, it would devour himself. Thereupon Master Sly suggested drowning it in sack; and one would have thought Hal was trying to do so. But the more he drank, the more was he engulfed in ideas of her who had charmed him. Still having a kind of delusion that she was in a manner present, he discoursed as if for her to overhear.

Ere he knew it, the other players were speaking of bed. Mr. Burbage had already slipped out to fulfil some mysterious engagement for the night within the city, which matter, whatever it was, had been the cause of his coming after supper from his home beyond the bars of Bishopsgate Street without the walls. Master Heminge's apprentices (for Master Heminge was a grocer as well as an actor) had come to escort him and Master Condell to their houses in Aldermanbury; and sturdy varlets were below to serve others of the company in like duty. At this late hour such guards against robbers were necessary in London streets. But Harry, who then lodged in the same house with Mr. Shakespeare, in St. Helen's, Bishopsgate,[14] was not yet for going home. He would make the cannikin clink for some hours more. Knowing the lad's ways, and his ability to take care of himself, Mr. Shakespeare left him to his desires; and at last Harry had no other companion than Will Sly, who still had head and stomach for another good-night flagon or two. When Sly in turn was shaky on his legs and half asleep, Harry accompanied him and his man to their door, reluctantly saw it close upon them, and then, solitary in night-wrapped London, looked up and down the narrow street, considering which way to roam in search of congenial souls, minded, like himself, to revel out the merry hours of darkness.

He loathed the thought of going to bed yet, and would travel far to find a fellow wassailer. His three shillings — though that sum then would buy more than a pound buys to-day — had gone at the Mermaid. He bethought himself of the taverns at which he might have credit. The list not offering much encouragement, he at last started off at random, leaving events to chance.

Plunging and swaying, rather than walking, he traversed a few streets, aimlessly turning what corners presented themselves. The creaking of the signs overhead in the wind mingled with the more mysterious sounds of the night. Once he heard a sudden rush of feet from a narrow lane, and instantly backed against a doorway, whipping out rapier and dagger. Two gaunt, ill-looking rascals, disclosed by a lantern hanging from an upper window, stood back and inspected him a moment; then, probably considering him not worth the risk, vanished into the darkness whence they had emerged.

More roaming brought Hal into Paternoster Row, and thence into Ave Maria Lane, giving him an occasional glimpse at the left, between houses, of the huge bulk of St. Paul's blotting darkly a darkness of another tone. At Ludgate, boldly passing himself off upon the blinking watchman as a belated page of Sir Robert Cecil's, he got himself let through, when he ought to have been taken before the constable as a night-walker; and so down the hill he went into Fleet Street. The taverns were now closed for the night to all outward appearance, the bells of Bow and other churches having rung the curfew some hours since, — at nine o'clock. But Hal knew that merriment was awake behind more than one cross-barred door-post or red lattice; and he tried several doors, but in vain. At last he found himself under the sign of the Devil, on the south side of the street, close to Temple Bar.

There was likelihood that Ben Jonson might be there, for Ben also was a fellow of late hours. Hal's heart suddenly warmed toward Master Jonson; he forgot the satire on the Globe plays, the apparent ingratitude to Shakespeare, and thought only of the convivial companion.

Much knocking on the door brought a servant of the tavern, by whom Hal, learning that Master Jonson was indeed above, sent up his name. He was at length admitted, and found his way to a large room in which he beheld the huge form and corrugated countenance of him he sought. Master Jonson filled a great chair at one side of a square table, and was discoursing to a group of variously attired gentlemen, Temple students, and others, this audience being in all different stages of wine. He greeted Master Hal in a somewhat severe yet paternal manner, beckoned him to his chair-side, and inquired in an undertone how Mr. Shakespeare fared. Manifestly the "war of the theatres," as it was called, had not destroyed the private esteem between the two dramatists. Hal's presence caused the talk to fall, in time, upon the new "Hamlet," which some of the then present members of the tribe of Ben had seen.

One young gentleman of the Temple, in the insolent stage of inebriety, spoke sneeringly of the play; whereupon Hal answered hotly. Both flashed out rapiers at the same instant, and as the table was between them Hal leaped upon it, to reach more quickly his opponent. Only the prompt action of Master Jonson, who mounted the table, making it groan beneath his weight, and thrust himself between the two, cut short the brawl. But now, each antagonist deeming himself the aggrieved person, and the Templar being upheld by several of the company, and a great noise of tongues arising, and the host running in to suppress the tumult, it was considered advisable to escort Master Marryott from the place. He was therefore hustled out by Master Jonson, the host, and a tapster ; and so found himself eventually in the street, the door barred against him.

He then perceived that he was without his rapier. It had been wrested from him at the first interference with the quarrel. Wishing to recover it, and in a wrathful spirit, he pounded on the door with his dagger hilt, and called out loudly for the return of his weapon ; but his efforts being misinterpreted, he was left to pound and shout in vain. Baffled and enraged, he started back toward Ludgate, with some wild thought of enlisting a band of ruffians to storm the tavern. But the wine had now got so complete possession of him that, when a figure emerging from Water Lane bumped heavily against him, all memory of the recent incident was knocked out of his mind.

"What in the fiend's name — " grumbled the newcomer; then suddenly changed his tone. "Why, od's-body, 'tis Master Marryott! Well met, boy! Here be thy two shillings, and never say Kit Bottle payeth not his debts. I've just been helping my friend to his lodging here at the sign of the Hanging Sword. 'Twas the least I could do for him. Art for a merry night of it, my bawcock? Come with me to Turnbull Street. There be a house there, where I warrant a welcome to any friend of Kit Bottle's. I've been out of favor there of late, but now my pockets sing this tune" (he rattled the coin in them), "and arms will be open for us."

Rejoiced at this encounter, Hal took the captain's arm, and strode with him through Shoe Lane, across Holborn Bridge, through Cow Lane, past the Pens of Smithfield, and so — undeterred by sleeping watchmen or by the post-and-chain bar — into Turnbull Street.[15] Kit knocked several times at the door of one of the forward-leaning houses, before he got a response. Then a second-story casement was opened, and a hoarse female voice asked who was below.

"What, canst not see 'tis old Kit, by the flame of his nose?" replied the captain.

The woman told him to wait a minute, and withdrew from the window.

"See, lad," whispered Bottle, "'tis late hours when Kit Bottle can't find open doors. To say true, I was afeard my welcome here might be a little halting; but it seems old scores are forgot. We shall be merry here, Hal!"

A sudden splash at their very feet made them start back and look up at the window. A pair of hands, holding an upturned pail, was swiftly drawn back, and the casement was then immediately closed.

Bottle smothered an oath. "Wert caught in any of that shower, lad?" he asked Hal.

"'Scaped by an inch," said Hal, with a hiccough. "Marry, is this thy welcome?"

Kit's wrath against the inmates of the house now exploded. Calling them "scullions," "scavengers," and names still less flattering, he began kicking and hammering on the door as if to break it down. Moved by the spirit of violence, Hal joined him in this demonstration. The upper windows opened, and voices began screaming "Murder!" and "Thieves!" In a short time several denizens of the neighborhood — which was a neighborhood of nocturnal habits — appeared in the street. Seeing how matters stood, they fell upon Kit and Hal, mauling the pair with fists, and tearing off their outer garments.

Soon a cry went up, "The watch!" whereupon Hal, with memories of restraint and inconvenience to which he had once before been put, called upon Kit to follow, and made a dash toward the end of the street. He speedily was out of pursuit, and the sound of Bottle's voice growling out objurgations, close behind him, satisfied him that the old soldier was at his heels. Hal, therefore, ran on, making no impediment of the bars, and passed the Pens without slack of speed. Stopping in Cow Lane he looked back, and to his surprise saw that he was now quite alone.

He went immediately back over his tracks in search of Bottle, but found no one. Turnbull Street had subsided into its former outward appearance of desertion. Thinking that Bottle might have passed him in the darkness, Hal returned southward. When he arrived in Fleet Street he retained but a confused, whirling recollection of what had occurred. Yet his mood was still for company and carouse. With great joy, therefore, he observed that a humble little alehouse to which he sometimes resorted, near Fleet Bridge, was opening for the day, as dawn was appearing. He went in and ordered wine.

The tapster, who knew him, remarked with astonishment that he was without hat or cloak; and the morning being very cold, and Hal unlikely to meet any person of quality at that hour, the fellow offered him a surcoat and cap, such as were worn by apprentices, to protect him from chill on the way homeward. Hal, who was now half comatose, passively let himself be thus fortified against the weather. With the sum repaid him by Bottle he was able to buy good cheer; his only lack was of company to share it with. He could not hope at this hour to fall in with another late-hour man; it was now time for the early rising folk to be abroad.

In from the street came half a dozen hardy looking fellows, calling for beer to be quickly drawn, as they had far to go to their work. Their dress was of leather and coarse cloth, and the tools they carried were those of carpenters. But to Hal, who now saw things vaguely, they were but fellow mortals, and thirsty. He welcomed them with a flourish and an imperative invitation to drink. This they readily accepted, grinning the while with boorish amusement. When they perforce departed, Hal, unwilling to lose new-found company so soon, attached himself to them; and was several times hindered from dragging them into taverns as they passed, by their promise, given with winks invisible to him, that they would drink on arriving at their destination.

So he went, upheld between a pair of them, and heeding not the way they took. Though it was now daylight, he was past recognizing landmarks. He had the dimmest sense of passing a succession of walled and turreted mansions at his left hand; then of catching glimpses of more open and park-like spaces at his right hand; of going, in a grave kind of semi-stupor, through two gateways and as many courtyards; of being passed on, with the companions to whom he clung, by dull warders, and by a busy, inattentive, pompous man of authority to whom his comrades reported in a body; of traversing with them, at last, a passage and a kind of postern, and emerging in a great garden. Here the carpenters seemed to become sensible of having committed a serious breach in sportively letting him be admitted as one of their own band. They held a brief consultation, looking around in a half frightened way to see if they were observed. They finally led him into an alley, formed by hedgerows, deposited him gently on the ground, and hastened off to another part of the garden. Once recumbent, he turned upon his side and went instantly to sleep.

When he awoke, several hours later, without the least knowledge what garden was this to which his eyes opened, or the least recollection how he had come into it, he saw, looking down at him in mild surprise, a slight, yellow-haired, pale-faced, highbrowed, dark-eyed, elderly lady, with a finely curved nose, a resolute mouth, and a sharp chin, and wearing a tight-bodied, wide-skirted costume of silvered white velvet and red silk, with a gold-laced, ermine-trimmed mantle, and a narrow, peaked velvet hat. Hal, in his first bewilderment, wondered where it was that he had previously seen this lady.

"Madam," he said, in a voice husky with cold,

"I seem to be an intruder. By your favor, what place is this?"

The lady looked at him sharply for a moment, then answered, simply:

"'Tis the garden of Whitehall palace. Who are you?"

Hal suppressed a startled exclamation. He remembered now where he had seen the lady: 'twas at the Christmas court performances. He flung into a kneeling posture, at her small, beribboned, cloth-shod feet.

"I am your Majesty's most loyal, most worshipful subject," he said.

"And what the devil are you doing here?" asked Queen Elizabeth.

CHAPTER III.

QUEEN AND WOMAN.

> "And commanded
> By such poor passion as the maid that milks."
> — *Antony and Cleopatra.*

THOUGH Queen Elizabeth often swore at her ladies and her favorite lords, it is not to be supposed that she would ordinarily address a stranger in such terms as she used but now toward Master Marryott.[16] Nor was it the surprise of finding asleep in her garden a youth, wearing an apprentice's surcoat over a gentleman's velvet doublet, — for Hal had moved in his sleep so as to disclose part of the doublet, — and silken hose, that evoked so curt an expression. Neither was it the possibility that the intruder might be another Capt. Thomas Leigh, who had been found lurking in the palace, near the door of the privy chamber, a day or two after the Essex rising, and had been subsequently put to death. Had a thought of assassination taken any root in the queen's mind at sight of the slumbering youth, she would, doubtless, have behaved as on a certain occasion at the time of the Babington conspiracy; when, walking in her garden, and being suddenly approached by one of the conspirators, and finding none of her guards within sight, she held the intruder in so intrepid a look that he shrank back — and the captain of her guard did not soon forget the rating she afterward gave him for that she had been left thus exposed. But on the present occasion she herself had petulantly ordered back the little train of gentlemen and ladies in waiting, guards, and pages, who would have followed her into the alley where she now was. They stood in separate groups, beyond the tall hedge, out of view but not out of call, and wondering what had put her majesty this morning into such a choleric desire for solitude. For that is what she was in, and what made her words to Hal so unlike those commonly used by stage royalty at the theatre.

What the devil *was* he doing there? Hal asked himself, as he gazed helplessly up at the queen. "I know not," he faltered. "I mean, I have no memory of coming hither. But 'tis not the first time, your majesty, I have waked up in a strange place and wondered at being there. I — I drank late last night."

He put his hand to his aching head, in a manner that unconsciously confirmed his confession; and then he looked at his coarse surcoat with an amazement that the queen could not doubt.

"What is your name?" asked the queen, who seemed to have her own reason for interrogating him quietly herself, instead of calling a guard and turning him over to some officer for examination.

"Harry Marryott, an it please your Majesty. A player in the lord chamberlain's company, though a gentleman by birth."

Elizabeth frowned slightly at the mention of the lord chamberlain's company; but a moment after, strange to say, there came into her face the sign of a sudden secret hope and pleasure.

"Being one of those players," said she, "you are well-wisher to the foolish men who partook in the late treason?" She watched narrowly for his answer.

"Not well-wisher to their treason, madam, I swear!"

"But to themselves?"

"As to men who have been our friends, we wish some of them whatever good may consist with your Majesty's own welfare, which is the welfare of England, the happiness of your subjects. But that wish makes no diminution of our loyalty, which for myself I would give my life for a chance of proving." He found it not difficult to talk to this queen, so human was she, so outright, direct, and to the point.

"Why," she replied, in a manner half careless, half significant, as if she were trying her way to some particular issue, "who knows but you may yet have that chance, and at the same time fulfil a kind wish toward one of those misguided plotters. An you were to be trusted — but nay, your presence here needs some accounting for. Dig your memory, man; knock your brains, and recall how you came hither. 'Tis worth while, youth, for you doubtless know what is supposed of men found unaccountably near our person, and what end is made of them."

Hal was horrified and heartstricken. "Madam," he murmured, "if my queen, who is the source and the object of all chivalrous thoughts in every gentleman's breast in England, one moment hold it possible that I am here for any purpose against her, let me die! Call guards, your Majesty, and have me slain!"

"Nay," said Elizabeth, convinced and really touched by his feeling, "I spoke not of what I thought, but of what others might infer. Now that I perceive your quality, it hath come to me that you might serve me in a business that needs such a man, — a man not known at court, and whom it would appear impossible I could have given audience to. Indeed, I was pondering on the difficulty of finding such a man in the time afforded, and in no very sweet humor either, when the sight of you broke in upon my thoughts."

"To serve your Majesty in any business would be

my supremest joy," said Hal, eagerly — and truly. His feeling in this was that of all young English gentlemen of his time.

"But this tells me not how came you into my private garden," said her Majesty.

"I remember some dispute at the Devil tavern," replied Harry, searching his memory. "And roaming the streets with one Captain Bottle, and being chased out of some neighborhood or other — and there I lose myself. It seems as if I went lugging forward through the streets, holding to an arm on either side, and then plunged quite out of this world, into cloud, or blackness, or nothing. Why, it is strange — meseems yonder workman, at the end of this alley, had some part in my goings last night."

The workman was a carpenter, engaged in erecting a wooden framework for an arched hedge that was to meet at right angles the alley in which the queen and Harry were. The man's work had brought him but now into their sight.

The queen, who on occasion could be the most ceremonial monarch in Christendom, could, when necessary, be the most matter-of-fact. She now gave a "hem" not loud enough for her unseen attendants to hear, but sufficient to attract the carpenter's attention. He stood as if petrified, recognizing the queen, then fell upon knees that the presence of Majesty had caused to quake. Elizabeth motioned him to her, and he approached, walking on his knees, in expectation of being instantly turned over to a yeoman of the guard. Hal himself remained in similar posture, which was the attitude Elizabeth required of all who addressed her.

"What know you of this young gentleman?" she asked the carpenter, in a tone that commanded like quietness in his manner of replying.

The fellow cringed and shook, begged huskily for mercy, and said that he had meant no harm; explained incoherently that the young gentleman, having fallen in with the carpenters when in his cups, had come with them to Whitehall in the belief that they were leading him to a drinking-place; that they had been curious to see his surprise when the porters, guards, or palace officers should confront him; that these functionaries had inattentively let him pass as one of the carpenters; that the carpenters had feared to disclaim him after having missed the proper moment for doing so. The fellow then began whimpering about his wife and eight children, who would starve if he were hanged or imprisoned. The queen cut him short by ordering that he and his comrades should say nothing of this young man's presence, as they valued their lives; hinted at dire penalties in case of any similar misdemeanor in future, and sent him back to his work.

"God's death!" she then said to Hal. "Watchful

porters and officers! I'll find those to blame, and they shall smart for their want of eyes. A glance at your hose and shoes, muddy though they be, would have made you out no workman. Yet perchance I shall have cause not to be sorry for their laxity this once. If it be that you are the man to serve me, I shall think you God-sent to my hand, for God he knows 'twas little like I should find in mine own palace a man not known there, and whom it should not seem possible I might ever have talked withal! Even had I sent for such an one, or had him brought to the palace for secret audience, there had needs been more trace left of my meeting him than there need be of my meeting you."

Hal perceived not why so absolute a monarch need conduct any matter darkly, or hide traces of her hand in it; but he said nothing, save that, if it might fall his happy lot to serve her, the gift from God would be to himself.

As for the queen, she had already made up her mind that he should serve her. It must be he, or no one. She had come to the garden from her privy council, with a certain secret act in her mind, an act possible to her if the right agent could be found; but in despair of finding in the given time such an agent, — one through whom her own instigation of the act could never be traced by the smallest circumstance. Here, as if indeed dropped from heaven, was a possible agent having that most needed, least expected, qualification. There need not remain the slightest credible evidence of his present interview with her. This qualification found so unexpectedly, without being sought, she was willing to risk that the young player possessed the other requisites, uncommon though they were. She believed he was loyal and chivalrous; therefore he would be as likely to keep her secret, at any hazard to himself, as to serve her with all zeal and with as much skill as he could command. By seeming to hold back her decision as to whether he might do her errand, she but gave that errand the more importance, and whetted his ambition to serve her in it.

"There is much to be said," replied the queen, "and small time to say it in. 'Tis already some minutes since I left my people without the hedge and came into this alley. They will presently think I am long meditating alone. They must not know I have seen you, or that you were here. So we must needs speak swiftly and quietly. As for those carpenters, who are all that know of your presence here, I have thrown that fellow into so great a fear, he and his mates will keep silence. Now heed. My privy council hath evidence of a certain gentleman's part in the conspiracy of your friends who abetted the Lord Essex. 'Tis evidence positive enough, and plenty enough, to take off his head, or twenty heads an he had them. He hath not the slightest knowledge that he is betrayed. 'Tis very like he sits at home, in the country, thinking himself secure, while the warrant is being writ for his arrest. The pursuivant to execute the warrant is to set out with men this afternoon. So much delay have I contrived to cause."

"Delay, your Majesty?" echoed Hal, thinking he might have wrongly heard.

"Delay," repeated Elizabeth, using for her extraordinary disclosures a quite ordinary tone. "I have delayed this messenger of the council for time to plan how the gentleman may escape before the arrest can be made."

She waited a moment, till Hal's look passed back from surprise to careful attention.

"You wonder that a queen, who may command all, should use secret means in such a matter. You wonder that I did not put my prohibition, at the outset, on proceedings against this gentleman. Or that I do not now order them stopped, by my sovereign right. Or that I do not openly pardon him, now or later. You do not see, young sir, that sometimes a monarch, though all-powerful, may have reason to sanction or even command a thing, yet have deep-hidden reason why the thing should be undone."

Hal bowed. He had little knowledge, or curiosity, regarding the mysteries of state affairs, and easily believed that the general weal might be promoted by the queen's outwardly authorizing a subject's arrest, and then secretly compassing his escape. And yet he might have known that a Tudor's motives in interfering with the natural course of justice were more likely to be private than public, and that a Tudor's circumstances must be unusual indeed to call for clandestine means, rather than an arbitrary mandate, for such interference. It was not till long afterward that, by putting two and two together, he formed the theory which it is perhaps as well to set forth now, at the opening of our history.

The Essex conspiracy was not against the person or supremacy of the queen, but against her existing government, which the plotters hoped to set aside by making her temporarily a prisoner and forcing her decrees. They avowed the greatest devotion to her Majesty's self. As a woman, she had little or no reason for bitter feelings against them. But the safety of the realm required that the principals should suffer. Yet she might have pardoned her beloved Essex, had she received the ring he sent her in claim of the promise of which it was the pledge.[17] But thinking him too proud even to ask the mercy he might have had of her, she let him die. As for his chief satellites, there were some for whom she cared nothing, some against whom there were old scores, and who might as well be dead or imprisoned as not, even were public policy out of the question. Southampton, for one, had offended her by marrying, and had later been a cause of sharp passages between her and Essex. But as to this mysterious gentleman, of whom she spoke to Master Marryott?

He was one of those who had contrived to get safe away from London, and who felicitated themselves that there existed no trace of their connection with the plot, but against whom evidence had eventually arisen in private testimony before the council. Of these men, it was decided by the council to make at least one capital example, and this particular gentleman was chosen, for his being a Catholic as well as a conspirator.

Now the fact seems to have been that Elizabeth, the woman, had softer recollections of this gentleman than Elizabeth, the queen, was fain to acknowledge to third parties. He was not alone in this circumstance, but he differed from Essex and other favored gentlemen in several particulars. Being a Catholic, he was not of the court. Once, many years before this March day, the queen, while hunting, sought refuge at his house from a sudden storm. She prolonged her stay on pretexts, and then kept him in attendance during one of her journeyings. Her association with him was conducted with unusual concealment. It was not violently broken off, nor carried on to satiety and natural death. It was merely interrupted and never resumed. Thus it remained sweet in her memory, took on the soft, idealizing tones that time gives, and was now cherished in her heart as an experience apart from, and more precious than, all other such. It was the one serene, perfect love-poem of her life. The others had been stormy, and mixed with a great deal of prose. This one might have been written by Mr. Edmund Spenser. And it was the dearer to her for its being a secret. No one had ever known of it but a tight-mouthed old manservant and a faithful maid of honor, the former now infirm, the latter dead.

She could not endure to mar this, her pet romance, by letting its hero die when it was in her power to save him. She had never put forth her hand, nor had he asked her to do so, to shield him from the smaller persecutions to which his religion had exposed him from neighbors and judges and county officers, and which had forced him to live most of the time an exile in France. But death was another matter, a catastrophe she liked not to think of as overtaking him through operations she could control; and this was none the less true though she had no hope of ever meeting him again.

Moreover, this lover had upon her affection one claim that others had forfeited: he had never married.[18] That alone entitled him at this time, in her eyes, to a consideration not merited by Essex or

Southampton. And, again, her fortitude had been so drawn upon in consigning Essex to the block, that she had not sufficient left to tolerate the sacrifice of this other sharer of her heart.

Now that fortitude had been greatly, though tacitly, admired by the lords to whom she wished to appear the embodiment of regal firmness, and she could not bring herself to confess to them that it was exhausted, or unequal to the next demand upon it. More than ever, in these later days, she desired to appear strong against her inner feelings, or indeed to appear quite above such inner feelings as she had too often shown toward her favorite gentlemen. That she, the Virgin Queen, leader of her people, conqueress of the great Armada, had entertained such feelings in the past, and been so foolish as to disclose them, was the greater reason why she now, when about to leave her final impression upon history, should seem proof against them. To refuse her sanction to the council's decision concerning this gentleman, when there was twofold political reason for that decision, and no political reason to interpose against it, would open the doors upon her secret. And she was as loath to expose her tenderly recollected love to be even suspected or guessed at, such was the ideal and sacred character it had taken in years of covert memory, as she was to be thought still prone to her old weakness. As for awaiting events and eventually saving the man by a pardon, such a course, in view of her having sanctioned the council's choice of him as an example, would disclose her as false to the council, and capricious beyond precedent, and would betray her secret as well."[19]

So here was one case in which she dared not arbitrarily oppose the council's proceeding, though her old lover's arrest meant his conviction, as sure as verdict was ever decided ere judge and jury sat, — as verdicts usually were in the treason trials of that blessed reign. For her peace as a woman, she must prevent that arrest. For her reputation as a queen, she must seem to favor it, and the prevention must be secret. One weakness, the vanity of strength and resolution, required that the indulgence of another weakness, undue tenderness of heart toward a particular object, should be covert. The queen's right hand must not know what the woman's left hand did. To get time for a plan, as she told Hal, she had requested that the pursuivant's men, while in quest of the gentleman, might bear letters to certain justices in his neighborhood; the preparation of these letters would delay, for a few hours, the departure of the warrant.

For her purpose she needed a man of courage, adroitness, and celerity; one who would be loyal to the secret reposed in him alone; one so out of court circles, so far from access to or by herself, that if he ever should betray her part in his mission none would believe him; a man who would take it on faith, as Hal really did, that deep state reasons dictated the nullification, secretly, of a proceeding granted openly, — for this strong queen would not have even the necessary confidant, any more than the lords of the council, suspect this weak woman.

"The man who is my servant in this," went on the queen, "must seem to act entirely for himself, not for me. There must be no evidence of his having served me; so he will never receive the credit of this mission for his sovereign, save in that sovereign's thoughts alone."

"Where else should he seek it, your Majesty?" replied Hal, brought to this degree of unselfish chivalry by the influence of her presence.

"Where else, truly?" echoed the queen, with a faint smile. "And he must never look to me for protection, should he find himself in danger of prison or death, in consequence of this service. Indeed, if pressure move him to say 'twas I commissioned him, I shall declare it a lie of malice or of deep design, meant to injure me."

"Your Majesty shall not be put to that shift, an I be your happy choice for the business," said Hal, thrilling more and more devotedly to the task as it appeared the more perilous and rewardless.

"You will be required to go from London," continued the queen, forgetting her pretence that he was not yet certainly her choice for the errand, "and to give your friends good reason for your absence."

"'Twill be easy," replied the player. "Our company goes travelling next week. I can find necessity for preceding them. One Master Crowe can play my parts till I fall in with them again."

"Even this gentleman," resumed the queen, after a moment's thought, and a consultation with pride and prudence, "must not know whom you obey in saving him. Your knowledge of his danger must seem to have come through spy work, or treachery in the palace, and your zeal for his safety must appear to spring from your friendship for the Essex party. The gentleman's mansion is near Welwyn, in Hertfordshire. He is a knight, one Sir Valentine Fleetwood."

Hal suppressed a cry. "Why, then," he said, "I can truly appear to act for myself in saving him. He is my friend, my benefactor; his father saved my grandfather's life in the days of papistry. I shall not be put to the invention of false reasons for saving Sir Valentine. There is reason enough in friendship and gratitude. I knew not he was back in England."

"That is well," said Elizabeth, checking a too hearty manifestation of her pleasure at the coincidence. "Now hear what you shall do. The pursuivant who is to apprehend him will ride forth this afternoon at about three o' the clock, with a body of men. You must set out earlier, arrive at Fleetwood house before them, warn Sir Valentine that they are coming, persuade him to fly, whether he will or no, and in every possible manner aid and hasten his safe departure from the country."

Hal bowed. His look betrayed some disappointment, as if the business were neither as difficult nor as dangerous as he had looked for.

The queen smiled.

"You think it a tame and simple matter," she said. "A mere business of fast riding 'twixt London and Welwyn, and thence to a seaport. But allow for the unexpected, young sir, which usually befalleth! Suppose impediments hinder you, as they hinder many on shorter journeys. Or suppose Sir Valentine be not at home when you arrive, and require seeking lest he by chance fall in with the pursuivant ere you meet him. Suppose he be not of a mind to fly the country, but doubt your warning, or choose to stay and risk trial rather than invite outlawry and confiscation. Suppose, in aiding him, you encounter the pursuivant and his men.[20] 'Twill be your duty to resist them to the utmost, even with your life. And should you be overcome and taken, you know what are the penalties of resisting officers on the queen's business, and of giving aid to her enemies. This business will make you as much a traitor, by statute, as Sir Valentine himself. Remember, if you be taken I shall not interfere in your behalf. It shall be that I know naught of you, and that I hold your act an impudent treason against myself, and call for your lawful death. So think not 'tis some holiday riding I send you on; and go not lightly as 'twere a-maying. Be ready for grave dangers and obstructions. Look to't ye be not taken! Perchance your own safety may yet lie in other countries for a time, ere all is done. Look for the unexpected, I tell you."

"I shall be heedful, your majesty. I crave your pardon, — 'tis shame I must confess it, — there will be horses to obtain, and other matters; I lack means —"

"By God's light, 'tis well I came by a purse-full this morning, and forgetfully bore it with me, having much on my mind," said Elizabeth, detaching a purse from her girdle and handing it to Hal. "I'm not wont of late to go so strong in purse." Pour these yellow pieces into your pocket — no need to count — and leave but two or three to make some noise withal." When Hal had obeyed her, she took back the purse and replaced it at her girdle. "Use what you need in the necessary costs; supply Sir Valentine an he require money, and let the rest be payment to yourself. Nay, 'twill be small enough, God's name! Yet I see no more reward for you — until all be smoothly done, and time hath passed, and you may find new access to me in other circumstance. Then I shall remember, and find way of favoring you."

Hal thereupon had vague, distant visions of himself as a gentleman pensioner, and as a knight, and as otherwise great; but he said only:

"The trust you place in me is bounteous reward, your Majesty!"

To which her Majesty replied:

"Bid yon carpenter lead you from the garden by private ways, that you may pass out as you entered, in the guise of a workman. Lose no time, thenceforth, — and God bless thee, lad!"

Hal was in the seventh heaven. She had actually thee'd him! And now she held out her hand, which he, on his knees, touched with reverential lips. It was a shapely, beautiful hand, even to the last of the queen's days; and a shapely, beautiful thing it was to remain in Hal's mental vision to the last of his. In a kind of dream he stepped back, bowing, to the alley's end. When he raised his eyes, the queen had turned, and was speeding toward the other end of the alley. A March wind was following her, between the high hedgerows, disturbing two or three tiny twigs that had lain in the frozen path.[22]

At that moment Hal counted his life a small thing

save where it might serve her; while she, who had read him through in five minutes, was thanking her stars for the miraculous timely advent of an agent so peculiarly suited to so peculiar a service, — a youth of some worldly experience, yet with all those chivalrous illusions which make him the greedier of a task as it is the more dangerous, the more zealous in it as it offers the less material reward. The romantic sophistries that youth cherishes may be turned to great use by those who know how to employ them. Indeed, may not the virtue of loyalty and blind devotion have been an invention of ingenious rulers, for their own convenience? May not that of womanworship be an invention of subtly clever women themselves, when women were wisely content with being worshipped, and were not ambitious of being elbowed and pushed about in the world's business; when they were satisfied to be the divinities, not the competitors, of men? Elizabeth knew that this player's head, heart, and hand were now all hers for the service engaged; and that by entrusting him with a large amount in gold, in advance, she but increased his sense of obligation to perform her errand without failing in a single point.

As he passed Charing Cross and proceeded eastward through the Strand, Hal became aware of the pains caused by his sleeping out-doors in March weather, and of the headache from last night's wine. In his interview with the queen, he had been unconscious of these. But he foresaw sufficient bodily activity to rid himself of them, with the aid of a copious warming draught and of a breakfast. He obtained the warming draught at the first tavern within Temple Bar, which was none other than the Devil. A drawer recognized him, despite the 'prentice's coat and cap, — no one who knew Master Marryott could be much surprised at his having got into any possible strange attire in some nocturnal prank, — and notified the landlord, who thereupon restored to Hal the rapier taken away the previous night. From the Devil tavern, Hal went to three or four shops farther in Fleet Street, and when he emerged from the last of these he wore a dull green cloth cloak, brown-lined, over his brown velvet doublet; a featherless brown hat of ample brim on his head, and high riding-boots to cover the nether part of his brown silk trunk-hose.

He had already looked his errand in the face, and made some plan for dealing with it. As he would be no match for a band of highway robbers, should he fall in with such between London and Welwyn, he must have at least one stout attendant. Fortunately, Paul's Walk, the place in which to obtain either man or woman for any service or purpose whatever, lay in his way to his lodging, where he must go before leaving London. He hastened through Ludgate, with never a glance at the prisoners whining through the iron grates their appeals for charity; and into Paul's Churchyard, and strode through the southern entrance of the mighty cathedral, making at once for the middle aisle.

It was the fashionable hour for the Paul's walkers, — about noon, — and the hubbub of a vast crowd went up to the lofty arches overhead. The great minster walk, with its column on which advertisements were hung, its column around which servingmen stood waiting to be hired, its other particular spots given over by custom to particular purposes, was to London at midday what the interior of the Exchange was by candle-light, — a veritable place of lounging, gossiping, promenading, trading, begging, pimping, pocket-picking, purse-cutting, everything. Hal threaded a swift way through the moving, chattering, multi-colored crowd, with an alert eye for the manner of man he wanted. Suddenly he felt a pull at his elbow; and turned instantly to behold a dismal attempt at gaiety on the large-boned red face of Captain Bottle. Beneath his forced grin, old Kit was in sadly sorry countenance, which made his attire look more poor and ragged than usual.

"What, old heart!" cried Kit. "Thou'rt alive, eh? Bones of Mary, I thought thee swallowed up by some black night-walking dragon in Cow Lane this morning!"

"We were together last night, I think," said Hal, not with positive certainty.

"Together, i' faith, till by my cursing and hard breathing I killed in mine ears the sound of thy steps, so I could not follow thee. Ah, Hal, there was the foul fiend's hand in the separating of us! For, being alone, and sitting down to rest me in the street, without Newgate, what should happen but I should fall asleep, and my purse be cut ere I waked? Old Kit hath not e'en a piece of metal left, to mimic the sound of coin withal!" Old Kit's look was so blue at this that Hal knew he was truly penniless, though whether the loss of his money had been as he related it, was a question for which Hal had no answer. The captain's eyes were already inclining toward that part of Hal's costume where his money was commonly bestowed.

"This evil town is plainly too much for thy rustical innocence, Kit," said Hal. "You need a country change. Come with me for a few days. Don't stare. I have private business, and require a man like thee. There's meat, drink, and beds in it, while it lasts; some fighting maybe, and perchance a residue of money when costs are paid. If there be, we shall divide equally. Wilt follow me?"

"To the other side of the round world, boy! And though old Kit be something of a liar and guzzler, and a little of a cheater and boaster, thou'lt find him as faithful as a dog, and as companionable a rascal as ever lived!"

"Then take this money, and buy me two horses in Smithfield, all equipped; and meet me with them at two o'clock, in St. John's Street, close without the bar. But first get thyself dinner, and a warm cloak to thy back. Haste, old dog o' war! There will be swift going for us, maybe, ere many suns set!"

The two left St. Paul's together by the north door, Bottle going on northward toward the Newgate,[23] Hal turning eastward toward St. Helen's, where he would refresh himself with a bath and food, and tell Mr. Shakespeare of news given him by a court scrivener in drunken confidence; of an imperative obligation to go and warn a friend in danger; of money won in dicing; of a willingness to resign his parts to Gil Crowe, and of his intention to rejoin the players at the first opportunity, wherever they might be.

As he turned out Bishopsgate Street, he thought how clear his way lay before him, and smiled with benignant superiority to his simple task. And then suddenly, causing his smile to fade a little, came back to him the words of the queen, "Allow for the unexpected, young sir, which usually befalleth!"

CHAPTER IV.

THE UNEXPECTED.

> "The affair cries haste,
> And speed must answer it." — *Othello.*

At two o'clock that afternoon, — it was Tuesday, the third day of March, — Master Marryott and Capt. Christopher Bottle rode northward from Smithfield bars, in somewhat different aspect and mood from those in which they had gone through their adventure in the same neighborhood the previous night. They were well mounted; for Kit Bottle was not the man to be gulled by the jinglers of the Smithfield horse-market, and knew, too well for his own good reputation, how to detect every trick by which the jockeys palmed off their jades on buyers who judged only by appearances.

They were fitly armed, too; for Hal, before rejoining the captain, had procured pistols as reinforcements to his rapier and dagger, and Kit had so far exceeded instructions as to do likewise. The captain as yet knew not what Hal's mission was, and he was too true a soldier to exhibit any curiosity, if he felt any. But there was always a possibility of use for weapons, in travelling in those days; even on the much-frequented road from London to St. Albans ("as common as the way between St. Albans and London," said Poins, of Doll Tearsheet), in which thoroughfare, until he should turn out beyond Barnet, Hal's course lay. It was a highway that, not far out of London, became like all other roads of the time narrow and rutty, often a mere ditch below the level of the fields, woods, or commons, at either side; rarely flanked, as in later times, by hedges, walls, or fences of any kind; passing by fewer houses, and through smaller villages, than it is now easy to imagine its doing.

On this, as on every English road, most passenger travel was by horseback or afoot, although the great, had their coaches, crude and slow-moving. Most transportation of goods was by pack-horse, the carriers going in numerous company for safety; though huge, lumbering, covered stage-wagons had already appeared on certain chief highways, with a record of something like two miles an hour. The royal post for the bearing of letters was in a primitive and uncertain state. Travelling by post was unknown, in the later sense of the term: such as it was, it was a luxury of the great, who had obvious means of arranging for relays of horses; and of state messengers, who might press horses for the queen's service. When ordinary men were in haste, and needed fresh horses, they might buy them, or trade for them, or hire them from carriers, or from stable-keepers where such existed. But the two animals obtained by Bottle in Smithfield, though neither as shapely nor as small as Spanish jennets, were quite sufficient for the immediate purpose, — the bearing of their riders, without stop, to Welwyn.

Islington and Highgate were passed without incident, and Hal, while soothed in his anxiety to perform his mission without a hitch, began to think again that the business was too easy to be interesting. As a young gentleman of twenty-two who had read "The Faerie Queen" for the romance and not for the allegory, he would have liked some opportunity to play the fighting knight in service of his queen. On Finchley Common he looked well about, half in dread, half in hope; whereupon Captain Bottle, as taking up a subject apropos, began to discourse upon highway robbers. From considering the possibilities of a present encounter with them, he fell to discussing their profession in a business light.

"An there must be vile laws to ruin gentlemen withal, and hard peace to take the bread out of true soldiers' mouths, beshrew me but bold robbing on the highway is choicer business than a parson's, or a lawyer's, or a lackey's in some great house, or even coney-catching in the taverns! When I was put to it to get my beef and clary one way or another, I stayed in London, thinking to keep up my purse by teaching fence; but 'tis an overcrowded vocation, and the rogues that can chatter the most Italian take all the cream. So old Kit must needs betake himself to a gentlemanly kind of gull-catching, never using the false dice till the true went against him, look you; nor bullying a winner out of the stakes when they could be had peaceably; and always working alone, disdaining to fellow with rascally gangs. But often I have sighed that I did not as Rumney did, — he that was mine ancient in the campaigns in Spain and Ireland. When the nation waxed womanish, and would have no more of war, Rumney, for love of the country, took to the highways, and I have heard he hath thrived well about Sherwood forest and toward Yorkshire. 'Twas my choice of a town life hindered me being his captain on the road as I had been in the wars. I hear he calleth himself captain now! Though he puts his head oftener into the noose than I, and runs more risk of sword and pistol, his work is the worthier of a soldier and gentleman for that. Yet I do not call Rumney gentleman, neither! A marvellous scurvy rogue! But no coward. Would that thy business might take us so far as we should fall in with the rascal! I should well like to drink a gallon of sack with the rascally cur, in memory of old times, or to stab him in the paunch for a trick he did me about a woman in the Low Countries!"

Finchley Common was crossed without threat of danger, the only rogues met being of the swindling, begging, feigning, pilfering order, all promptly recognized and classified by the experienced captain. Nor did Whetston or Barnet or Hatfield, or the intervening country, yield any event, save that a clock struck six, and the day — gray enough at best — was on the wane when they passed through Hatfield. They had made but five miles an hour, the road, though frozen, being uneven and difficult, and Hal assuming that the pursuivant, ignorant of a plan to forewarn Sir Valentine, would not greatly hasten. He relied on the hour's start he had taken out of London, and he saved his horses to meet any demand for speed that might suddenly arise. At the worst, if the officer and his men came up behind him, he could increase his pace and outride them to Welwyn. And thus it was that he let no northbound riders pass him, and that when such riders, of whatever aspect, appeared in the distant rear, he spurred forward sufficiently to leave them out of sight.

On the hill, two or three miles beyond Hatfield, he stopped and looked back over the lower country, but could make out no group of horsemen in the gathering darkness. His destination was now near at hand, and he was still unsettled between opposite feelings, — satisfaction that his errand seemed certain of accomplishment, regret that there seemed no prospect of narrow work by which he might a little distinguish himself in his own eyes. The last few miles he rode in silence, Bottle having ceased prattling and become meditative under the influence of nightfall.

It was seven o'clock when they rode across the brook into close view of Welwyn church at the left of the road, and a few minutes later when they drew up before the wall in front of Fleetwood house, — of which Hal knew the location, through visits in former years, — and began to pound on the barred gate with their weapons, and to call "Ho, within!"

The mansion beyond the wall was a timbered one, its gables backed by trees. It had no park, and its wall enclosed also a small orchard at the rear, and a smaller courtyard at the front. At one side of the gate was a porter's lodge, but this was at present vacant, or surely the knocking on the wooden gate would have brought forth its occupant. It seemed as if the house was deserted, and Hal had a sudden inward sense of unexpected obstacle, perhaps insuperable, in his way. His heart beat a little more rapidly, until Kit, having ridden to where he could see the side of the house, reported a light in the side window of a rear chamber. Hal thereupon increased his hallooing, with some thought of what might occur if the pursuivants should come up ere he got admission.

At length there appeared a moving nebula of light amidst the darkness over the yard; it approached the gate; steps were heard on the walk within; finally a little wicket was opened in the gate, and a long, bearded, sour face was visible in the light of a lanthorn held up by its owner.

"Who is it disturbeth the night in this manner?" asked a nasal voice, in a tone of complaint and reproof.

"'Tis I, Master Underhill," spoke Hal, from his horse, "Master Harry Marryott, Sir Valentine's friend. I must see Sir Valentine without a moment's delay," and he started to dismount.

"I know not if thou canst see Sir Valentine without delay, or at all whatsoever," replied the man of dismal countenance. His face had the crow's feet and the imprinted frown of his fifty years, and there was some gray on his bare head.

"Not see him!" blurted out Hal. "What the devil — open me the gate this instant or I'll teach thee a lesson! Dost hear, Anthony?"

"Yield not to thy wrath nor call upon the foul fiend, Master Marryott," said Anthony, severely. "I shall go decently and in order, and learn if thou mayst be admitted." And he leisurely closed the wicket to return to the house.

Hal could scarce contain himself for anger. Being now afoot he called after the man, and hammered on the gate, but with no effect of recalling or hastening him.

"A snivelling Puritan, or I'm a counterfeit soldier!" observed Kit Bottle, in a tone of contempt and detestation.[24]

"Ay," said Hal, "and all the worse whiner because, out of inherited ties, he serveth a Catholic master. The old groaner,— that he should put me to this delay when Sir Valentine's life is at stake!"

This was Hal's first intimation to Kit of the real nature of his business. The captain received it without comment, merely asking if he should dismount.

"No," said Hal, tying his own horse to the gate; "but when I am admitted, ride you back to the village, and listen for the sound of hoofs from the direction of London; if you hear such, come swiftly back, hallooing at the top of thy voice, and get off thy horse, and hold him ready for another to mount in thy stead. A hundred curses on that Tony Underhill! He hath been Sir Valentine's steward so long, he dareth any impertinence. And yet he never stayed me at the gate before! And his grave look when he said he knew not if I might see Sir Valentine! 'Twas a more solemn face than even he is wont to wear. Holy Mary! can it be that they are here already,— that they have come before me?"

"An it be men in quest of Sir Valentine, you mean," said Kit, who was of quick divination, " where be their horses? They would scarce stable them, and make a visit. Nor would all be so quiet and dark."

"And yet he looked as something were amiss," replied Hal, but partly reassured.

The faint mist of light appeared again, the deliberate steps were heard, and this time the gate was unbarred. and slowly drawn a little space open. In the lanthorn's light was seen the spare, tall figure that went with the long, gloomy face.

"I will conduct thee to Sir Valentine," said Anthony. Hal stepped forward with an exclamation of relief and pleasure, and Kit Bottle instantly started his horse back toward the village.

Hal followed the Puritan steward through a porched doorway, across a hall, up a staircase that ascended athwart the rear, and thence along a corridor, to the last door on the side toward the back of the house. Anthony softly opened this door.

Hal entered a chamber lighted by two candles on a table, and containing in one corner a large high-posted bed. On the table, among other things, lay an ivory crucifix. A plainly dressed gentleman sat on a chair between the table and the bed. To this gentleman, without casting a look at his face, Hal bowed respectfully, and began, "I thank God, Sir Valentine —"

"Nay, sir," answered the gentleman, quietly, as if to prevent some mistake; and Hal, looking up, perceived that this was not Sir Valentine, but a pale, watchful-looking man, with fiery eyes; while a voice, strangely weakened, came from the bed:

"Thou'rt welcome, Harry."

"What!" cried Hal, striding to the bed. "Sir Valentine, goest thou to bed so early?"

"Ay," replied Sir Valentine, motionless on his back, "and have been abed these two days, with promise from my good physician here of getting up some six days hence or so."

"Thou'lt not move for another week, at least, Sir Valentine," said the physician, the gentleman whom Hal first addressed.

"'Tis a sword wound got in a quarrel, Harry," explained Sir Valentine, feebly, and paused, out of breath, looking for a reply.

But Hal stood startled and speechless. Not move for a week, and the state officer likely to arrive in an hour! "And in every possible manner aid and hasten his departure from the country," her Majesty had said; and Hal had taken her money, and by his promise, by her trust in him, by every consideration that went to the making of a gentleman, a man of honor, or an honest servant, stood bound to carry out her wish.

The errand was not to be so simple, after all.

CHAPTER V.

THE PLAYER PROVES HIMSELF A GENTLEMAN.

"Warrants and pursuivants! Away! warrants and pursuivants!" — The Wise Woman of Hogsdon.

SIR VALENTINE FLEETWOOD was a thin man, with regular features and sunken cheeks, his usually sallow face now flushed with fever. His full round beard was gray, but there were yet streaks of black in his flowing hair.

"Sir Valentine," Hal began, suppressing his excitement, "there is private news I must make known to you instantly." And he cast a look at the doctor, who frowned, and at Anthony, who remained motionless near the door, with his lanthorn still in hand, as if expecting that he should soon have to escort Hal out again.

"Sir Valentine is not in a condition to hear —" broke in the doctor, in a voice of no loudness, but of much latent authority.

"But this is of the gravest import —" interrupted Hal, and was himself interrupted by Sir Valentine, who had gathered breath for speech.

"Nay, Harry, it may wait. I am in no mind for business."

"But it requireth immediate action," said Hal, who would have told the news itself, but that he desired first the absence of the doctor and the steward.

"Then 'twill serve nothing to be told," said Sir Valentine, lapsing into his former weakness, and with a slight shade of annoyance upon his face. "As thou see'st, boy, I am in no state for action. A plague upon the leg, I can't stir it half an inch."

"But —" cried Harry.

The physician rose, and Anthony, with an outraged look, took a deprecatory step toward Harry.

"No more, young sir!" quoth the physician, imperatively. "Sir Valentine's life —"

"But that is what I have come to speak of," replied Hal, in some dudgeon. "Zounds, sir, do you know what you hinder? There are concerns you wot not of!"

"Tut, Master Marryott," said Sir Valentine. "As for my life, 'tis best in the doctor's hands; and for concerns, I have none now but my recovery. Not for myself, the blessed Mary knoweth! But for others' sakes, in another land. Oh, to think I should be drawn into an unwilling quarrel, and get this plagued hurt! And mine opponent — hast heard yet how Mr. Hazlehurst fares, Anthony?"

"No, your honor," said the Puritan; but he let his glance fall to the floor as he spoke, and seemed to suffer an inward groan as of self-reproach. Sir Valentine could not see him for the bed-curtains.

"'Tis a lesson to shun disputes, boy," said Sir Valentine, to Hal. "Here were my old neighbor's son, young Mr. Hazlehurst, and myself, bare acquaintances, 'tis true, but wishing each other no harm. And two days ago, meeting where the roads crossed, and a foolish question of right of way occurring, he must sputter out hot words at me, and I must chide him as becometh an elder man; and ere I think of consequences, his sword is out, and I have much to do to defend myself! And the end is, each is carried off by servants, with blood flowing; my wound in the groin, his somewhere in the breast. I would fain know how he lies toward recovery! You should have taken pains to inquire, Anthony."

"Sir Valentine," said the physician, "thou art talking too much. Master Marryott, you see how things stand. If you bear Sir Valentine friendship, you have no choice but to go away, sith you have paid your respects. He would have it that you be admitted. Pray, abuse not his courtesy."

"But, sir, that which I must tell him concerns—"

"I'll hear naught that concerns myself," said Sir Valentine, with the childish stubbornness of illness. "Tell me of thine own self, Harry. 'Tis years since I saw thee last, and in that time I've had no word of thee. Didst go to London, and stay there? My letter, it seems, availed thee nothing. How livest thou? What is thy place in the world?"

Hal decided to throw the physician and Anthony off guard by coming at his news indirectly. So he answered Sir Valentine:

"I am a stage player."

Sir Valentine opened eyes and mouth in amazement; he gasped and stared.

"A stage player!" he echoed, horrified. "Thy father's son a stage player! A Marryott a stage player! Sir, sir, you have fallen low! Blessed Mary, what are the times? A gentleman turn stage player!"

Old Anthony had drawn back from Hal, vastly scandalized, his eyes raised heavenward as if for divine protection from contamination; and the physician gazed, in a kind of passionless curiosity.

"A stage player," said Hal, firmly, having taken his resolution, "may prove himself still a gentleman. He may have a gentleman's sense of old friendship shown, and a gentleman's honesty to repay it, as I have when I come to save thee from the privy council's men riding hither to arrest thee for high treason! And a gentleman's authority, as I have when I bid this doctor and this Anthony to aid thy escape, and betray or hinder it not, on pain of deeper wounds than thine!" And Hal, having drawn his sword, stood with his back to the doorway.

Sir Valentine himself was the first to speak; he did so with quiet gravity:

"Art quite sure of this, Harry?"

"Quite, Sir Valentine. We stage players consort with possessors of state secrets, now and then. The warrant for thy apprehension was signed this day. A council's pursuivant was to leave London at three o'clock, with men to assure thy seizure. I, bearing in mind my family's debt to thine, and mine own to thee, started at two, to give thee warning. More than that, I swear to save thee. This arrest, look you, means thy death; from what I heard, I perceive thy doom is prearranged; thy trial is to be a pretence."

"I can believe that!" said Sir Valentine, with a grim smile.

"'Tis not my fault that these two have been let into the secret," said Hal, indicating the physician and Anthony.

"And it shall not be to Sir Valentine's disadvantage, sir, speaking for myself," said the physician.

"His honor knows whether I may be trusted," said Anthony, swelling with haughty consciousness of his fidelity, as if to outdo the physician, toward whom his looks were always oblique and of a covert antipathy.

"I know ye are my friends," said Sir Valentine. "I could have spoken for you. But what is to be done? 'Tis true I cannot move. Think it no whimsy of the doctor's, Harry. Blessed Mary, send heaven to my help! Think not, Harry, 'tis for myself I moan. Thou knowest not how my matters stand abroad. There are those awaiting me in France, dependent on me —"

"And to France we must send you safe, Sir Valentine!" said Harry. "You could not be supported on horseback, I suppose?"

The physician looked amazed at the very suggestion, and Sir Valentine smiled gloomily and shook his head.

"Or in a coach, an one were to be had?" Hal went on.

"'Twould be the death of him in two miles," said the physician. "Moreover, where is a coach to be got in time?"

"Is there no hiding-place near, to which you might be carried?" asked Hal, of Sir Valentine, knowing how most Catholic houses were provided in those days.

Sir Valentine exchanged looks with the physician and Anthony, then glanced toward the wall of the chamber, and answered:

"There is a space 'twixt yon panelling and the outer woodwork of the house. It hath air through hidden openings to the cracked plaster without; and is close to the chimney, for warmth. In a hasty search it would be passed over, — there is good proof of that. But this pursuivant, not finding me, would sound every foot of wall in the house. He would, eventually, detect the hollowness of the panelling there, and the looseness of the boards that hide the entrance. Or, if he did not that, he and his men would rouse the county, and occupy the house in expectation of my secret return; they would learn of my quarrel and wound, and would know I must be hid somewhere near. While they remained in the house, searching the neighborhood with sheriff's and magistrate's men, keeping watch on every one, how should I be supplied and cared for in that hole? It would soon become, not my hiding-place, but my grave, — for which 'tis truly of the right dimensions!"

"But if, not finding you in the first search, they should suppose you gone elsewhere?" said Hal, for sheer need of offering some hope, however wild.

"Why, they would still make the house the centre of their search, as I said."

"But if they were made to believe you had fled afar?"

"They would soon learn of my wound. It hath been bruited about the neighborhood. They would know it made far flight impossible."

"But can they learn how bad thy wound is? Might it not be a harmless scratch?"

"It might, for all the neighborhood knoweth of it," put in Anthony; and the physician nodded.

"Then, if they had reason to think you far fled?" pursued Hal.

"Why," replied Sir Valentime, "some of them would go to make far hunt; others would wait for my possible return, and to search the house for papers. And the constables and officers of the shire would be put on the watch for me."

"Need the search for papers lead to the discovery of yon hiding-place?"

"No. The searchers would find papers in my study to reward a search, though none to harm any but myself. The other gentlemen concerned are beyond earthly harm."

"But," quoth Hal, the vaguest outlines of a plan beginning to take shape before him, "were the pursuivant, on arriving at your gate, to be checked by certain news that you had fled in a particular direction, would he not hasten off forthwith on your track, with all his men? Would he take time for present search or occupancy of your house, or demand upon constable's or sheriff's men? And if your track were kept ever in view before him, would he not continue upon it to the end? And suppose some of his men were left posted in thy house.

These would be few, three or four at most, seeing that the main force were close upon thy trail. These three or four would not look for thy return; they would look for thy taking by their comrades first. They would keep no vigil, and being without their leader, — who would head the pursuing party, — they would rest content with small search for papers; they would rather be industrious in searching thy wine-cellar and pantry. Thus you could be covertly attended from this chamber, by nurse or doctor, acquainted with the house. And when you were able to move, these men, being small in force, might be overpowered; or, being careless, they might be eluded. And thus you might pass out of the house by night, and into a coach got ready by the doctor, and so to the sea; and the men in thy house none the wiser, and those upon thy false track still chasing farther away."

"Harry, Harry," said Sir Valentine, in a kindly but hopeless tone, "thou speak'st dreams, boy!"

"Ne'ertheless," said Hal, "is't not as I say, an the false chase were once contrived?"

"Why," put in the physician, "that is true enough. Send me away the pursuivant and most of his men, and let those who stay think Sir Valentine thus pursued, and I'll warrant the looking to Sir Valentine's wants, and his removal in nine days or so. Nine days he will need, not an hour less; and yet another day, to make sure; that is ten. But should the pursuers on the false chase discover their mistake, and return ere ten days be gone, all were lost. E'en suppose they could be tricked by some misguidance at the gate, which is not conceivable, they'd not go long on their vain hunt without tangible track to follow. Why, Master Marryott, they'd come speeding back in two hours!"

"But if a man rode ahead, and left tangible track, by being seen and noted in the taverns and highways? He need but keep up the chase, by not being caught; the pursuivant may be trusted to pick up all traces left of his travels. These messengers of the council are skilled in tracing men, when there are men to leave traces."

"What wild prating is this?" cried Sir Valentine, somewhat impatiently. "I know thou mean'st kindly, Harry, but thy plan is made of moonshine. Let a man, or a hundred men, ride forth and leave traces, what shall make these officers think the man is I?"

"They shall see him leave thy gate in flight when they come up. And, as for his leading them a chase, he will be on one of thy horses, an there be time to make one ready, otherwise on mine, — in either case, on a fresher horse than theirs. So he shall outride them at the first dash, and then, one way and another, lead them farther and farther, day after day."

"But, man, man! Wilder and wilder!" exclaimed Sir Valentine, as if he thought himself trifled with. "Know you not their leader will be one that is well acquainted with my face?"

"So much the better," cried Hal; "for then he will take oath it is you he sees departing!"

"I he sees departing?" echoed Sir Valentine, and began to look at Hal apprehensively, as if in suspicion of madness, a suspicion in which the physician and Anthony seemed to join. "I departing, when I am in yon narrow hole between timbers? I departing, when I am hurt beyond power of motion, as their leader will doubtless learn at the village alehouse, on inquiring if I be at home."

"Yes, sir," said Hal, "he shall think it is you, and the more so if he have heard of your wound. For, in the lanthorn's light, as he comes in seeing distance, he shall perceive that you sit your horse as a lame man doth. And that thy head is stiffly perched, thy shoulders drawn back, in the manner peculiar to them. And that thy left elbow is thrust out as is its wont. And that thy hat, as usual, shades thy brow thus. But more than all else, sir, that thy face is of little breadth, thy beard gray and round, as they have been these many years."

And Hal, having realized in attitude each previous

point in his description, took from his pocket the false beard that had lain there since the first performance of "Hamlet," and tying it on his face, which he had thinned by drawing in his cheeks, stood transformed into the living semblance of Sir Valentine Fleetwood.

CHAPTER VI.

AND THE GENTLEMAN PROVES HIMSELF A PLAYER.

"Let the world think me a bad counterfeit, if I cannot give him the slip at an instant." — Every Man in His Humor.

THERE was a moment's silence in the chamber. Then —

"Play-acting!" muttered Anthony, with a dark frown, followed by an upturning of the eyes.

"Thou'lt pass, my son!" said the physician, his eyes alight with approval and new-found hope. "Truly, I think he will, Sir Valentine, — with a touch of the scissors to shape his beard more like!" And he took up from the table a pair of scissors, doubtless used in cutting bandages for the wounded man, and striding toward Master Marryott, applied them with careful dexterity. "Behold," said he, when he had finished. "Thou'lt surely fool them in the lanthorn's light and the haste. By close work thou mightst truly lead them off in the night, but in daylight the falseness of thy beard may easily be seen, for the strings 'tis tied withal."

"But the officers shall not see my face after the

starting. I'll not stay near enough to them for that. 'Tis by word of innkeepers and townspeople and country-folk, of my passage through the country, that I shall be traced. And mark: save to officers that keep note of Catholics, Sir Valentine is scarce known ten miles hence, so much hath he lived abroad. And I'm not known out of London and Oxfordshire. So who's to set the pursuers right?"

"But what then?" said the physician. "Those same innkeepers and such can but report the passage of a man with a false beard, at best. More like, they will cause thy detention as a questionable person, till the council's men come up to thee. Either way, the pursuivant will see the trick, and speed hotfoot back to this house."

"Why, look you," said Hal, "early in the morning I will hastily enter some inn, my face muffled as for cold. There, in a private chamber, I will take off the beard, and come forth as if I had but shaved. And so report will remain of me, that I came bearded and departed shaven; and the men in pursuit will take this very shaving as a means of disguise. They'll be the more convinced I'm the man."

"Ay, but there you risk their losing trace of you; for the absence of the beard will show your youth, and make you at odds with their description of you."

"Why, the loss of a beard will sometimes give an elder man a look of youth. And the same companion shall ride with me,— he that now keeps watch without. By the description of him as my attendant, 'twill be known I am the gentleman that rode from Fleetwood house. And to make my trace the more certain, let a second accompany me,— one of Sir Valentine's servants that live here constantly and are better known than their master is. And he shall also guide me on the roads hereabouts, in my first dash from the gates; for, look you, there will be fleet riding for an hour or two!"

"Thou hearest, Sir Valentine," said the physician, turning to the wounded gentleman.

"Ay," replied the knight, "and being weak of breath, have waited for a breach to put my word in. 'Tis all madness, this ye talk of! E'en were't possible, I should let no man risk life for me as this young gentleman offereth. Why, lad, they'd catch thee, of a surety —"

"I make question of that, Sir Valentine," quoth Hal.

"Some time or other, they would," said the knight. "And thou knowest the penalty of aiding the escape of one accused of treason! The act itself is treason."

"And what if I have already incurred penalties as grievous, on mine own account? And what if I have some running away to do, for myself? May not one flight suffice for both? While I lead these men on a false chase from thee, I but put distance 'twixt myself and danger," said Hal, with less regard for truth than for leading Sir Valentine into his plans.

"What, Harry?" cried Sir Valentine. "Is it true? But still, thou'rt yet in good way to make thine own escape. To wait for these officers, and to keep them at thy tail, will doubly imperil thee. Thou shalt not multiply thine own danger for me, — by Mary, thou shalt not!"

"But I mean not to be caught, Sir Valentine. Have I no skill, no hardihood? Shall youth serve nothing, and strong arms, and hard legs? I will elude them, I swear! But first I will keep them on my tail time enough for thy removal. Ten days, the doctor said. An I lead off these fellows a five days' ride from Fleetwood house, straight north toward Scotland, and then drop them, 'twill take five days for them to ride back. And there, of but five days' work on my part, come the ten days' delay thou needest!"

"But thou canst not do it, Harry," persisted Sir Valentine, while the physician silently paced the floor in thought, and the Puritan looked on with outward indifference. "Why, bethink you! To escape thy pursuers, and yet not to let them lose trace of thee; to outride them ever, yet never ride too far away from them; to elude them, yet not to drop them; this for five days, and then to break off the track and leave them baffled, at the last! 'Tis impossible!"

"'Tis a glorious kind of sport, Sir Valentine!" cried Hal, his eyes aglow. "'Tis a game worth playing! Nay, 'tis a stage play, wherein I undertake to act the part of Sir Valentine Fleetwood in flight and disguise! Ods-body, I shall prove I am a player! Thou shalt not refuse, Sir Valentine! Do as thou wilt, I am for the gate, and when the officers come up, the devil seize me an I do not lead them off again!"

"Sir Valentine doth not refuse," cried the physician, who had manifestly made up his mind. "Thou need'st fresh horses? Anthony shall fetch them to the gate. And one of Sir Valentine's known servants, to show the road and leave the better trace? Anthony shall go. Continual residence here, in his master's absence, hath made him as well known for Sir Valentine's man as Sir Valentine is little known for Anthony's master. On your way to the stable, Anthony, send Mary hither, and John. They shall help me house Sir Valentine yonder, with store of food and drink. Straight north toward Scotland, sayest thou, Master Marryott? The right road for thy wild-goose chase. We shall do our part, my son. Only gain us the ten days."

And the physician strode to the side of the chamber, put aside some faded hangings, and began to loosen a section of the panelling.

Anthony, frowning haughtily at the physician's giving him orders, looked inquiringly at Sir Valentine.

"But, my good father," began the knight, addressing the physician. Hal shot a glance of discovery at the latter. My father! This "doctor" was a doctor of other than the body, then! Hal had wondered to see a physician of such mien and manner in this country place, and had thought he might have been summoned from London. But now all was clear. He was a popish priest, disguised in ordinary habit, to escape the severity of the Elizabethan statutes; though, doubtless, he knew enough of surgery and medicine for the treatment of Sir Valentine's wound.

"There is no time for talk, my son," said this doctor, interrupting Sir Valentine. "Remember those in France. And let Anthony do as I said."

"Thou hast heard, Anthony," said the knight, compliantly, after a moment's reflection. "Lead out the horses —"

"Three, Sir Valentine," put in Hal, to whom time was beginning to appear extremely precious, "as Anthony is to go with us. I shall leave my two for thy use."

"And take money, Anthony," went on Sir Valentine, while the priest continued to open the way to the secret closet.

"I have money, sir," said Hal.

"But Anthony shall take some, — the half of what is in the chest, Anthony. The rest will serve me to France, an this plan indeed be not madness."

"You have sure ways of going to France, I doubt not," said Hal to Sir Valentine.

"Ay," said the knight, with a smiling side glance at the busy priest, "we have made that voyage when ports were e'en closer watched than now. And hear this, Anthony, before you go, — Anthony will show thee, Harry, how to make for France on thine own account, if indeed thou dost ride free of these messengers. And he will tell thee where in Paris I am to be found. When we meet there, — the saints intercede that we may! — I shall have a way of thanking thee, perchance. Go, Anthony!"

The servant left the room, with a glumness belonging rather to a general habit of surly disapproval than to any particular objection to the task before him.

"This house and land," Sir Valentine went on, "will be confiscate, of course, and myself outlawed. But thou see'st how this estate hath fallen, Harry. I keep here but two servants besides Anthony, where once I kept twenty. But in all these years I have built up some means of living, across the narrow seas; and thou shalt not want in France, Harry!"

"Think not of me, but of thyself, Sir Valentine. I'd best leave thee now, and hasten Anthony with the horses. I can find him by his lanthorn's light. We have lost much time."

But Sir Valentine would embrace him ere he left, as well as a man so wounded might; and the knight, touched with gratitude, wept as the youth bent over him. Hal then turned to take swift leave of the priest, who had now caused a dark hole to gape in the wooden panelling. The latter, at this, took up a cloak from a chair, detached Hal's own shorter cloak, and put the other over the youth's shoulders, saying :

"'Tis Sir Valentine's own cloak, and more befitting the part thou hast to play, Master Actor! Take my blessing, and the saints watch over thee!"

With no more ado, Hal hastened from the room, and down to the hall, where Anthony, bearing the lanthorn, was ordering the two other servants to their master's chamber. Hal held his cloak over his face till they were gone up the stairs; then he bade Anthony show him quickly to the stables, adding :

"As for the money, if you must obey orders, you may get it while I am saddling the horses."

The steward gave a grunt, and led the way out to the stables, where he indicated the three best horses. He then returned to the house, leaving the lanthorn; but presently reappeared, in time to help Hal with the horses, and to receive at the same time the player's explicit directions for the conduct of matters on the arrival of the officers.

The two men then led the horses to the front gate, where Anthony tied a pair of them, that he might take Hal's London horse to the stable. Master Marryott mounted and rode toward the village to acquaint Captain Bottle with what was to be done. On perceiving Kit's stalwart figure, black against the dim night, Hal called out to him to follow back to the mansion. While the two were covering the distance thereto, Hal briefly put the soldier in possession of what it was needful for the latter to know. Anthony had now returned from the stable, and the lanthorn revealed Hal's transformation, which the captain viewed with critical approval while transferring himself from his tired horse to one of the fresh ones.

"And the Puritan rides with us?" queried Bottle, while Anthony was gone with the second horse to the stable. "Sad company, sad company! An the dull rogue sermon me upon the sins of the flesh, I'll knock in his teeth to shut up his throat withal! Well, well! This mixing in matters of state maketh strange bedfellows. I mind me once — lend ear, Hal! Hoofs yonder, or I'm an owl else!"

Hal listened. Yes, horses were crossing the wooden bridge of the brook on the Londonward side of the village.

"Should these be the men?" whispered Hal in a low voice. "They come slowly."

"Who else should be on the road at this hour?" replied Kit. "They know not any reason for haste."

"A red murrain on that Puritan, then!" said Hal. "What holds him so long at the stable? All is lost, without his lanthorn. I'll ride in and fetch him."

"Nay, they must use time enough in coming hither. Hark! They have halted in the village. Mayhap they must needs ask the way to Fleetwood house."

"'Tis well, then. They will learn of Sir Valentine's hurt."

There was then a very trying time of silence and waiting, during which Hal's heart beat somewhat as it had beaten in the tiring-room before the performance of "Hamlet."

"Hear them again," he said at last, through his teeth. "And that rascal Puritan —"

"Save thy breath! Here he comes."

Anthony indeed now appeared with the light, crossing the yard with longer strides than he had previously taken; he, too, had heard the approaching horses.

"Into thy saddle, dog!" muttered Hal. "And a plague on thee for thy slowness! Now do as I bid, or I'll give thee a bellyful of steel!"

The steward having got on horseback, Hal led the way back into the yard. The three then wheeled about, and stood just within the now wide-open gate, Anthony at Hal's right and bearing the lanthorn in his left hand, Kit at Hal's left. Hal measured with his ears the constantly decreasing distance of the hoof-beats on the hard road, as they advanced at a steady walking pace. Through the silence came the sound of a far-off clock striking eight, and then of the approaching horsemen talking to one another in low tones.

At last Hal said, "Now!" and rode forth into the road, which was here of exceptional width. The three, riding abreast, turned toward London, as if intending to ride southward. Had they continued, they would soon have met the approaching horsemen face to face. But suddenly Hal, as if he now for the first time discovered the presence of newcomers, stopped short, as did also his two attendants. Anthony, in pretence of enabling the make-believe Sir Valentine to perceive who the horsemen were, held the lanthorn up, a little to the right and rear of Hal's body, so that it revealed his attitude and left his face in shadow. Leaning forward, as in pain, yet with head stiffly set, shoulders forced back, hat low on brow, left elbow thrust out, and beard well outlined against the light, Hal peered anxiously into the gloom. Out of that gloom there came, after a startled exclamation and a hush of low voices, the clear greeting:

"Give you good even, Sir Valentine!"

Hal uttered a swift order to his men. Anthony instantly wheeled around, to take the lead, and rode northward. Hal did likewise, and was immediately followed by Captain Bottle. As soon as Hal made sure that Kit had turned, he called to the steward ahead to make speed; and a moment later the three were galloping over the frozen road at the devil's gait.

"Halt! In the queen's name!" rang out of the darkness behind, in the voice that had been heard before.

"Go to hell, Roger Barnet!" shouted back Kit Bottle, to Hal's astonishment.

"You know him?" queried Hal, as the horses flew onward.

"Yes, and a taker of traitors he is, sure enough!" growled Kit through the night. "A very hell-hound, at a man's heels! Hear him cursing, back yonder, for his pistol will not go off! They have whipped up; the whole pack is on the scent!"

"Good!" cried Hal. "Sir Valentine and the priest will have plain sailing. The chase is begun, old Kit! Five days of this, and the hounds must neither lose nor catch us! Ods-body, the Puritan's lanthorn is out! I hope he knows the road in the dark!"

CHAPTER VII.

MISTRESS ANNE HAZLEHURST.

"I have got the start;
But ere the goal, 'twill ask both brain and art."
— *The English Traveller.*

MANIFESTLY the Puritan knew the road, and manifestly it was known to the horses, also; for without decrease of swiftness the few black objects at the roadside — indistinct blurs against the less black stretches of night-sky — seemed to race back toward the men in pursuit. Soon the riders had a wood at their right, a park at their left. Then there was perforce a slowing up, for a hill had to be ascended. But by this time the enemy was left almost out of ear-shot. Hal, knowing his party to be the more freshly mounted, took heed to make no further gain at present. While in the vicinity of Fleetwood house, the chase must be so close that the officers would not for a moment drop it to consider some other course of action. As long as they were at his heels, and saw imminent possibility of taking him, it was not probable that they would separate for the purpose of searching Sir Valentine's house, or of causing proclamation to be sent broadcast by which port wardens might be put on guard, or of taking time to seek the aid of shire officers, justices, and constables. It was not for himself that Hal had most to fear a hue and cry of the country, for by keeping ahead of the officers by whom that hue and cry must be evoked, he should keep ahead of the hue and cry itself; but such a raising of the country would direct to Fleetwood house an attention which might hinder Sir Valentine's eventual removal. Once the pursuers were drawn into another county, Hal might gain over them sufficient time for his own rest and refreshment, and for his necessary changes of horse. When committed to the hunt by several hours' hard riding, the officers, for their own reputation, would be less likely to abandon it for a return to Fleetwood house; and though, as the hunt should develop into a long and toilsome business, they would surely take time to enlist local authorities in it, those authorities would not be of Hertfordshire, and their eyes would be turned toward Hal himself, not toward Fleetwood house.

"Tell me more of this Barnet," said Hal to Captain Bottle, as the three fugitives rode up a second hill. The sound of the pursuers, galloping across the level stretch between the two heights, came with faint distinctness to the ears of the pursued, in intervals of the noise made by their own horses, — noise of breathing, snorting, treading the rough earth, and clashing against the loose stones that lay in the ditch-like road.

"Why, he is a chaser of men by choice," answered Kit. "I knew him years agone, in Sir Francis Walsingham's day. Beshrew me if he is ever happy without a warrant in his pouch. I'm a bottle-ale rascal an he hath not carried the signature of the secretary of state over more miles than any other man! A silent, unsocial rogue! When I knew him first, he was one of Walsingham's men; and so was I, i' faith! We chased down some of the Babington conspirators together, — that was fifteen years ago. For, look you, this raising of the country against a traitor is well enough, when he is a gentleman of note, that openly gathers his followers and fortifies his house and has not to be hunted out like a hare. But when traitors are subtle fellows that flee and disguise themselves, these loutish constables' knaves, that watch for hunted men in front of alehouses, are sad servants of the state, God wot! — and I have seen with these eyes a letter to that effect, from Lord Burleigh to Sir Francis, when this same Barnet and I were a-hunting the Babington rascals." [25]

"Then this Barnet is like to keep on our track?" interrogated Hal.

"Yea, that he is! 'Tis meat and drink to the

rogue, this man-hunting! He takes a pride in it, and used to boast he had never yet lost his game. And never did he, to my knowledge, but once, and that was my doing, which was the cause of our falling out. When Sir Francis Walsingham died, we remained in service as pursuivants — to attend the orders of the council and the high commission. That was a fat trade! Great takings, rare purse-filling! Old Kit had no need of playing coney-catcher in those days! We would be sent to bring people up to London, to prison, and 'twas our right to charge them what we pleased for service and accommodation; and when they could not pay, it went hard with them. Well, Roger Barnet and I disagreed once about dividing the money we meant to squeeze out of a Gloucestershire gentleman, that some lord his neighbor had got a council's order against, for having troubled his lordship with a lawful suit in the courts. Rather than take the worse of it from Roger Barnet, I got up when he was asleep, at the inn we were staying overnight, and set the gentleman free. Roger would have killed me the next day, had he been as good a swordsman as he is a man-hunter. But, as it was, he had to be content with my losing so fat a service. For he was in favor with Mr. Beal, the clerk of the council, and might have made things hard for me but that I took forthwith to the wars."

"God look to it he may not have chance of making things hard for thee in this business!" said Hal.

"Why, one thing is sure," replied Kit, "he will stick to our heels the longer for my being of the party. 'Twould warm his heart to pay off old scores. He'll perchance think 'twas I that got word of Sir Valentine's danger and brought warning. And, certes, he finds me aiding an accused traitor, which brings me, too, under the treason statutes. 'Twould be a sweet morsel to Roger Barnet to carry me back prisoner to London! An thy plan be to keep Roger on our track, 'tis well I made myself known by word of mouth, as I did. Though, for that matter, I say it again, Roger is not the dog to quit any scent, let him once lay his nose to the earth."

Ahead rode the Puritan, in a silence as of sullenness, his figure more clearly drawn against the night as Hal's eyes were the better accustomed to the darkness. Hal now spoke so that both Anthony and Kit might hear, saying:

"My men, ye are to plant it in your minds that I am Sir Valentine Fleetwood, none other; but ye will seem to wish to hide from people that I am he. Hence ye will call me by some other name, it matters not what; and the better 'twill be an ye blunder in that name, and disagree in it from time to time. The more then will it appear that I, Sir Valentine, am trying to pass myself off as another. But sometimes seem to forget, and call me Sir Valentine, and then hastily correct yourselves as if ye had spoke incautiously."

"The lie be on your own head, though my mouth be forced to speak it," replied Anthony Underhill, dismally.

"Willingly," said Hal; and Kit Bottle put in:

"An the weight be too heavy on thy head, Master Marryott, let old Kit bear some of it. Ods-body, some folk be overfearful of damnation!"

Anthony muttered something about scoffers, and rode on without further speech. So they traversed a hamlet, then a plain, then more hills and another sleeping village. Varying their pace as the exigencies of the road required, they were imitated in this — as they could hear — by Barnet's party. The narrowness of the highway, which hereabouts ran for a good distance between lines of wooden fence, compelled them to ride in single file. They had been on the road an hour, perhaps, and made about five miles, so that they were probably a mile from Stevenage, when Anthony called back to Hal:

"There be riders in front, sir, coming toward us."

"So my ears tell me," said Hal, after a moment's listening. "Who the devil can be abroad at this hour? I hope we suffer no delay in passing them."

Barnet's men were now a half mile behind, evidently nursing the powers of their horses for a timely dash. A stoppage of any kind might nip Hal's fine project in the bud. Hence it was with anxiety that he strained his eyes forward. The newcomers were approaching at a fast walk. One of them, the foremost, was carrying a light. As they drew nearer, riding one behind another, they took a side of the road, the more speedily to pass. But the leader, as he came opposite Anthony Underhill, and saw the Puritan's face in the feeble light, instantly pulled up, and called out to one behind in a kind of surprise:

"Here's Sir Valentine's steward, Anthony Underhill!"

"Give ye good even, Dickon, and let us pass," said Anthony, sourly; for the other had quickly turned his horse crosswise so as to block most of the narrow road.

"Is that thy master I see yonder?" he asked, holding his light toward Hal, who had promptly ridden up abreast of Anthony.

"What is that to you, fellow?" cried Hal.

"'Tis something to me!" called out a voice behind the fellow,—a voice that startled Hal, for it was a woman's. "Are you Sir Valentine?"

"Who wishes to know?" inquired Hal, putting some courtesy into the speech.

"I do—Anne Hazlehurst!" was the quick

answer. And the light-bearer having made room for her, she rode forward.

Hazlehurst! Where, Hal asked himself, had he recently heard that name?

"Well, are you Sir Valentine?" she demanded, impatiently.

"I do not deny it," said Hal.

"Then here's for you, — slayer of my brother!" she cried, and struck him full in the face with the flat of a sword she had held beneath her cloak. In doing this she thrust her hooded head more into the lanthorn's light, and Hal recalled two things at the same instant, — the name Hazlehurst as that of the gentleman with whom Sir Valentine had fought, and the woman's face as that with which he, Master Marryott, had fallen in love at the theatre during the play of "Hamlet."

CHAPTER VIII.

"A DEVIL OF A WOMAN."

"*From all such devils, good Lord, deliver us!*" — *The Taming of the Shrew.*

"And now, my men, upon him!" cried Mistress Hazlehurst, backing to make room in which her followers might obey.

These followers tried to push forward; the horses crowded one another, and there ensued much huddling and confusion. But the lantern-bearer, holding his light and his bridle in one hand, caught Mr. Marryott's bridle with the other. Hal struck this hand down with one of his pistols, which were not prepared for firing. He then drew his sword, with a gesture that threw hesitation into the ranks of his opposers.

"Madam," he cried, in no very gentle tone, "may I know what is your purpose in this?"

"'Tis to prevent your flight," she called back, promptly. "The officers of justice are slow; I shall see that you forestall them not."

For a moment Hal, thinking only of the officers behind him, wondered if she could have heard of the council's intention, and whether it was to the royal messengers that she alluded.

"What have officers of justice to do with me?" he asked.

"To call you to account for the killing of my brother!"

Sir Valentine's fight, in which wounds had been given on both sides, again recurred to Hal's mind.

"Your brother is dead, then?" he inquired.

"I am but now from his funeral!" was her answer.

In that case, Hal deduced, her brother must have died two days before, that is to say, on the very day of the fight. The news must have come belated to the sister, for she had been at the performance of "Hamlet," yesterday. And here was explanation of her departure from the theatre in the midst of the play. The summons to her dead brother's side had followed her to the playhouse, and there overtaken her. Afterward, Hal found these inferences to be correct.

For a second or two of mutual inaction, he marvelled at the strange ways of circumstance which had brought this woman, whom he had yesterday admired in the crowded London playhouse, to confront him in such odd relations on this lonely, night-hidden road in Hertfordshire. But a sound that a turn of the wind brought — the sound of Roger Barnet's men riding nearer — sharpened him to the necessity of immediate action against this sudden hindrance. Yet he felt loath to go from this woman. Go he must, however, though even at the possible cost of violence to her people.

The Puritan retained his place at Marryott's side. Kit Bottle was close behind, and with horse already half turned so that he might face Barnet's men should they come up too soon; he had drawn his sword, and was quietly making ready his pistols.

"Madam," said Hal, decisively, "I did not kill your brother. Now, by your favor, I will pass, for I am in some haste."

"What!" she cried. "Did you lie just now, when you said you were Sir Valentine Fleetwood?"

Now, Hal might tell her that he was not Sir Valentine; but, doubtless, she would not believe him; and thus the situation would not be changed. And, on the other hand, if she should believe him, so much the worse, — she would then bend her energies toward the hindrance of the real Sir Valentine; would ride on toward Fleetwood house, be met and questioned by Roger Barnet, and set him right, or at least cause him to send a party back to Fleetwood house to investigate. So Hal's purpose would be speedily frustrated. His only course was to let her think him really the man he was impersonating; indeed that course would make but another step in the continued deception of Roger Barnet, and Hal was bound to take such steps — not avoid them — for the next five days.

"Mistress Hazlehurst," replied Hal, taking a kind of furtive joy in using her name upon his lips for the first time, "I do not deny that I am Sir Valentine Fleetwood; but I did not kill your brother. I wish you heaven's blessing and a good night, for I am going on!" With that he started his horse forward.

"Take him!" she shouted to her men. "Ye shall pay for it an he escape!"

The threat had effect. The attendants crowded upon Hal, some with swords drawn, some with clubs upraised; so that his horse, after a few steps, reared wildly upon its haunches, and sought a way out of the press.

"Back, dogs!" commanded Marryott, striking right and left with sword and pistol. There were cries of pain from men and horses; the men wielded their weapons as best they could; but a way was somehow opened. Mistress Hazlehurst herself was forced against the fence at the roadside, one of her followers — a slender, agile youth — skilfully interposing his horse and body between her and the crush. She would have pressed into the midst of the blows and of the rearing beasts, had not this servant restrained her horse by means which she, in her excitement, did not perceive. But she continued calling out orders, in a loud, wrathful voice.

As Hal opened way, Anthony and Bottle followed close, preventing the enemy from closing in upon his rear. The Puritan used a short sword with a business-like deliberation and care, and with no word or other vocal sign than a kind of solemnly approbative grunt as he thrust. Bottle, who rode last, handled his long rapier with great swiftness and potency, in all directions, swearing all the while; and finally let off his two pistols, one after the other, at two men who hung with persistence upon Hal's flanks, while Hal was forcing the last opposition in front. One of these two fell wounded or dead, the other was thrown by his maddened horse; and finally the three fugitives were free of the mass of men and beasts that had barred the way. One of the horses was clattering down the road ahead, without a rider. Hal informed himself by a single glance that Anthony and Kit were free and able, and then, with an "On we go!" he spurred after the riderless horse toward Stevenage.

"After him, you knaves!" screamed Mistress Hazlehurst, in a transport of baffled rage; but her servants, some unhorsed, some with broken heads or pierced bodies, one with a pistol wound in his side, and the rest endeavoring to get the horses under control, were quite heedless of her cries.

"A sad plight to leave a lady in!" said Hal, who had heard her futile order. He and his two men were now riding at a gallop, to regain lost advantage.

"A devil of a woman!" quoth Captain Bottle, in a tone of mere comment, void of any feeling save, perhaps, a little admiration.

"Why did she not know me, either as Sir Valentine, or as not being Sir Valentine?" asked Hal, calling ahead to Anthony, who had resumed his place in front.

"She hath dwelt most time in London with a city kinswoman," was the answer, "and Sir Valentine hath lived usually in France since she was born."

"'Tis well Master Barnet knew Sir Valentine better, or knew him well enough to take me for him in my disguise," said Hal.

"Trust Roger Barnet to know every papist in the kingdom," called out Kit Bottle, "and to know every one else that's like to give occasion for his services. It is a pride of his to know the English papists wherever they be. Roger is often on the Continent, look you. He is the privy council's longest finger!"

"Tell me of this Mistress Hazlehurst," said Hal to the Puritan, to whose side he now rode up. "Is't true she is the sister of the gentleman Sir Valentine fought?"

"His only sister," returned Anthony. "His only close kin. She is now heiress to the Hazlehurst estate, and just old enough to be free of wardship."

"A strong love she must have borne her brother, to fly straight from his funeral to see him avenged!"

"Nay, I know not any great love betwixt 'em. They could not live in the same house, or in the same county, for their wrangles — being both of an ungodly violence. 'Twas her brother's unrighteous proneness to anger that forced the brawl on Sir Valentine. 'Twas that heathenish quarrelsomeness, some say, that kept Mr. Hazlehurst a bachelor. 'Tis a wonder the evil spirit of wrath in him brought him not sooner to his death. He fought many duels, — not hereabouts, where men were careful against provoking him, but in France, where he lived much. 'Twas there, indeed, that he and Sir Valentine best knew each other."

"And yet this sister must have loved him. Women are not commonly so active toward punishing a brother's slayer," insisted Hal.

"Why," replied Anthony, "methinks this woman is a hothead that must needs do with her own hands what, if she were another woman, she would only wish done. 'Tis a pride of family that moveth her to look to the avenging of her brother's death. A blow at him she conceiveth to be a blow at herself, the two being of same name and blood. This sister and brother have ever been more quick, one to resent an affront against the other from a third person, than they have been slow to affront each other. I am not wont to speak in the language of the lost, or to apply the name of the arch-enemy to them that bear God's image; but, indeed, as far as a headstrong will and violent ways are diabolical, yon profane man spoke aptly when he named Mistress Anne a devil of a woman!"

"All's one for that," said Hal, curtly. "But, certes, as far as a matchless face and a voice of music are angelical, I speak as aptly when I name this Mistress Anne an angel of a woman! It went against me to leave her in the road thus, in a huddle of bleeding servants and runaway horses."

"'Tis a huddle that will block the way for Roger Barnet a while," put in Captain Bottle.

"Doubtless he and his men have ridden up to her by now," replied Marryott. "I'd fain see what is occurring betwixt them." Then lapsing into silence, Hal and his two attendants rode on, passing through slumbering Stevenage, and continuing uninterruptedly northward.

Barnet's party had indeed come up to Mistress Hazlehurst's, and the scene now occurring between them was one destined to have a strange conclusion.

Anne's followers, — raw serving men without the skill or decision to have used rightly their numerical superiority over the three fugitives, — all were more or less hurt, except two, — the slight one who had personally shielded her, and the lantern-bearer, who had been taken out of the fray by the intractability of his horse. Not only was her escort useless for any immediate pursuit of the supposed Sir Valentine, but the condition of its members required of her, as their mistress and leader, an instant looking to. The necessity of this forbade her own mad impulse to ride unaided after the man who had escaped her, and whom she was the more passionately enraged against because of his victory over her and of his treatment of her servants. Nothing could have been more vexatious than the situation into which she had been brought; and she was bitterly chafing at her defeat, while forcing herself to consider steps for the proper care of her injured servants, when Barnet's troop came clattering up the road.

Mistress Hazlehurst's horses, except the runaway, had now been got under command; some of her men, merely bruised in body or head, stood holding them; others, worse hurt, lay groaning at the roadside, whither she had ordered their comrades to drag them. Anne herself sat her horse in the middle of the road, the little fellow, still mounted, at her left hand. Such was the group that caused Barnet and his men to pull up their horses to an abrupt halt. Peering forward, with eyes now habituated to the darkness, the royal pursuivant swiftly inspected the figures before him, perceived that Sir Valentine and his two attendants were not of them, wondered what a woman was doing at the head of such a party, dismissed that question as none of his business, and called out:

"Madam, a gentleman hath passed you, with two men. Did he keep the road to Stevenage, or turn out yonder?"

"Sir Valentine Fleetwood, mean you?" asked Anne, with sudden eagerness.

"The same. Way to pass, please you. And answer."

Roger Barnet was a man of middle height; bodily, of a good thickness and great solidity; a man with a bold, square face, a frown, cold eyes, a short black beard; a keeper of his own counsel, a man of the fewest possible words, and those gruffly spoken. Anne, because her mind was working upon other matter, took no offence at his sharp, discourteous, mandatory style of addressing her. Without heeding his demand for way, she said:

"Sir Valentine hath indeed passed! See how he dealt with my servants when I tried to stay him! Are you magistrate's men?"

"I am a messenger of the queen," said Barnet, deigning an answer because, on looking more closely at her horses, a certain idea had come to him.

"In pursuit of Sir Valentine?" she asked.

"With a warrant for his apprehension," was the reply.

"What! For my brother's death? Hath her Majesty heard—"

"For high treason; and if these be your horses, in the queen's name—"

But Mistress Hazlehurst cut short his speech, in turn.

"High treason!" she cried, with jubilation; and this thought flashed through her mind: that if taken for high treason, her enemy, a Catholic of long residence in France, was a doomed man; whereas a judicial investigation of his quarrel with her brother might absolve Sir Valentine from guilt or blame. True, the state's revenge for an offence against itself would not, as such, be her revenge for an offence against her family, and would not in itself afford her the triumph she craved; but Sir Valentine was in a way to escape the State's revenge; she might be an instrument to effect his capture; in being that, she would find her own revenge. She could then truly say to her enemy, "But for me you might be free; of my work, done in retaliation for killing my brother, shall come your death; and so our blood, as much as the crown, is avenged." All this, never expressed in detail, but conceived in entirety during the time of a breath, was in her mind as she went on:

"God's light, he shall be caught, then! He went toward Stevenage. I will ride with you!"

"Nay, madam, there are enough of us. But your horses are fresher than ours. I take some of yours, in the queen's name, and leave mine in your charge," And he forthwith dismounted, ordering his men to do likewise. But ere he made another movement, his hand happening to seek his pouch, he uttered an oath, and exclaimed:

"The queen's letters! There's delay! They must be delivered to-night. Madam, know you where Sir William Crashaw's house is? And Mr. Richard Brewby's?"

"Both are down the first road to the right."

"Then down the first road to the right I must go, and let Sir Valentine Fleetwood gain time while I am about it. Which is your best horse, mistress? And one of your men shall guide me to those gentlemen's houses." And, resigning his horse to a follower, he strode into the midst of the Hazlehurst group.

"But why lose this time, sir?" said Anne. "Let my man himself bear these letters."

"When I am charged with letters," replied Roger Barnet, "they pass not from me save into the hands for which they are intended. I shall carry these letters, and catch this traitor. By your leave, I take this horse — and this — and this. Get off, fellow! Hudsdon, bring my saddle, and saddle me this beast. Change horses, the rest of you."

"But will you not send men after this traitor,

while you bear the letters?" queried Anne, making no protest against the pressing of her horses into the queen's service, — a procedure in which no attempt was made to include the horse she herself was on.

Barnet gave a grunt of laughter, to which he added the words, "My men go with me!" Perhaps he dared not trust his men out of his sight, perhaps he wished no one but himself to have the credit of taking the fugitive, perhaps he needed the protection of his complete force against possible attack.

"But, man," cried Anne, sharply, "you will lose track of Sir Valentine! You will take two hours, carrying those letters!"

"Why, mistress," replied Barnet, as the change of horses from one party to the other went rapidly on, "will not people in farmhouses and villages hear his three horses pass?" Though he assumed a voice of confidence, there was yet in it a tone betraying that he shared her fears.

"He ought to be followed while he is yet scarce out of hearing," said Anne, "and overtaken, and hindered one way or another till you catch up."

Barnet cast a gloomy look at her, as if pained at the mention of a course so excellent, but in the present case so impossible.

"My horse is the best in the county," she went on. "I can catch him, — hang me if I cannot! I can delay him, too, if there be any way under heaven to do so! Dickon, look to thy wounded fellows! See them taken home, and show this gentleman the way to Sir William Crashaw's and Mr. Brewby's. Come, Francis!" — this to the small attendant who kept always near her — "God be praised, you are well-mounted, too!" And she turned her horse's head toward Stevenage.

"But, Mistress Anne," cried Dickon, in dismay, "you will be robbed — killed! Ride not without company!"

"Let go, Dickon, and do as I bid! I shall ride so fast, the fiend himself cannot catch me, till I fall in with that traitor; and then I shall have him and his men for company till this officer come up to him. Master Messenger, for mine own reasons I promise to impede Sir Valentine; to be a burden, a weight, and a chain upon him, holding him back by all means I can devise, till you bear your letters and o'ertake him. Dickon, heed my orders! Follow me, Francis! Ods-daggers, must I be a milksop, and afraid o' nights, because I wasn't born to wear hose instead of petticoats?" And having by this time got her horse clear of the group in the road, she made off toward Stevenage, followed by her mounted page, Francis.

"It may turn out well for us that Sir Valentine Fleetwood happened to kill her brother," was the only comment of Roger Barnet, as he mounted the horse his man Hudsdon had newly saddled. He had seen much and many, in his time, and was not surprised at anything, especially if it bore the shape of a woman.

CHAPTER IX.

THE FIRST DAY OF THE FLIGHT.

"That wench is stark mad, or wonderful froward." — *The Taming of the Shrew.*

THE object of this double chase, Master Marryott, rode on with his two men, through the night, beyond Stevenage, at what pace it seemed best to maintain. The slowness, incredible to a bicyclist or horseman who to-day follows the same route, was all the greater for the darkness; but slowness had good cause without darkness. English horse-breeding had not yet shown or sought great results in speed. An Elizabethan steed would make a strange showing on a twentieth century race-track; for the special product of those days was neither horses nor machines, but men. And such as the horses were, what were the roads they had to traverse! When a horse put his foot down, the chances were that it would land in a deep rut, or slide crunching down the hardened ridge at the side thereof, or find lodgment in a soggy puddle, or sink deep into soft earth, or fall, like certain of the Scriptural seed, upon stony places. It is no wonder, then, that on a certain occasion, when

Queen Elizabeth was particularly impatient for a swift answer to a letter she caused sent to the keepers of Mary Stuart, the messenger's time from London to Fotheringay and back was at the rate of less than sixty miles a day. As for travel upon wheels, an example thereof will occur later in this narrative. But there was in those days one compensatory circumstance to fugitives flying with a rapidity then thought the greatest attainable: if they could not fly any faster, neither could their pursuers.

The night journey of our three riders continued in silence. As no sound of other horses now came from behind or from anywhere else, and as the objects passed in the darkness were but as indistinct figures in thick ink against a ground of watered ink, Hal's senses naturally turned inward, and mainly upon what was then foremost in the landscape of his mind. This was the face of Mistress Anne Hazlehurst; and the more he gazed upon the image thereof, the more he sighed at having to increase the distance between himself and the reality. His reluctance to going from the neighborhood of her was none the less for the matter-of-fact promptness with which he did go therefrom. The face was no less a magnet to him for that he so readily and steadily resisted its drawing powers. Those drawing powers would, of course, by the very nature of magnets, decrease as he went farther from their source; but as yet they were marvellously strong. Such is the charm exerted upon impressionable youth by a pair of puzzling eyes, a mysterious expression, a piquant contour, allied to beauty. All the effect of his first sight of that face was revived, and eked to greater magnitude by his strange confrontation with her, proud and wrathful in the poor lantern rays that fell intermittently and shiftingly upon her in the dark road.

He wondered what would be her subsequent proceedings that night; tried to form a mental panorama of her conduct regarding her wounded servants; of her actions now that she saw her design upset, the tenor of her life necessarily affected by this new catastrophe to her household. He pitied her, as he thought of the confused and difficult situation into which she had been so suddenly plunged. And then he came to consider what must be her feelings toward himself. Looking upon him as her brother's slayer, she must view him with both hate and horror. His violent treatment of her servants would augment the former feeling to a very madness of impotent wrath.

Yet it was not Hal Marryott that she hated, — it was the make-believe Sir Valentine Fleetwood; not the player, but the part he played. Still, a dislike of a character assumed by an actor often refuses to separate the actor from the character; moreover, she must necessarily hate him, should she ever come to know him, for having assumed that part, — for being, indeed, the aider of her enemy against herself. Hal registered one determination: should the uncertain future — now of a most exceeding uncertainty in his case — bring him in his own person into the horizon of this woman, he would take care she should not know he had played this part. What had passed between them should be blotted out; should be as if indeed Sir Valentine, not Hal Marryott, had escaped her in the road. And Hal bethought himself of one gain that the encounter had yielded him: it had acquainted him with the name and place of the previously unknown beauty. Some day, when he should have gone through with all this business, he might indeed seek her.

When he should have gone through with this business? The uncertain future came back to his thoughts. What would be the outcome of this strange flight? So strange, that if he should tell his friends in London of it, they would laugh at the tale as at a wild fiction. Fool a trained man-hunter, a royal messenger grown old in catching people for the council, and fool him by such a device as Hal had employed! Act a part in real life, even for a moment, to the complete deception of the spectator intended to be duped! To be sure, Dick Tarleton had done so, when he pretended in an inn at Sandwich to be a seminary priest, in order to be arrested and have the officers pay his score and take him to London, where, being known, he was sure to be discharged. But Dick Tarleton was a great comedian, and had essayed to represent no certain identifiable seminary priest; whereas Master Marryott, who had dared impersonate a particular known man, was but a novice at acting.

But Hal soon perceived this fact: that playing a part on the stage and playing a part in real life are two vastly different matters. A great actor of the first may be a great failure in the second, and the worst stage player may, under sufficient stress, fill an assumed character deceptively in real life. The spectator in a theatre expects to see a character pretended, and knows that what he sees is make-believe, not real. A spectator in real life, chosen to be duped, expects no such thing, and is therefore ready to take a pretence for what it purports to be. Whatever may occur eventually to undeceive him, he is in proper mind for deception at first contact with the pretence. And the very unlikelihood of such an attempt as Hal's, the very seeming impossibility of its success, was reason for Roger Barnet's not having suspected it.

These thoughts now occurred to Hal for the first time. Should he succeed in his novel adventure, he might congratulate himself upon the achievement, not of a great feat of stage-playing, indeed, though to his stage training he owed his quick perception and imitation of Sir Valentine's chief physical peculiarities, but of a singular and daring act, in which he both actually and figuratively played a part.

But was he destined to succeed? Was Roger Barnet still upon his track? Or was he fleeing from nothing, leaving a track for nobody to follow? Well, he must trust to those at Fleetwood house to keep Sir Valentine's actual whereabouts from discovery, and to Barnet's skill in picking up the trace that a fugitive *must* leave, willy-nilly. But what if fate, so fond of playing tricks on mortals, should conceive the whim of covering up the track of this one fugitive who desired his track to be seen? Hal cast away this thought. He must proceed, confidently, though in blindness as to what was doing behind him. At present, silence was there; no sound of far-off horse-hoofs. But this might be attributed to Barnet's interruption by Anne's party; to measures for procuring fresh horses, and to the necessary delivery of the letters of which the queen had told him. And so, fleeing from cold darkness and the unknown into cold darkness and the unknown, deep in his thoughts, and trusting to his star, Master Marryott rode on through Baldock and toward Biggleswade. Kit Bottle presently called his attention to their having passed out of Hertfordshire into Bedfordshire.

The captain had been hard put to it for a fellow talker. His remarks to Hal had elicited only absent monosyllables or silence. At last, with a gulp as of choking down an antipathy, he had ridden forward to Anthony and tried conversation with that person. Master Underhill listened as one swallows by compulsion a disagreeable dose, and gave brief, surly answers. Kit touched with perfect freedom upon the other's most private concerns, not deeming that a despised dissenter had a right to the ordinary immunities.

"Marry, I know not which astoundeth me the more," said the soldier; "that a papist should keep a Puritan in's household, or that the Puritan should serve the papist!"

Anthony was for a moment silent, as if to ignore the impudent speech; but then, in a manner of resignation, as if confession and apology were part of his proper punishment, he said, with a lofty kind of humility:

"The case no more astoundeth you than it reproacheth me. It biteth my conscience day and night, and hath done so this many a year. Daily I resolve me to quit the service of them that cherish the gauds and idolatries of papistry. But the flesh is weak; I was born in Sir Valentine's household, and I could not find strength to wrench me from it."

"Ay," said Kit, "no doubt it hath been in its way a fat stewardship, though the estate be decreased. The master being so oft abroad, and all left to your hands, I'll warrant there have been plump takings, for balm to the bites o' conscience."

"I perceive you are a flippant railer; but you touch me not. What should they of no religion understand of the bites of conscience?"

"No religion! Go to, man! Though I be a soldier, and of a free life, look you, I've practised more religions than your ignorance wots of; and every one of them better than your scurvy, hang-dog, vinegar-faced nonconformity! Nay, I have been Puritan, too, when it served my turn, in the days when I was of Walsingham's men. He had precisian leanings, and so had the clerk o' the council, Mr. Beal. But you are an ingrate, to fatten on a good service, yet call it a reproach!"

"Fatten!" echoed the Puritan, glancing down at his spare frame. "Mayhap it hath been a good service formerly, by comparison with its having this night made me partaker in a five days' lie, abettor of a piece of play-acting, and associate of a scurrilous soldier!"

With which Anthony Underhill quickened his horse so as to move from the captain's side; whereupon Kit, too amazed for timely outward resentment, lapsed into silent meditation.

They rode through Biggleswade. Fatigue was now telling on them. Hal's latest sleep had been that of the previous morning, in the cold open air of Whitehall garden, — an age ago it seemed! Kit's most recent slumbers, taken even earlier, had been, doubtless, in equally comfortless circumstances. Hal learned, by a question, that Anthony had passed yesternight in bed, warm and sober. So Hal decided that when the three should stop at dawn for rest, food, change of horses, and the removal of the false beard, himself and Kit should attempt an hour's repose while Anthony should watch. The Puritan should be one of the sleepers, Kit the watcher, at the second halt. Hal planned and announced all details for assuring an immediate flight on the distant advent of the pursuers. A system of brief stops and of alternate watches could be employed throughout the whole flight without loss of advantage, for Barnet also would have to make similar delays for rest, food, and the changing or baiting of horses.

On wore the night. They passed through Eaton Socon, and continued northward instead of turning into St. Neots at the right. They took notice here, as they had taken at previous forkings of the road, that there were houses at or near the junction, —

houses in which uneasy slumberers would be awakened by their passing and heed which way their horses went. Roger Barnet would have but to ride up noisily, and, perchance, pound and call at a house or two, to bring these persons to windows with word of what they had heard. Hal marvelled as he thought of it the more, how the nature of things will let no man traverse this world, or any part of it, without leaving trace of his passage. He saw in this material fact an image of life itself, and in the night silence, broken only by the clatter of his horses and by some far-off dog's bark or cock's crow, he had many new thoughts. So he rode into Huntingdonshire, and presently, as the pallor of dawn began to blanch the ashen sky, he passed Kimbolton, whose castle now seemed a chill death-place for poor Catherine of Aragon; and, four miles farther on, he drew up, in the dim early light, before the inn at Catworth Magna, and set Kit bawling lustily for the landlord.

A blinking hostler came from the stable yard, and the beefy-looking host from the inn door, at the same time. But the travellers would not get off their mounts until they were assured of obtaining fresh ones. Captain Bottle did the talking. The new horses were brought out to the green before the inn. Kit dismounted and examined them, then struck a bargain with the inn-keeper for their use, dragging the latter's slow wits to a decision by main force. This done, Hal leaped to the ground, called for a room fronting on the green, a speedy breakfast served therein, a razor and shaving materials taken thither, and some oat-cakes and ale brought out to Anthony, who should stay with the horses.

Hal then strode up and down the green, while Anthony ate and Kit and the hostler transferred the saddles and bridles. He kept well muffled about the face with his cloak, in such manner as at once to display his beard and yet conceal the evidence of its falseness. The new horses ready, Anthony mounted one, and, under pretence of exercising them, moved off with them toward the direction whence Barnet would eventually come. Hal, to forestall hindrance in case of a necessarily hasty departure, handed the inn-keeper gold enough to cover all charges he might incur, and was shown, with Kit, to a small, bare-walled, wainscoted, plastered, slope-roofed room up-stairs. He threw open the casement toward the green, and promptly fell upon the eggs, fish, and beer that were by this time served upon a board set on stools instead of on trestles. Finishing simultaneously with Kit, Hal took off his false beard, strewed its severed tufts over the floor, and then submitted his face, which had a few days' natural growth of stubble, to a razor wielded by the captain. After this operation, the two stretched themselves upon the bed, in their clothes, their heads toward the open window.

A dream of endless riding, varied by regularly renewed charges against a wall of plunging horses that invariably fled away to intervene again, and by the alternate menacings and mockings of a beautiful face, culminated in a clamorous tumult like the shouting of a multitude. Hal sprang up. Bottle was bounding from the bed at the same instant.

The sound was only the steadily repeated, " Halloo, halloo!" of Anthony Underhill beneath the open window. Hal looked out. The Puritan sat his horse on the green, holding the other two animals at his either side, all heads pointed northward. On seeing Hal, he beckoned and was silent.

Hal and Kit rushed to the passage, thence down the stairs, and through the entrance-way, to horse. The landlord, called forth by Anthony's hullabaloo, stared at them in wonder. Hal returned his gaze, that an impression of the newly shaven face might remain well fixed in the host's mind ; and then jerked rein for a start. Neither Hal nor Kit had yet taken time to look for the cause of Anthony's alarm. As they galloped away from the inn, Hal heard the patter of horses coming up from the south. He turned in his saddle, expecting to see Roger Barnet and his crew in full chase.

But the horses were only two in number, and on

them were Mistress Hazlehurst, in a crimson cloak and hood, and the page in green who had attended her at the theatre. Hal's heart bounded with sudden pleasure. As he gazed back at her, he caught himself smiling.

She saw him, noted his two companions, and seemed to be in doubt. The landlord was still before the inn. She reined up, and spoke to him. Hal could see the innkeeper presently, while answering her, put his hand to his chin. "Good!" thought Hal; "he is telling her that, though I depart smooth-faced, I arrived bearded."

The next moment, she and the page were riding after the three fugitives.

Without decreasing his pace, Hal asked Anthony:

"Was it she only that you saw coming? Are Barnet's men behind?"

"'Twas she only. But she is enough to raise the country on us!"

"Think you that is her purpose?"

"Ay," replied Anthony. "She hath heard of the treason matter from the pursuivant, and hath shot off, like bolt from bow, to denounce you. 'Tis her method of vengeance."

"'Tis like a woman — of a certain kind," commented Kit Bottle, who had taken in the situation as promptly as the others had.

"'Tis like a Hazlehurst," said Anthony.

"Well," said Master Marryott, for a pretext, "'tis doubtless as you say; but I desire assurance. It may serve us to know her intentions. She cannot harm us here." (They were now out of the village.) "Though she would raise hell's own hue and cry about us, she might halloo her loudest, none would hear at this part of the road. We shall wait for her."

Anthony cast a keen glance at Hal, and Kit Bottle thrust his tongue in his cheek and looked away, — manifestations at which Hal could only turn red and wish that either of the two had given some open cause for rebuke. He was determined, however; the temptation to play with fire in the shape of a beautiful woman was too alluring, the danger apparently too little. So the three horses dropped to a walk, and presently the two that followed were at their heels. Hal looked back as she came on, to see if she still carried the sword she had used on the previous night; but he saw no sign of it about her. In fact, she had given it to Francis, who bore at his girdle a poniard also.

"Mistress, you travel ill-protected," was Hal's speech of greeting.

"So my brother must have done when he met you last," was her prompt and defiant answer.

She let her horse drop into the gait of Hal's, and made no move to go from his side. The Puritan resumed his place at the head, and Francis, in order to be immediately behind his mistress, fell in with Kit Bottle. In this order the party of five proceeded northward, their horses walking.

"I did not harm your brother," reiterated Marryott, with a sigh.

"I perceive," she replied, ironically, "you are not the man that hurt my brother. You have made of yourself another man, by giving yourself another face! God 'a' mercy, the world is dull, indeed, an it is to be fooled with a scrape of a razor! You should have bought the silence of mine host yonder, methinks! And changed your company, altered your attitude, rid yourself of the stiffness from the wound my brother gave you, and washed your face of the welt my sword left! You have a good barber, Sir Valentine; he hath shaved a score of years from your face; he hath renewed your youth as if with water from that fountain men tell of, in America!"

"The loss of a long-worn beard indeed giveth some men a strange look of youth," assented Hal, as if humoring her spirit of bitter derision against himself. He was glad of her conviction that he could look youthful and yet be the middle-aged Sir Valentine.

"'Twas so in the case of an uncle of mine," she said, curtly, "which the more hindereth your imposing on me with a face of five and twenty."

"Five and twenty?" echoed Hal, involuntarily,

surprised that he should appear even so old. But a moment's reflection told him that his age must be increased in appearance by the assumed stiffness of his attitude; by the frown and the labial rigidity he partly simulated, partly had acquired since yesterday; by the gauntness and pallor, both due to nervous tension and to lack of sleep and food. He was indeed an older man than the "Laertes" of two days ago, and not to be recognized as the same, for in the play he had worn a mustache and an air little like his present thoughtful mien.

"And I'll warrant this new face will serve you little to throw them off that are coming yonder," she went on, indicating the rearward road by a slight backward toss of the head.

"Certain riders from London, mean you?" said Hal. "By your leave, madam, sith you be in their secrets, I would fain know how far behind us they ride?"

"Not so far but they will be at your heels ere this day's sun grow tired of shining."

"Ay, truly? They will do swift riding, then!"

"Mayhap 'twill come of their swift riding," she replied, taunted by his courteous, almost sugary, tone. "And mayhap, of your meeting hindrance!"

"Prithee, what should put hindrance in my way?" he inquired, with a most annoying pretence of polite surprise and curiosity.

"I will!" she cried. "I have run after you for that purpose!"

"God's light, say you so? And what will you do to hinder me?"

"I know not yet," she answered, with high serenity. "But I shall find a way."

"No doubt you will choose the simplest way," said Hal.

"What is that, I pray you?" she asked, quickly.

But Hal merely smiled. She followed his glance, however, which rested upon a gabled country-house far across the open field at their right, and she read his thought.

"Nay," she said, her chin elevated haughtily, "I disdain help. 'Tis my humor to be alone the means of throwing you into the hands that bring the warrant for you. Nor shall I lose sight of you time enough to seek rustic officers and set them on you."

"You are wise in that," said Hal; "for, indeed, if you took but time to cry out against me to some passing wayfarer, I and my men would be up-tails-and-away in a twinkling. For my own interest, I tell you this; sith I'd fain not have you do aught to deprive me of your company as fellow traveller."

She colored with indignation at this compliment, and Hal, thereby reminded that she saw in him her brother's slayer, and sensible how much affront lay in the speech in the circumstances, reddened as deeply. If he could but find a way, without making her doubt that he was Sir Valentine, of convincing her that he had not been her brother's opponent! He had thought vaguely that, by his reiterated denials of a hand in the killing, he might finally implant in her mind the impression that, though he was Sir Valentine, he had not given the mortal thrust; that there was some mystery about the fight, to be explained in time. But he now perceived that if such an idea could be rooted into her mind, its effect must be to make her drop the chase and go back to Sir Valentine's neighborhood. There she might find conclusive evidence of Sir Valentine's responsibility for her brother's death, and make upon Fleetwood house some kind of invasion that would endanger the real Sir Valentine. Moreover, Hal took a keen, though disturbed, joy in her presence, despite the bar of bloodshed that in her mind existed between them; and though to retain that joy he must let her continue in that supposition, he elected to retain it at the price.

After a pause, during which she acquired the coolness of voice to answer Hal's thoughtlessly offensive words, she said:

"I pray God to hasten the hour when I shall be your fellow traveller toward London!"

"An Roger Barnet, with his warrant of the council, were left out, I should pray God to be your fellow traveller anywhere!" was Hal's reply,—and again he had to curse his heedlessness, as again he saw how odious to her was the truth that had slipped so readily out of him. "You rode fast, else you had not overtaken me," he said, in hope of changing her thoughts.

"And having overtaken you, I shall not lose you," she answered.

"And you have not slept nor eaten! Marry, you must be weary and faint, mistress!"

"Neither too weary nor too faint to dog you to your undoing," she said, resolutely throwing off all air of fatigue.

"And you risked the dangers of the road. Odsdeath, if you had fallen in with robbers!"

"That danger is past," she said. "Henceforth, till the officers be with us, I shall go in your company, and the appearance of you and your men will be my guard against robbers."

"Nay, an you were threatened, I and my men would offer more than mere appearance in your protection, I do assure you!"

"Be that as it may," she answered, coldly. "Appearance would serve. I take protection of you while I have need of it, and not as a favor or a courtesy, but as a right—"

"From a gentleman to a lady, yes," put in Hal.

"From an enemy," she went on, ignoring his

interruption, "sith it be a practice in war to avail oneself of the enemy without scruple, in all ways possible!"

Hal sighed. He would rather let his protection be accepted otherwise. But he inwardly valued her unconscious tribute to the gentlemanhood she divined in him, — the tribute apparent in her taking for granted that he would act her protector even on a journey in which her declared object was to hold him back for the death he was flying from. There were such gentlemen in those days; and there have been such women as Anne — women who will avail themselves of the generosity of men they are seeking to destroy — in all days.

He was glad of the assurance received from her that Roger Barnet was still on his track. Thus far, all was going well. If this woman, from pride or caprice or a strange jealousy of keeping her vengeance all to herself, did indeed think to impede him by other and more exclusive means than public denunciation or hue and cry, he felt that he had little to fear from her. To put her declaration to the test, he held the horses down to an easy gait in passing through the next villages, though he was ready to spur forward at a sign; but she indicated no thought of starting an outcry. She kept her eyes averted in deep thought. Hal would have given much to read what was passing within that shapely head.

Without doubt, she was intent upon some plan for making a gift of him to his pursuers, some device for achieving that revenge which she craved as a solitary feast, and which she was not willing to owe to any one but herself. What design was she forming? Hal imagined she could not be very expert in designs. A crafty nature would not have declared war openly, as her proud and impulsive heart had bade her do. He admired her for that frankness, for that unconscious superiority to underhand fighting. It showed a noble, masterful soul, and matched well her imperious beauty.

They rode through Clapton and Deane. Her fatigue became more and more evident, though pride and resolution battled hard against it. Her only food during the forenoon was some cold ham she got at a country inn in Northamptonshire, at which Hal paused to bait the horses. They proceeded into Rutlandshire. Before entering Glaiston she swayed upon her side-saddle, but instantly recovered herself. At Manton she was shivering, — the day was indeed a cold one, though the sun had come out at eight o'clock, but she had not shivered so before.

"We shall have dinner and a rest at Oakham," said Master Marryott, softly. "'Tis but three miles ahead."

"All's one, three miles or thirty!" she answered.

As they stopped before an inn at the farther end of Oakham, — an inn chosen by Hal for its situation favorable to hasty flight northward, — the clocks in the town were sounding noon; noon of Wednesday, March 4, 1601; noon of the long first day of the hoped-for five days' flight.

CHAPTER X.

THE LOCKED DOOR.

"When I was at home, I was in a better place: but travellers must be content."
—*As You Like It.*

BEFORE alighting from her horse, Mistress Hazlehurst waited to see what her enemy should do. The enemy's first proceedings were similar to those taken upon his arrival at Catworth Magna. That is to say, through the expeditious offices of Captain Bottle, new horses were placed ready before the inn, ere the party dismounted from the tired ones; dinner and a room were bespoken; and all possible charges were forestalled by advance payment. Anne imitated this whole arrangement precisely, causing no little wonder on the part of the inn people, that she should give her orders independently, though they were exactly like those of the three men with whom she and her page were manifestly travelling. It was mentally set down by the shrewd ones that here were man and wife, or brother and sister, not on speaking terms, yet obliged to perform a journey together.

Hal remained outside the inn with Anthony, till

Bottle should ride back to keep watch. Anne stood near him, not irresolute, but to observe his actions. Refreshed with a stirrup-cup and some cakes, Bottle soon rode off, with two led horses. Perceiving the object of this movement, Anne dismissed the captain from her observation, that she might concentrate it upon the supposed Sir Valentine. As her boy Francis was in no less need of food and sleep than herself, she gave a coin to one of the hostlers, with orders to walk her horses up and down before the inn till she should come for them.

Hal counted on her fatigue to reinforce her proud determination that she would not resort to the local authorities against him. Yet he would not go to his chamber ere she went to hers. Deducing this from his actions — for no speech passed between them while they tarried before the inn — and being indeed well-nigh too exhausted to stand, she finally called for a servant to show her to her room. Francis followed her, to wait upon her at dinner and then to lie on a bench outside her door.

Hal watched her into the entrance-hall of the inn. At the foot of the stairs leading to the upper floor, she stopped, handed a piece of money to the attendant, and spoke a few words in a low tone. The fellow glanced toward the inn porch in which Hal was standing, and nodded obedience. Hal inferred that she was engaging to be notified instantly in case of his departure. A moment later Hal beckoned Anthony to follow, and went, under the guidance of the landlady herself, up to his own room.

As he turned from the stair-head into the upper passage, he saw a door close, which he divined to be that of his fair enemy. A moment later an inn servant appeared with a bench, and placed it outside this door. On reaching his own room, in the same passage, Hal noticed that this bench, on which Francis was to rest, stood in view of his own door, and also — by way of the stairs — of the entrance-hall below. He smiled at the precautions taken by the foe.

Examining his room, he saw that it had the required window overlooking the front inn yard and the road beyond. Immediately beneath this window was the sloping roof of the inn porch. Having opened the casement, and moved the bed's head near it, Hal turned to the dinner that a servant was placing on a small trestle-table, for which there was ample free space in the chamber. The English inns of those days were indeed commodious, and those in the country towns were better than those in London. Hosts took pride in their tapestry, furniture, bedding, plate, and glasses. Some of the inns in the greater towns and roads had room for three hundred guests with their horses and servants. Noblemen travelled with great retinues, and carried furniture with them. It was a golden age of inns, — though, to be sure, the servants were in many cases in league with highway robbers, to whom they gave information of the wealth, destinations, routes, and times of setting forth of well-furnished guests. The inn at which Hal now refreshed himself, in Oakham, was not of the large or celebrated ones. He had his own reasons for resorting to small and obscure hostelries. Yet he found the dinner good, the ale of the best, and, after that, the bed extremely comfortable, even though he lay in his clothes, with his hand on his sword-hilt.

He had flung himself down, immediately after dinner, not waiting for the platters and cups to be taken away. Anthony, who had been as a table-fellow sour and monosyllabic, but by no means abstemious, for all his Puritanism, was as prompt as Hal to avail himself of the comfort of the bed. His appreciation was soon evinced by a loud snoring, whose sturdy nasality seemed of a piece with his canting, rebuking manner of speech when he allowed himself to be lured into conversation. There was in his snore a rhythmic wrestling and protesting, as of Jacob with the angel, or a preacher against Satan, that befitted well his righteous non-conformity. From this thought — for which he wondered that he could find place when his situation provided so much other matter for meditation — Hal's mind lapsed into the incoherent visions of slumber, and soon deep sleep was upon him.

Hal had arranged that Kit Bottle should return to the inn and call him, after four hours, in the event of no appearance of the pursuit. When Hal awoke with a start, therefore, and yet heard no such hallooing as Anthony had given at Catworth, he supposed that Kit must have summoned him by a less alarming cry. His head shot out of the window, but he beheld no Kit. Turning to Anthony, he saw that the Puritan had just opened his eyes.

"Didst hear anything?" queried Hal.

"Not sith I awoke," was the answer. "Yet meseems in my sleep there was a loud grating sound and a terrific crash."

"In our dreams we multiply the sounds that touch our ears," said Hal. "It must have been a sound of omen, to have waked us both. So let us think of a small grating sound —"

At that instant his eyes alighted on the door. He would have sworn a key had been in that door, though he had not locked it before sleeping. He had noticed the key for its great size and rustiness. But no key was there now, at least on the inside. Hal strode from the bed, and tried the door. It was locked.

"How now?" quoth he. "Some one has robbed

us of our key, and used it on the wrong side of the door!"

"I warrant it should be no far seeking to find that some one," growled Anthony, rising to his feet.

"Ay," said Hal, "'tis just the shallow, childish stop-nobody thing a woman would do, and think she hath played a fine trick! Come, Anthony,"—Hal spoke the Puritan's name not superciliously now, for he was beginning to like a fellow who could toil forward so uncomplainingly through fatigue and danger, yet make such full use of comforts when they fell to him,—"I see Captain Bottle riding hither, at a walk. That means 'tis four o'clock, though Master Barnet hath not yet shown his face. We must be taking horse again."

And he dropped out of the window to the porch roof, let himself down a corner-post, and stood in the inn yard. Anne's horses were still there. As soon as Anthony was beside him, Hal stepped into the entrance-passage. At the stair-foot stood Mistress Hazlehurst, her back to the door, giving some swift and excited commands to her page, Francis, who was ready to ride.

She turned to see who had entered the inn. On perceiving it was Hal, and that his face wore an involuntary quizzical smile, she caught her breath, and became the very picture of defeat and self-discovered foolishness.

"Have you seen aught of a key I lost?" said Hal, ere he thought. "I need it to unlock my door and get out of my room, as I am in some haste!"

She turned deep crimson at the jest; her eyes shot a glance of fire, her lips closed tight; and, without a word, she glided past him, and out to her horses. He saw in her look a new sense of the insufficiency of easy and obvious means, and a resolution to rise to the needs of her purpose.

"Her eyes are opened," mused Hal, following her and Francis to the yard. "Her next step is like to be more considerable!"

Meeting Kit and the horses just within the inn yard gate, Hal and Anthony mounted. Anne and her page were prompt to follow their example. With courtesy, Hal held back his horses for her to precede him out to the road. A minute afterward the five riders, so strangely brought into a single group, were pushing northward in the cold, waning afternoon.

She had slept some, and was the better for the food she had taken. Yet this riding was manifestly a wearier business than it could have been at the time of her setting out. It was a chilly business, too, for March had begun to turn out very January-like, and was steadily becoming more so. The look of dogged endurance that mingled on her face with the new resolution there, continually touched Hal's tender and pitying side. His countenance as continually showed his feelings, and she perceived them with deep and ill-concealed resentment.

But she at last attained a degree of stolid iciness at which she remained. It imposed upon Hal, riding at her side, a silence that became the harder to break as it became the less bearable. And the further she tried to put herself out of his pity, the greater his pity grew, for the effort she was required to make. The more his admiration increased, too; and if pity is ever akin to love, it is certainly so when united to admiration. Her determination had not the mannish mien, nor her dislike the acrid, ill-bred aspect that would have repelled; they were of the womanly and high-born character that made them rather pique and allure. Partly to provoke her feelings to some change of phase, partly to elicit relief from the impassiveness in which she had sought refuge, partly for the cruel pleasure sometimes inexplicably found in torturing the tender and beautiful, — a pleasure followed by penitence as keen, — he made two or three delicate jests about the locked door; these were received with momentary glints of rage from her dark eyes, succeeded by coldness more freezing than before.

The silence created — and diffused — by her enveloped the whole party, making the ride even more bleak than it was already from the wintry day and the loneliness of the road. It was bad weather for travelling, less by reason of the present cold than of the signs of impending storm. "There is snow in the air," growled Anthony Underhill to himself, as if he smelled it. Of the country through which they passed, the most was open, only the pasture-land and the grounds pertaining immediately to gentlemen's houses being fenced. Enclosures were a new thing in those days, defended by the raisers of sheep and cattle, bewailed by the farmers who tilled the soil. Where the road did not run between woods or over wild moors, it gave views of far-off sheep-cotes, of mills, and here and there of distant castle-towers, or the gables of some squire's rambling manor-house; or it passed through straggling villages, each with a central green having a may-pole and an open pool.

But most human life was indoors upon this evening of belated winter; still and brown was the landscape. Once, soon after they had passed from Rutlandshire into Leicestershire, a burst of yokelish laughter struck their ears from among some trees, like a sudden ray of light and warmth in a cold, dead world. It came from some yeomen's sons who were destroying the eggs of birds of prey. The population of Melton Mowbray was housed and at supper, as they rode through that town in the early dusk without stop.

On into Nottinghamshire they went; and at last, checked alike by darkness and by weariness, they came to a halt before a little, low, wobbly-looking wood-and-plaster inn at the junction of the Nottingham road with the cross-road to Newark.

CHAPTER XI.

WINE AND SONG.

"He's in the third degree of drink; he's drowned." — *Twelfth Night.*

THE inn people coming forth with a light, Hal made similar arrangements to those effected at his two previous stopping-places, with this difference, that he himself was to watch for two hours, and then be succeeded by Anthony. Anne could not exactly repeat her precautions taken at Oakham, for Hal procured the only available fresh horses before she applied for any; nor could she arrange that her own horses should be held in readiness before the inn. She caused them, however, to be fed and kept in an unlocked shed, from which her page might speedily take them out; and she was successful in bespeaking information in case of the enemy's departure.

Though Hal left her sight in riding back to keep watch, she now knew that he would not flee without calling his attendants, nor could he continue his flight in either practicable direction — toward Nottingham or toward Newark — without passing the inn. So she went to her room — one of the few with which the low upper story of the house was provided — in confident mind, stationing Francis on a bench where he might, in a state of half slumber, watch the door of Kit and Anthony. As for the window of the room taken by these two, it was not far from her own, and by keeping the latter open she counted upon hearing any exit made through the former. She lay down, and dozed wakefully.

Hal's watch was without event. As he moved up and down the silent road with his horses, he continued to ask himself whether she might yet have formed a plan of action against him; and from this question he fell to considering what plan might be possible. He tried to devise one for her, but could invent none that he saw himself unable to defeat.

He returned to the inn at the end of his two hours, and summoned Anthony by a whistle previously agreed upon. Anthony came down by the stairs, and went silently on guard. Hal, who had not yet eaten, now entered the inn with a ready appetite for the supper he had previously ordered. As he stepped from the outer wind into the passage, he noticed that the door was open which led thence to the inn parlor. Just within that door stood a figure. He glanced at it. By the light of the candles farther in the room, he saw that it was Mistress Hazlehurst.

"Sir," she said to him, in a dry tone, which, as also her face, she tried to rob of all expression save that of ordinary, indifferent civility, "I learn you bespoke supper to be sent to your room. I am having mine own served here. We have full understanding of each other's intent. There is open warfare between us. Yet while we be fellow travellers, each set upon the other's defeat, meseems we should as well comport ourselves as fellow travellers till one win the other's undoing. Though writ down in blood as bitter foes, in birth we are equal, and our lands are neighbor. So I do offer that we sup together, as becometh people of civility upon the same journey, though enemies they be to the death."

To this proposal, so congenial with his inclinations, what could Master Marryott do but forthwith assent, too dazzled by the prospect to torture his brain for a likely motive on her part? With a "Right readily, mistress!" he hastened to give the necessary orders, and then entered the parlor, which had no occupant but Mistress Anne. The last tippler of the night had sought his bed.

At one side of the low room was a fire in a wide hearth. At another side, beneath a deep, long, horizontal window was a table, on which some dishes were already set. The floor was covered with stale rushes. There were no hangings on the besmoked, plastered, timbered walls. The poor candles shed a wavering light. This was no Mermaid tavern, indeed. Yet Hal felt mightily, dangerously comfortable here.

He opened a casement a little, that he might hear any alarm from Anthony, and then he sat down at the table, opposite Anne. He saw that Francis, who seemed of wire, and proof against fatigue and lack of sleep, stood ready to wait upon his mistress. He saw, too, that her wine was placed on a rude kind of sideboard, to be served from thence each time a sip might be wanted, as in the private houses of gentlefolk. When a tapster came, sleepy and muttering to himself, with Hal's wine, Master Marryott ordered it put as the lady's was; and then Mistress Hazlehurst proposed, in the manner she had used before, that the inn servant be dismissed and Francis wait upon them both.

"It is but fair repayment," she added, "for the protection I receive upon the road by the presence of your men."

Hal was nothing loath. He would not show suspicion, if he felt any, at being invited to be left alone with his enemy and her servant. Francis was but a slip of a boy, — and yet, in his tirelessness, his reposeful manner, his discreet look, the closeness of his mouth, there was sufficient of the undisclosed, of the possibly latent, to put a wise man on his guard. Hal kept a corner of his eye upon the page, therefore, while with the rest of it he studied the fine face and graceful motions — motions the more effective for being few — of the page's mistress.

The early part of the meal went in silence, Francis attending to the dishes and serving the wine noiselessly, with neither haste nor tardiness. Hal saw in the looks of both lady and page the reviving effects of a short sleep and of cold water. Anne ate, not as if hungry, but as if providing against possible exposure and fasting. That Francis might not have to depart unfed, she bade him partake of certain dishes as he bore them from before her. He contrived to do this, and yet to see that Master Marryott never wanted for wine.

And, indeed, Master Marryott, warmed, comforted, made to see things rosily, put into mood of rare good-feeling and admiration, kept Francis busy and busier between the sideboard and the wine-cup at Hal's hand. Finally, the page, when he should have taken the flagon back to the sideboard, set it down on the table, that he might thereafter fill the cup without even the loss of time involved in traversing the rush-covered floor. Was this the boy's own happy thought, or was it in obedience to a meaning glance from his mistress? Hal did not query himself on this point; he had observed no meaning glance. He was entering the seventh heaven of wine; it seemed the most natural thing in the world that he should find the flagon constantly at his elbow. And suddenly this silence, so long maintained, appeared absurd, unaccountable. God-'a'-mercy! why should people sit tongue-tied in this manner? Wherefore he spoke:

"Truly 'twas well thought on that we might use civil courtesy between us, enemies though you will have us! 'Tis like the exchange of gentleness 'twixt our noblest soldiers and those of Spain, in times of truce, or even in the breathing moments 'tween sword-thrusts. Truly, courtesy sweeteneth all transactions, even those of enmity and warfare! 'Tis like this wine that giveth a soft and pleasing hue, as of its own color, to all one sees and hears when one has drunk of it. Taste it, madam, I pray. Your glass hath not been once refilled. Nay, an you spare the wine so, I shall say you but half act upon your own offer!"

She drank what remained in her cup, and let Francis fill it again.

"No doubt the ladies of France drink more wine than we of England," she said, as if at the same time to account for his importunity and her moderation. He perceived the allusion to Sir Valentine's long residence in France, and was put on his guard against betraying himself. He ought to have taken more into mind that she regarded him as her brother's slayer, and that her tone was strangely urbane for such regarding, even though courtesy had been agreed upon. But by this time he had too much wine in. He had long since exhausted the contents of his own flagon, and was now being served from hers.

"The ladies of France," he replied, "are none the better of the ladies of England for that."

"I have heard there is a certain facility and grace in them, that we lack," she answered, having noticed that he drank at the end of each speech he made.

"It may be," he said, "but 'tis the facility and grace of the cat, with claws and teeth at the back of it." He had to speak of French ladies entirely from hearsay. "For softness, united with strength and candor, for amplitude and warmth of heart, commend me to the English ladies." Euphuism was still the fashion, and people of breeding had the knack of conversing offhand in sentences that would now seem studied.

The cup-lifting that followed this remark was accompanied by so direct a look at her that she could not but know for which particular English lady the compliment was intended. She gave no outward sign of anger.

"The French excel us in their wine, at least," she replied, sipping from her cup as if to demonstrate the sincerity of her words, — an action that instantly moved Master Hal to further and deeper potations.

"SHE GAVE NO OUTWARD SIGN OF ANGER."

"Why, I should be an ingrate to gainsay that," said he. "'Tis indeed matter for thanks that we, sitting by night in this lone country ale-house, — 'tis little better, — with the March wind howling wolf-like without, may imbibe, and cheer our souls with, the sunlight that hath fallen in past years upon French hillsides. But we should be churls to despise the vineyards of Spain or Italy, either! Or the Rhenish, that hath gladdened so many a heart and begot so many a song! Lovest thou music, madam?"

She kept a startled silence for a moment, at a loss how to receive the change from "you" to "thou" in his style of addressing her. In truth the familiarity was on his part unpremeditated and innocent. But, for another reason than that, she speedily decided to overlook it, and she answered, in words that gave Hal a sudden thrill, for they were those of one of Master Shakespeare's own comedies, often played by the company:

> "The man that hath no music in himself,
> Nor is not moved with concord of sweet sounds
> Is fit for treasons, stratagems, and spoils."

She paused here, as if struck with the thought that the speech might not be known to the Catholic knight.

"'Tis Lorenzo's speech in 'The Merchant,'" said

Hal, quite ecstatic. "I —" he caught himself in time to avoid saying, "know the part by heart, having studied it in hope of some day playing it," and added, instead, "saw the comedy in London when 'twas first played, and a friend sent me a book of it last year, that he bought in Paul's Churchyard. Thou'st seen the play, I ween."

"And read it," she answered, this time filling his glass herself, for Francis had stolen from the room with a flagon in quest of more wine at the bar.

"Know'st thou the full speech," said he, "beginning, 'How sweet the moonlight sleeps upon this bank'?" Without waiting for an answer, and being now in the vinous rage for reciting, he went on through the scene to its interruption by the entrance of Portia and Nerissa. It was nothing wonderful, in those days, that a gentleman should speak verse well; yet she viewed him with some astonishment, in which was a first faint touch of regret that circumstance made this man, in whom otherwise she might find certain admirable qualities, irrevocably her foe, to become inevitably her victim. This regret she instantly put from her, and set herself the more to plying him with wine.

"I'll warrant thou hast music at the end of thy tongue, and of thy fingers also," said Hal. "Would there were an instrument here! Heavenly must be the offspring, when such hands wed string of lute, or key of virginal! But thy lips are here. Wilt sing? All are abed. I prithee, a song!"

"Nay, 'twere better you should sing," she answered, by way of evading a course of importunities, and seeing that he was in ripe mood for compliance.

"Willingly, an thou'lt engage to sing in thy turn," he replied.

She gave her promise, thinking she would not have to keep it; for when a gentleman in wine becomes vocally inclined, he is apt to go on like a wound-up clock till he be stopped, or till he run down into slumber.

So Hal began, with Shakespeare's "O mistress mine, where are you roaming?" as a song whose line, "That can sing both high and low," was appropriate to their recent subject. And this led naturally to the song "It was a lover and his lass," which in turn called up Ben Jonson's song on a kiss, from the masque of "Cynthia's Revels." Then something gave a convivial shift to Hal's thoughts, and he offered King Henry VIII.'s "Pastime with good company," from which he went to the old drinking song from "Gammer Gurton's Needle."

Mistress Hazlehurst, having perceived that singing hindered his drinking, though each lapse between songs was filled with a hasty draught, was now willing enough to keep her promise; and she made bold to remind him of it. He was quite eager to hear her, though it should require silence on his own part. She sang Shakespeare's "When icicles hang by the wall," in a low and melodious voice, of much beauty in a limited range,— a voice of the same quality as her ordinary speaking tones. Seeing that Hal, who gazed in admiration, broke his own inaction by constant applications to the flagon, which the clever Francis had succeeded in filling at the bar, she followed this song immediately with "Blow, blow, thou winter wind."

Hal was now ready to volunteer with "Under the greenwood tree," but she cut him short, and drove him to repeated uses of the cup, by starting John Heywood's song of "The green willow," which she selected as suiting her purpose by reason of its great length.

When this was at last finished, Hal, who had been regarding her steadily with eyes that sometimes blinked for drowsiness, opened his mouth to put in practice a compliment he had for some minutes been meditating,— that of singing "Who is Sylvia?" in such manner as should imply that Mistress Hazlehurst embodied all the excellences of her who "excelled each mortal thing upon the dull earth dwelling." She silenced him at the outset by taking up Heywood's "Be merry, friends," at which, despite how much he admired her face and was thrilled by her voice, he sat back in resignation; for the old song she had this time hit upon was as nearly endless as it was monotonous. Hal's nurse had many times droned him to sleep with it, in his infancy.

And now its somnolent effect was as great as ever. Save for her voice, in the unvarying rhythm of the countless four-line stanzas marked by the refrain, "Be merry, friends!" at the end of each, and for a frequent moan or whine of the wind without, the utmost stillness reigned. Francis had effaced himself on a high-backed seat in a dark corner of the fireplace. The candles burned dimly for want of snuffing, and they were just so far from Hal's arm that, in his drowsy state, it was too great an effort to reach them. Indeed, it had now become too great an effort to draw the wine flagon toward him. His brain swam a little. He sat back limp in his oaken settle, his head fell more and more heavily toward his breast. Things became vaguer and vaguer before him; the face from whose lips the soporific melody proceeded was blended more and more with the ambient shadows. His eyelids closed.

She continued the song more softly, a triumphant light slowly increasing in her eyes. At last her voice was still. The supposed Sir Valentine moved not, lifted not his head, opened not his eyes. Only his regular breathing, the heavy breathing of vinous stupor, was heard in the room.

Mistress Hazlehurst rose without noise.

"He will not be in riding mood for ten hours to come," she said, quietly, to Francis. "An his men waken him, he'll be for calling them hard names, and off to sleep again! God-'a'-mercy, what an ocean of wine hath he swallowed in three short hours! Come, Francis, we may sleep with ease of mind to-night. He is stayed beyond even the will to go on. And I thank heaven, for I am well-nigh as drowsy, and as loath to ride in this weather, as he must be!"

It was sleepily indeed that she stepped, with as little sound as could be, over the crackling rushes to the door. To keep her enemy in the drinking mood, and to dissemble her purpose, she had taken an unusual quantity of wine herself. Ladies did not drink as much in Elizabeth's outwardly decent reign as they came to drink a few years later, under Scottish Jeames, when, if Sir John Harrington lied not in 1606, those of the court did "abandon their sobriety" and were "seen to roll about in intoxication." And Mistress Hazlehurst was the last woman in the world to violate the prevalent seemliness under the virgin queen. But she had sipped enough to augment the languor induced by her recent exertions. She put a hand upon the door-post to support herself as she approached it.

There was a wild, swift beating of horses' hoofs on the road outside; an abrupt stoppage just before the inn; a shrill whistle, and this shout from Anthony Underhill:

"What, ho! Halloo, halloo!"

Hal raised his head, and looked drowsily around with blinking eyes. There was a noise overhead of a heavy tread, — that of Captain Bottle, responding to the alarm. In a trice old Kit was heard clearing the stairs at a bound, and then seen dashing through the passage and out into the darkness. He had unbarred the outer door with a single movement.

Hal stared inquiringly at Mistress Hazlehurst. Her eyes had a glow of confident expectation. That was her blunder.

Her look told him all, — that she had supped with him, sung for him, incited him to drink, in order that he might be unfit for flight or action. He sprang to his feet, clapped on his hat, threw off his tipsiness with one backward jerk of the shoulders; was himself again, with clear eyes and strong, steady limbs.

"To horse, madam, if you would still ride with us!" he cried. "I have some thirty miles or so to go to-night!"

And he strode past her, and out after Kit Bottle.

"'Tis Barnet's men, methinks, by the sound of the horses yonder," said Anthony, composedly, pointing southward, as Hal rose into the saddle.

Hal looked back toward the open door of the inn.

In a moment Anne came out with Francis, who ran at once to the shed wherein her horses were.

In the doorway between parlor and passage she had undergone a moment of sickening chagrin. Not only had she failed ridiculously a second time, but she must now abandon her clutch upon her enemy, or face with him that thirty miles of night ride in biting weather! Francis looked at her for commands. She tightened her lips again, imitated Hal's own motion of casting away lassitude, drew her cloak close around her, put up her hood, and hastened out to the windy night.

Hal made great stir with his horses before moving off, that the inn people might be awakened and some of them note which road he took. This precaution, used for the benefit of Roger Barnet, gave Anne time to join Hal's party.

When the pursuivant and his fellows rode up, soon afterward, on half dead horses, that stumbled before the inn, the fugitives were well forward on the Nottingham road. It was a bitter, black night.

"Fellow travellers still!" quoth Master Marryott, to the dark figure that rode galloping, with flying cloak, beside him.

"And shall be till I see you caught, though I must ride sleepless till I drop!" was the reply.

CHAPTER XII.

THE CONSTABLE OF CLOWN.

"I am a wise fellow; and, which is more, an officer; . . . and one that knows the law, go to." — *Much Ado about Nothing.*

IT was one hour after midnight, when the fellow travellers left the lone inn near the Newark crossroad. They had arrived there at eight o'clock in the evening. During their stay, Hal had obtained no sleep but that which he had taken at the table, and which had lasted but a few minutes. Anne had slept perhaps an hour before going down to the parlor. The reader will remember the fatigued condition in which both had come to the inn. Their next rest could not be had until a long and hard ride should achieve for them a probable gain of some hours over the horsemen whom Anthony Underhill had heard. For this gain, Hal counted on the fact that Barnet's horses, more recently ridden, could not be as fresh as his own, and on Barnet's constant necessity of pausing at each branching of the road, to make inquiries. Such were the conditions under which the second full day of the flight began.

It was now a time for drawing on that reserved energy which manifests itself only in seasons of strait. Hal was aware, from past experience, of this stored-up stock of endurance, that serves its possessor on occasions of extremity. To Anne, its existence within her must have come as a new disclosure. Hal, as a man of gentle rearing, had for her a man's compassion for a woman to whom this discovery is made by hardship undergone for the first time. And yet, so does human nature abound in apparent contradictions, he had a kind of satisfaction, almost gleeful, at the toils she had brought upon herself by attempting to overreach him. For, had she used in sleep the time she had spent in that attempt, had she not taken sufficient of the wine to enervate herself somewhat, she would now have been in fresh vigor for the wearing ride before her.

The riders had a slight check at Nottingham, owing to a difference of opinion between Master Marryott and the watch, as to the propriety of their passing through the town at such an hour of the night. Hal was in instant readiness for any outcry on the part of Mistress Hazlehurst. But he looked so resolute, Kit Bottle so formidable, Anthony Underhill so rigid with latent fighting force, that Anne doubtless saw little to be gained from a conflict between her enemy and the unaided dotards of the night watch. A gold piece, to reinforce a story explaining their early riding, proved the magic opener it commonly proves, and obtained a lantern from one of the watchmen, as well; and the fugitives rode free, northward into Sherwood forest.

It was lone riding, and toilsome, through the greenwood where Robin Hood and his outlaws had made merry, and past Newstead Abbey; and would have been next to impossible but for the lantern, with which the Puritan lighted up a few inches of the tree-roofed road ahead. Dawn found them near Mansfield, through which town they soon after passed without stay, and proceeded into Derbyshire.

At seven o'clock, having covered twenty-nine miles in the six hours since their last setting out, and all but Kit Bottle being ready to fall from their saddles, they stopped before a humble hostelry at Scardiff.

They could get but one fresh horse here. Bottle took this one, upon which to ride back to a suitable spot for watching the road behind. The others of the party had to be content with giving their nearly used-up animals what rest might be had in saddle and bridle, and under a penthouse roof at one end of the inn. Hal, before entering the inn, bought the vigilance of a hostler toward keeping his horses in readiness for further going, and against any attempt on Anne's part, through Francis, to disable them while he slept; though, indeed, he saw little likelihood of her employing such means, both she and her page being in the utmost need of immediate sleep; and she unable to purchase treachery of the inn folk, for, as he observed when she paid the hostess in advance, her purse was now sadly fallen away. Hal foresaw, from this last circumstance, two things: a certainty of her resorting soon to desperate measures against him, and an opportunity for his chivalry to display itself in an offer to pay her charges while she continued with deadly purpose to accompany him.

As Hal was about to follow Anne into the house, he was greeted by a pleasant-eyed old fellow who had been sitting on a bench by the door, with a mug of ale at his side; an old fellow whose frieze jacket and breeches proclaimed a yeoman, and whose presence on the outer bench on so cold a morning betokened a lively curiosity as to the doings of his fellow-men.

"God save your worship!" said he, in a mild little voice, rising and bowing with great respect for gentility. "I dare say your honor hasna' fell in with the rascals, on your worship's travels?"

Seeing but a rustical officiousness and news-hunger in this speech, Hal paused, and asked:

"What rascals, goodman?"

"Them that ha' pestered travellers, and householders, too, so bad of late, on roads hereabout. Marry, 'tis well to go in plenty company, when robbers ride in such number together! They make parlous wayfaring for gentlefolk, your worship!"

"You mean that a band of highway robbers, more than common bold, hath been in the neighborhood?"

"Ay, and I would any man might say the rogues were yet out of it! They have terrified constables, and the justices sleep over the matter, and the sheriff hath his affairs elsewhere; so God look after honest travellers, say I, sir!"

"You say well," replied Marryott, casting a glance at Anne, who also had stopped to listen to the countryman's words. She took from Hal's countenance a sense of the further obligation she must needs be under for his protection, now that a particular known danger was at hand; but this sense only moved her to the inward resolve of ending alike that obligation and their northward travel, by some supreme effort to entrap him. He read her thought in her face, and his look defied her. She hastened to her room, he to his; she, attended by Francis, he by Anthony Underhill.

Marryott and Anthony soon despatched the scant meal brought to their chamber. Before placing himself for sleep, Harry looked into the passage. The boy Francis was at his customary post outside his mistress's door.

Hal and the Puritan were asleep before eight o'clock. At ten, Hal awoke. After he had glanced out of the window, and seen no one about the inn, something — he knew not what — impelled him to take another view of the passage. He did so; and this time he beheld no Francis.

He awakened Anthony, and the two stepped softly into the passage. They stood for an instant before Mistress Hazlehurst's door, but heard no sound from within. Down-stairs they went, surveying the public room of the house as they passed out to the open air. The room was empty. They hastened to the shed where the horses were. The horses were now but two, — Marryott's and Anthony's. Those of Mistress Hazlehurst and her page were gone.

With Hal's quick feeling of alarm, there came also a chilling sense of sudden loneliness. A void seemed to have opened around him.

"The devil!" was all that he could say.

"She cannot have given up, and gone back," volunteered Anthony. "She would have had to pass your man Bottle, and he would have ridden hither to tell you she was stirring."

"Ay, 'tis plain enough she hath not fled southward, where Kit keeps watch for Barnet's men. She hath ridden forward! Ho, John Ostler, a murrain on you!" cried Hal. "The lady — whither hath she gone, and when? Speak out, or 'twill fare hard with you!"

"'Twas but your own two beasts your honor bade me guard," said the hostler, coming from the stables. "As for the lady, her and the lad went that way, an hour since or so!" And the fellow pointed northward.

"Haste, Anthony!" muttered Hal, untying his own horse. "Ride yonder for Kit Bottle, and then you and he gallop after me! She hath gone to raise the country ahead of us! Failure of other means hath pushed her to belie her declaration."

"A woman's declaration needeth little pushing, to be o'erthrown," commented Anthony, sagely, as he mounted.

"Tut, knave, 'tis a woman's privilege to renounce her word!" replied Master Marryott, sharply, having already leaped to saddle.

"It may be so; I know not," said Anthony, with sour indifference; and the two made for the road together.

"Well, see that Kit and you follow speedily, while I fly forward to stay that lady, lest we be caught 'twixt Barnet's men behind us, and a hue and cry in front!" Whereupon, without more ado, Hal spurred his horse in the direction that Anne had taken, while Anthony turned southward in quest of Bottle.

As Hal sped along, he did not dare confess which of the two motives more fed his anxious impatience: solicitude for his own cause, or fear that Anne might meet danger on the road, — for he recalled what the countryman had told him of highway robbers infesting the neighborhood.

He put four miles behind him, neither winning glimpse of her nor being overtaken by Kit and Anthony. Seeking naught in the forward distance but her figure — now so distinct in his imagination, so painfully absent from his real vision, — he paid no heed, until he had galloped into the very midst of it, to a numerous crowd of heavy-shod countrymen that lined both sides of the road at the entrance to the village of Clown.

So impetuous had been Hal's forward movement, so complete the possession of his mind by the one image, that he had seen this village assemblage with dull eyes, and with no sense of its possibly having anything to do with himself; yet it was just such a gathering that he ought to have expected, and against which he ought to have been on his guard. Not until it closed about him, not until a huge loutish fellow caught the rein of his suddenly impeded horse, and a pair of rustics drew across the road — from a side lane — a clumsy covered coach that wholly blocked the way, and a little old man on the edge of the crowd brandished a rusty bill and called out in a squeaky voice, "Surrender!" did Hal realize that he had ridden right into the hands of a force hastily gathered by the village constable to waylay and take him prisoner.

Hal clapped hand to sword-hilt, and surveyed the crowd with a sweeping glance. The constable had evidently brought out every able-bodied man in the near neighborhood. Three or four were armed with long bills, hooked and pointed, like that borne by the constable himself. Others carried stout staves. Emboldened by the example of the giant who had seized Hal's rein, the clowns pressed close around his horse. Ere Hal could draw sword, his wrist was caught in the iron grasp of one of the giant's great brown paws. Two other burly villagers laid hold of his pistols. With his free hand, Hal tried to back his horse out of the press, but was prevented both by the throng behind and by the big fellow's gripe of the rein. Marryott thereupon flashed out his dagger, and essayed to use it upon the hand that imprisoned his wrist. But his arm was caught, in the elbow crook, by the hook of a bill that a yeoman wielded in the nick of time. The next instant, a heavy blow from a stave struck the dagger from Hal's hand. His legs were seized, and he was a captured man.

All this had occurred in short time, during the plunging of Hal's horse and the shouting of the crowd. It had been a vastly different matter from the night encounter with Mistress Hazlehurst's servants. These yokels of Clown, assembled in large number, led by the parish Hercules, bearing the homely weapons to which they were used, opposing afoot and by daylight a solitary mounted man to whom their attack was a complete surprise, were a force from whom defeat was no disgrace. Yet never did Master Marryott know keener rage, humiliation, and self-reproach — self-reproach for his heedless precipitancy, and his having ridden on without his two men — than when he found himself captive to these rustics; save when, a moment later, his glance met an open casement of an ale-house at one side of the road, and he saw Anne Hazlehurst! Her look was one of triumph; her smile like that with which he had greeted her after the incident of the locked door at Oakham. And, for the space of that moment, he hated her.

"Sir Valentine Fleetwood," cried the constable, in his senile squeak, pushing his way with a sudden access of pomposity from his place at the crowd's edge, "I apprehend you for high treason, and charge you to get down from your horse and come peaceably to the justice's house."

"Justice's house!" cried Hal, most wrathfully. "Of what do you prate, old fool? What have I to do with scurvy, rustical justices?"

"To Justice Loudwight's, your honor," replied the constable, suddenly tamed by Hal's high and mighty tone. "In good sooth, his house is pleasant lodging, even for a knight, or lord either, and his table and wine —"

"Devil take Justice Loudwight's table and wine, and a black murrain take yourself!" broke in Hal, from his horse. "Give me my weapons, and let me pass! What foolery is this, you rogue, to hinder one of her Majesty's subjects travelling on weighty business?"

"Nay, sir, I know my duty, and Mr. Loudwight shall judge. I must hold you till he come back from Chesterfield, whither he hath gone to —"

"I care not wherefore Mr. Loudwight hath gone to Chesterfield, or if every other country wight in Derbyshire hath gone to visit the foul fiend! Nor can I tarry for their coming back," quoth Hal, truly enough, for such tarrying meant his detention for the arrival of Roger Barnet. "Let me pass on, or this place shall rue this day!"

"I be the constable, and I know my duty, and I must apprehend all flying traitors, whether they be traitors or no, which is a matter for my betters in the law to give judgment on."

The constable's manner showed a desire to prove himself an authoritative personage, in the eyes of the community and of Mistress Hazlehurst. He was a quailing old fellow, who pretended boldness; a simple soul, who affected shrewdness.

"Know your duty, say you?" quoth Hal. "Were that so, you would know a constable may not hold a gentleman without a warrant. Where is your writ?"

"Talk not of warrants! I'll have warrants enough when Justice Loudwight cometh home. Though I have no warrant yet, I have information," and the constable glanced at the window from which Anne looked down at the scene.

Hal thought of the surely fatal consequences of his remaining in custody till either Justice Loudwight should come home or Roger Barnet arrive. His heart sank. True, Kit Bottle and Anthony Underhill might appear at any moment; but their two swords, unaided by his own, would scarce avail against the whole village toward effecting a rescue. He pondered a second; then spoke thus:

"Look you, Master Constable! You have information. Well, information is but information. Mine affairs so press me onward that I may not wait to be judged of your Mr. Loudwight. Hear you, therefore, the charge against me, and mine answer to't. While the justice is away, is not the constable the main pillar of the law? And shall not a constable judge of information that cometh to him first? Odslight, 'tis a pretty pass when one may say this-and-that into the ears of a constable, and bid him act upon it as 'twere heaven's truth! Hath he no mind of his own, by which he may judge of information? If he have authority to receive information, hath he not authority to receive denial of it, and to render opinion 'twixt the two?"

The constable, flattered and magnified — he knew not exactly why — by Hal's words and mien, expanded and looked profound; then answered, with a sage, approving nod:

"There is much law and equity in what you say, sir!"

Quick to improve the situation, Hal instantly added:

"Then face me with your informer, Master Constable, and judge lawfully between us!"

"Bring this worshipful prisoner before me!" commanded the constable, addressing the giant and the others in possession of Hal's horse, legs, and weapons; and thereupon walked, with great authority, into the ale-house. Hal was promptly pulled from his saddle, and led after him. The constabulary presence established itself behind a table at one side of the public room. The giant and another fellow held Hal, while a third tied his hands behind with a rope.

The villagery crowded into the room, pushing Hal almost against the constable's table. But, after a moment, the crowd parted; for Anne Hazlehurst, having witnessed the course of events from her window, had come down-stairs without being summoned, and she now moved forward to Hal's side, closely followed by Francis. Meanwhile, at the constable's order, a gawkish stripling, whose looks betokened an underdone pedagogue, took a seat at the table's end, with writing materials which the officer of the peace had commanded from the ale-house keeper in order to give an imposing legal aspect to the proceedings.

"Now, sir," began the constable, with his best copy of a judicial frown, "there is here to be examined a question of whether this offender be in truth a pursued traitor —"

"Pardon me, Master Constable," objected Hal. "Sith it is questionable whether I be that traitor, I may not yet be called an offender."

"Sir," replied the constable, taking on severity from the presence of Anne, "leave these matters to them that stand for the laws. Offender you are, and that's certain, having done offence in that you did resist apprehension."

"Nay, if I be the pursued traitor I am charged with being," said Hal, "then might that apprehension have been proper, and I might stand guilty of resistance; but if I be no such traitor, the apprehension was but the molesting of a true subject of the queen, and my resistance was but a self-defence, and the offence was of them that stayed me."

The constable began to fear he was in deep waters; so cleared his throat for time, and at last proceeded:

"There is much can be said thereon, and if it be exhibited that there was resistance, then be sure justice will be rendered. If it be proven you are no traitor, then perhaps it shall follow that there was no resistance. But yet I say not so for certain. What is your name, sir?"

Before Hal could answer, Mistress Hazlehurst put in:

"His name is Sir Valentine Fleetwood, and he is flying from a warrant—"

"Write down Sir Valentine Fleetwood," said the constable, in an undertone, to the youth with quill, ink-horn, and paper.

"Write down no such name!" cried Hal. "Write down Harry Marryott, gentleman, of the lord chamberlain's company of players!" And Hal faced Anne, with a look of defiance. Ere any one could speak, he went on, "This lady, whom I take to be your informer, will confess that, if I be not Sir Valentine Fleetwood, I am not the person she doth accuse."

During the silence of the assemblage, Anne regarded Hal with a contemptuous smile, as if she thought his device to escape detention as shallow and foolish as had been her own first attempt to hinder him.

"What name shall I put down?" asked the puzzled scribe, of the constable.

"Write Sir Valentine Fleetwood!" repeated Anne, peremptorily. "This gentleman's sorry shift to evade you, Master Constable, is scarce worthy of his birth."

"Write down Sir Valentine Fleetwood," ordered the constable. "Is not this the examination of Sir Valentine Fleetwood, and whose name else — ?"

"If it be the examination of Sir Valentine Fleetwood," interrupted Hal, "then 'tis not my examination, and I demand of you my liberty forthwith; for I do not acknowledge that name! I warn you, constable!"

Taken aback by Hal's threatening tone, the constable looked irresolute, and glanced from Hal to Anne and back again.

Mistress Hazlehurst opened her eyes in a mixture of amazement and alarm, as if it might indeed be possible that her enemy's device should have effect upon this ignorant rustic. She took the supposed Sir Valentine's denial of that name to be a pitiful lie, employed on the spur of the moment. It was not less important to Hal that she should so take it, than it was that the constable should receive it as truth; and he now had to wear toward the officer a manner of veracity, and toward Anne the mien of a ready and brazen liar. This could not but make her loathe him the more, and it went against him to assume it. But in his mind he could hear the steady hoof-beats of Roger Barnet's horses coming up from the south, and so he must stick firmly to the truth which made him in her eyes a liar.

Her momentary look of alarm died away as the constable continued to gaze in stupid indecision. She waited for others to speak; she had no interest in hastening matters; her hopes were served by every minute of delay. But Hal's case was the reverse.

"Well, man," he said, to the slow-thinking constable, "I am here to answer to any charge made against me in mine own name. If you have aught to say concerning Mr. Harry Marryott, of the lord chamberlain's players, set it forth, for I am in haste. I swear to you, by God's name, and on the cross of my sword if yon fellow hand it back to me, that I am not Sir Valentine Fleetwood, and that there is no warrant for my apprehension!"

"Perjurer!" cried Anne, with scorn and indignation.

"Nay, madam," quoth the constable, somewhat impressed by Hal's declaration, "an oath is an oath. There be the laws of evidence—"

"Then hear my oath!" she broke in. "I swear, before God, this gentleman is he that the royal officers are in pursuit of, with proper warrant,—as you shall soon know, when they come hither!"

The constable sat in bewilderment; frowned, gulped, and hemmed; gazed at Hal, at Anne, at the table before him, and into the open mouth of the lean clerk, who waited for something to write down. At last he squeaked:

"'Tis but oath against oath — a fair balance."

"Then take the oath of my page," said Anne, quickly, drawing Francis forward. "He will swear this is the gentleman of whom I told you."

"That I do," quoth Francis, sturdily, "upon this cross!" And he held aloft his dagger-hilt.

The constable heaved a great sigh of relief, and looked upon Hal with an eased countenance.

"The weight of evidence convicts you, sir," he said. "Let the name of Sir Valentine Fleetwood be taken down, and then his oath, and then the names of these two swearers, and their two oaths —"

"Stay a moment, Master Constable!" cried Hal, his eye suddenly caught by the dismounting of two men from horseback, outside the ale-house window, which had been opened to let fresh air in upon the crowd. "There be other oaths to take down! Ho, Kit Bottle, and Anthony, tie your horses and come hither! Nay, gripe not your swords! Let there be no breach of the peace. But hasten in!"

The general attention fell upon the newcomers, who had ridden hotly. With a dauntless air Kit Bottle strode through the crowd, handling men roughly to make a way, and followed close by Anthony.

"What a murrain hath befallen — ?" Kit was beginning; but Hal stopped him with:

"No time for words! Captain Bottle, you and worthy Master Underhill, testify to this officer my name, the name half London knows me by as a player of the lord chamberlain's company! This lady will have it I am one Sir Valentine Fleetwood. Speak my true name, therefore, upon your oath."

Hal had said enough to inform both Kit and Anthony what name was wanted on this occasion, and the captain instantly answered:

"I will swear to this officer — an thou call'st him such — and maintain it with my sword against any man in England, that thou art no Sir Valentine Fleetwood, but art Master Harry Marryott, and none other, of the lord chamberlain's servants!"

"'Tis the simple truth," said Anthony Underhill, glowering coldly upon the constable. "I will take oath thereto."

The constable held up three fingers of one hand, on Hal's side, and two fingers of the other hand, on Anne's side, and said to her:

"Mistress, here be three oaths against two; thou'rt clearly outsworn!"

"Perjurers!" said Anne, facing Master Marryott and his men.

"Nay, nay, madam!" quoth the constable, becoming severe on the victorious side. "An there be charge of perjury in the case, look to thyself!

Since these three have sworn truly, it followeth that thy two oaths be false oaths!"

"Rascal!" cried Hal. "Do you dare accuse this lady of false swearing?"

"Why, why, surely your three oaths be true —"

"True they are, and see you to't my horse and weapons be rendered up to me straightways! But this lady swore what she thought true. She had good reason for so thinking, and village rogues would best use fair words to her!"

He cast a side-glance at Anne, as he finished speaking; but at that instant she turned her back upon him, and went from the room, as swiftly as the crowd could let her. Hal, perforce, stayed to be unbound by the rustics that had held him. At the further orders of the constable, who speedily dwindled into obsequious nothingness under the swaggering disdain of Captain Bottle, Hal's weapons were restored to him. When he went out to the road, he found his horse ready, with Kit's and Anthony's. The huge coach, recently used by the rustics to obstruct the way, had been moved back into the lane. Hal remarked aloud upon this, as he made ready to mount.

"Ay, your worship," said a villager, who had overheard him, "we opened the way again, when the lady rode off a minute ago."

"The lady!" cried Hal, and exchanged a blank

look with Kit and Anthony. He had lost sight of her, while being released and repossessed of his weapons. "A plague on my dull wits!" he added, for the ears of his two men alone. "She hath gone to try the same game in the next parish, and fortune will scarce favor me with such another choice organ of the law as this constable!"

Meanwhile, in the ale-house, the constable, after some meditation, called for ale to be brought to the table at which he had been sitting, and said, thoughtfully, to his ally of the pen and inkhorn:

"Thou mayst tear what thou hast taken down of the examination, William."

And William, muddled by participation in the recent rush of events, absently tore to pieces his sheet of paper, on which he had written nothing.

CHAPTER XIII.

THE PRISONER IN THE COACH.

"It smites my heart to deal ungently with thee, lady."— The Fair Immured.

"She is like to find some magistrate of knowledge and resources next time!" continued Hal, alluding to Anne. "Well, there's naught to do but ride after her!"

"But what then?" put in Kit. "What shall hinder her from crying out?"

Hal, just mounted, happened to glance at the coach in the lane. He had, in one moment, a swift series of thoughts.

"Would that a dozen horses were to be had!" quoth he.

"Why, now," said Kit, "here come a score of horses, but with men upon their backs."

Hal turned a startled look southward. No, the riders were not Barnet's men; they rode together in too great disorder. Something impelled Hal to wait their coming up. In a few minutes it could be seen that they were a diverse company, some bravely dressed, some raggedly, some in both bravery and rags at once. Some had reckless faces, some uneasy, some stealthy, some sheepish. Their leader, a tall man, who would have been handsome but for his low brow and an inequality between the two halves of his visage, looked a mixture of insolent boldness and knavish servility.

"Why, God's body!" ejaculated Kit Bottle, with sudden astonishment and gladness. "'Tis that same rascal, the very rogue himself, and none else! I had thought we might fall in with him hereabouts!"

"Of whom speak you?" asked Hal, curtly.

"Of that villain Rumney, — mine old comrade that turned robber; him I once told you of. Ho, Rumney, thou counterfeit captain! Well met, thou rogue, says Kit Bottle!"

And while the one "captain" rode out to welcome the other, Hal remembered what the yeoman at Scardiff had told him of the highway robbers; he scanned the villainous faces of these men, and was thankful in his heart that Anne Hazlehurst had not ridden their way; and then he thought of her on the road ahead, and looked again at the coach, and at the horses of the newcomers.

By the time the two former companions in arms had finished their first salutations, Hal had formed his plan. He called Kit back to him, and said:

"If thy friend hath a mind to put himself and his

company in my service for three days, there shall be fair pay forthcoming."

"I know not how Rumney will take to honest service," replied Kit, doubtfully. "But leave the handling of the matter to me — and the fixing of the pay, too." And he rode back to the robber captain, who with his band had remained awaiting Kit's return at the place where they had stopped, some distance from Hal and Anthony. The villagers, now joined by the constable himself, stood gaping before the ale-house, exchanging a curious inspection with the questionable-looking newcomers.

Kit and Captain Rumney whispered together for a long time, gravely and mysteriously. Rumney was at first of a frowning and holding-off disposition; looked askance at Hal several times, and shook his head skeptically, as if he could see no advantage in what was proposed. Kit, as his face and gestures showed, waxed eloquent and urgent. There were moments when wrathful looks and words passed between the two, and old matters were raked up, and recriminations cast. But in the end, Rumney showed a yielding countenance, and Kit came back to Hal in triumph. The rate of hire being within Hal's limits, the robber captain rode up, at Kit's motion, and was introduced to Hal as to Sir Valentine Fleetwood.

Hal, on viewing this new ally more closely, mentally set him down as good for two or three days' fidelity if tactfully dealt with. Rumney, on his part, looked Hal over searchingly, with half closed gray eyes, as if to see what might be made out of him. The rascal had a fawning manner that might become insolent, or threatening, or cruel, upon the least occasion.

Rumney now went back to his men, and briefly acquainted them with what he had done, — a disclosure whose only outward effect was to make them gaze with a little more interest at Master Marryott. At this time, Hal was questioning the constable regarding the coach. He learned that, when bogged in mire during a prolonged rain, it had been abandoned by its former owners, who had taken to horseback and left it with the ale-house keeper in lieu of other payment of a large score run up while they were storm-stayed. Hal promptly bought it from the landlord, with what harness belonged to it, and with all the carriers' gear that remained about the stables.

At Hal's order, Rumney now had his men hitch their horses to the great vehicle, and thereupon remount, so that the animals might serve at once to bear and to draw. Master Marryott put Kit Bottle in charge of the robbers and the coach, with instructions to follow at the best possible speed, and then spurred off, with Anthony Underhill, in hope of overtaking Mistress Hazlehurst.

It was his intention to catch her if he could do so without entering any inhabited place or putting himself at risk of a second capture. Should he find himself approaching any such place or risk, he would wait for, or return to, Kit and the robbers. With his so greatly augmented force of fighting men, he could overawe or rout such a crowd as he had met at Clown; and, should the necessity arise, he might even offer a hopeful resistance to Roger Barnet's party. But against a general hue and cry, or an effectual marshalling of magistrate's officers and servants, either or both of which Anne might cause in front of him, he could not long contend. Hence the speed at which he now urged his horse in pursuit of her.

He had ridden seven miles from Clown, and met with no impediment in any of the intermediate hamlets, — a fact which convinced him that she would not again rely on such inferior agents of the law as she had first fallen in with, — when at a sharp turn of the road he suddenly came in sight of her. She and her page were at a standstill, she mounted, he afoot. It was a miry place, sheltered by trees and thickets from the drying effect of sun and the freezing effect of wind; and Francis stood in deep mud, examining the stone-bruised forefoot of her horse.

"This is good fortune, madam!" cried Hal, his

eyes sparkling as well with the pleasure of seeing her as with relief of mind.

"If it be so, enjoy it while you may," she answered, scorning his elation. "My hindrance here is but for a time."

"I know it well, madam," replied Hal, courteously; "for I, myself, have provided for your going forward."

"*You* have provided?" she said, regarding him with astonishment.

"Yes, mistress; for look you: if I thought to send you anywhere under escort, I could not afford what escort I might trust, or trust what escort I might afford. If I left you here, without escort, you would be in danger from rogues and vagabonds of the road, and you would be free to raise the country about me,—as you tried yonder, and rode on to try again. If I committed you to the hospitality of gentlefolk hereabouts, you would have that same freedom. Even though you gave up your design against me, and would start back for Hertfordshire or elsewhere—"

"No fear of that!" she said, defiantly.

"If there were hope of it," Hal went on, "your safety, and another reason, would forbid my allowing it."

The other reason, which he dared not tell her, was this: if permitted to return southward, she might meet Roger Barnet and incidentally give such description of Hal as would beget a doubt whether, after all, the right man was being chased.

"Therefore," concluded Hal, who had so opened his mind to her for his own justification, "it behoveth me to take you with me."

"To *take* me!" said she, with the emphasis of both query and correction on the verb.

"As a prisoner," added Hal, quietly.

She looked at him as a queen might look at a madman.

"I your prisoner!" she said. "By God's light, never!"

"My prisoner," said Hal, gently, "now and for three days to come. Anthony, look to the boy, and to his horse tied yonder; and follow this lady and me into the woods, that we may wait my men without scrutiny of passing travellers. Madam, be so good, I pray you, to ride betwixt yon thickets."

"That I will not!" cried Anne, with eyes afire.

Hal waited for one drawing of his breath; then rode to her side, grasped her bridle, and led her unwilling horse after him through the fairly clear way that he had pointed out. She showed herself too amazed for action, and made no resistance with her hands; but if looks could have smitten, Master Marryott would have found himself sorely belabored.

Hal stopped in the woods, within easy hearing distance of the road. Anthony, having lifted the small page to his own saddle-bow, disarmed him of weapons, and taken the other horse in leading, came after. When the little group was finally stationary among the trees and underbrush, Anne's face betrayed some falling away of defiance. She looked around in a kind of momentary panic, as if she would leap from her horse, and flee afoot. But on every side she saw but dark pools, damp earth, moist roots, and brush. She gave a shiver, and stayed in her saddle.

"Have no fear, mistress," said Hal. "No harm will come to you. While you go yieldingly, no hand shall touch you; and in any case, no hand but mine own, which is a gentleman's."

"Would you dare use force?" she cried, somewhat huskily, her eyes — half threatening, half intimidated — turned full upon him.

"If I must," said he, meeting her gaze with outward calmness.

She dropped her glance, and was silent. Anthony now placed Francis on the latter's own horse, but kept a stern eye upon him, and a firm hand upon his bridle. The four sat perfectly still, save for the restless movements of their shivering horses, in the chill and sombre forest. No one was heard to pass in the road.

"For what are you waiting?" asked Anne, after awhile.

"For my men to come up, with the coach you are to occupy," Hal replied.

She answered him with a look of surprise, but said nothing.

After a weary length, the tread of many horses and the noise of cumbrous wheels was heard from the uneven and miry road. Hal, retaining Anne's bridle, and motioning Anthony to follow, led the short but toilsome ride back to the highway. The strange crew, headed by Kit Bottle and Captain Rumney, came into view around the turn. Losing no time for greetings, Hal ordered the men to ride on at their best pace to a dryer part of the road, that the coach might not become fixed in the mire. This was done, the robbers looking with some curiosity at Anne as they passed. Hal and his immediate party followed. At an open place, where the earth was hard, he called a halt; then dismounted, and led Anne's horse close to the coach.

The vehicle was as crude as may be supposed when it is remembered that the use of coaches in England was then scarce thirty-five years old. It was springless, heavy of wheel, and with a cover having the entrance-opening at the side. An occupant of it, unless he sat by this opening, was concealed from view; and his cries, if he made any, might be drowned by the various noises of the creaking and rumbling vehicle, the heavily harnessed horses, and the boisterous escort. Once an inmate of this moving prison, Anne might try in vain to communicate with the outside world through which her captors might convey her.[26]

"Mistress," said Hal, with great respect, "be so gracious as to exchange your lame horse for the coach." And he offered his hand to assist her.

"I will not stir!" she replied, to the additional curiosity of Rumney and such of his men as could witness the scene by looking back from their horses.

Knowing how much slower must be his future progress, with this coach to be dragged along, and how much less he could afford to suffer delay, he forthwith abandoned words for acts. With all possible gentleness, but all necessary force, he deliberately grasped her foot and took it from the stirrup. He then directed Kit Bottle to dismount, and unfasten the saddle-girth of her horse. This done, Hal drew the saddle down, on his side, until he could clasp her waist. He then had Bottle lead her horse away, so that, the saddle sliding to the ground, she could not but set foot upon the earth. She held, however, to the bridle, until Hal, by a steady compulsion, which he made as painless as possible, loosened her hands from it, one at a time.

He had been in some slight fear of a more active resistance from her; but she proved herself of a dignity above that of women who bite and scratch.

She was of too great a stateliness to put herself into ungraceful or vixenish attitudes. So she neither clawed nor pounded, though she would have struck with her dagger had Hal not taken it from her in time. But she exerted all her strength in holding back from whatever motion he sought to compel from her. He saw that he should have difficulty in making her enter the coach.

He had a rude, bench-like seat taken out of the vehicle, and placed beneath the opening, to serve as a step. As she would not budge, even to approach the carriage, he lifted her with both arms, carried her forward, and placed her in a standing position on the bench. He then paused for breath, still keeping one arm about her. Commanding Kit to hold the bench steady, Hal stepped upon it, for the purpose of lifting her into the vehicle. He saw that she was taller by far than the opening through which she would have to pass, and saw, at the same moment, that she made herself rigid, so that, in forcing her into the coach, he might be put to the use of violence.

He gathered strength for his final effort, and grasped her waist again. At this instant, he noticed an amused grin on the faces of some of Rumney's ruffians, and was conscious that, perspiring and red-faced from his exertions, he doubtless made a somewhat ridiculous figure. Perhaps this knowledge acted as a stimulant, and also made him a little less considerate toward his prisoner. He stiffened his muscles, changed her direction from the perpendicular to the oblique, and stepped up into the coach, her diagonal position permitting her admission, headforemost, through the opening. He then caused the seat to be returned, and placed her, full-length, upon it; and ordered Francis to be put into the coach with her.

His own horse being brought close to the opening, Hal transferred himself to the saddle, his intention being to ride at the side of the coach wherever the width of the road should allow. Anthony was to follow close behind him. Captain Bottle was sent forward to lead the caravan. Anne's side-saddle was placed in the coach; her horse, being lame, was turned loose; that of Francis was hitched, with the animals ridden by the robbers, to the vehicle. Captain Rumney was left to choose his own place, Hal supposing he would elect to be near his old-time gossip, Bottle. But Rumney preferred to ride behind the coach. Hal thereupon called to Bottle to start, the robbers whipped their horses, the coach-wheels began to turn, and the flight was at last resumed.

Why should Rumney have placed himself at the rear? Hal wondered, and a vague misgiving entered his mind; nor was he reassured when, at a place where a hard heath permitted Anthony to ride for a moment at Hal's side, the Puritan muttered to him :

"Saw'st thou the look of that robber captain when he first set eyes on the lady? I liked it not!"

With which, Anthony fell behind again to Rumney's side.

Nor — now that he recalled that look, a greedy lighting up of wicked eyes — did Hal himself like it, and the future seemed dubious.

CHAPTER XIV.

HOW THE PAGE WALKED IN HIS SLEEP.

"I spy a black, suspicious, threatening cloud." — *Henry VI., Part III.*

MASTER MARRYOTT had lost nearly two hours at Clown, through his detention by the constable, his waiting to enlist the highway robbers, and his measures for putting the coach into service. And such was the badness of the road, that he had consumed more than an hour in covering, with alternate dashes and delays, the seven miles from Clown to the place where he had overtaken Anne. Almost another hour had been used in awaiting the coming of the coach, and lodging the prisoner therein. It was, thus, between two and three in the afternoon when the northward journey was again taken up.

Hal, as he rode beside the coach, considered his situation with regard to his pursuer, Roger Barnet. The latter, arriving with tired horses at the scene of Hal's wine-drinking, and thereafter compelled to stop often for traces of the fugitives, must have been as great a loser of time as Hal had been; and this accounted for his non-appearance during either of the recent delays. But, by this time, he was probably not very far behind; and hereafter Hal's rate of speed must be, by reason of the coach, considerably slower. The latter circumstance would offset, in Barnet's favor, the two disadvantages under which he labored. Moreover, upon learning at Clown what company Hal had reinforced himself with, the pursuivant would find the track easier, and hence speedier, to follow; the passage of so numerous and ill-looking a band being certain to attract more attention than would that of a party of three or five.

But Hal counted upon one likelihood for a compensating gain of a few hours, — the likelihood that Barnet, to strengthen himself for possible conflict with Hal's increased force, would tarry to augment his own troop with men from the neighborhood, and that, in his subsequent pursuit, as well as in this measure, his very reliance on his advantages would make him less strenuous for speed.

Cheering himself with the best probabilities, though not ignoring the worst, Master Marryott pressed steadily on, after the manner of the tortoise. When bad spots in the road appeared, Kit Bottle, at the head of the line, caused the robbers to whip up their horses; and if this did not avail to keep the coach from being stayed, Hal had the men dismount and put their shoulders to the wheels. A grumbling dislike to this kind of service evinced itself, but Captain Rumney, flattered by the courteous way in which Hal gave him the necessary orders for transmission, checked with peremptory looks the discontent. Hal conceded a short stop, at a solitary tavern, for a refection of beer and barley-cakes. During this pause, and also while passing through villages, Hal remained at the coach-opening, ready to close its curtain with his own hand, on the least occasion from the inmates.

But Anne and her page, whose flight from Scardiff that morning had shortened their sleeping-time, were too languid for present effort. In attitudes best accommodated to the movements of the coach, they sat — or half reclined — with their backs against the side of the vehicle for support. With changeless face and lack-lustre eyes, Anne viewed what of the passing country she could see through the opening; heedless whether Hal's figure interrupted her vision or not; whether she passed habitations, or barren heath, or fields, or forest. Yet she did not refuse the repast that Hal handed into the coach, which, when resort was had to the lone tavern, he had caused to stop at some distance from the house.

Only once during the afternoon did he take the precaution of shutting the coach entrance; it was while passing through the considerable town of Rotherham.

Night fell while the travellers were toilsomely penetrating further into the West Riding of Yorkshire. When at last Hal gave the word to halt, they found themselves before a rude inn with numerous mean outbuildings, on a hill about six miles beyond Rotherham.

Hal had now to provide, because of new conditions, somewhat otherwise than he had done at his previous stopping-places. Anne and Francis were to be closely guarded, a repressive hand held ready to check the least hostile act or communication. Fresh horses could not be obtained in number equal to the company. Ere he had ordered the halt, Master Marryott had formed his plans.

At first it seemed that he might not unopposedly have his way with the frowsy-headed landlord who appeared in the doorway's light in response to his summons. But when the blinking host became aware of the numerousness of the company, and when Captain Rumney rode forward into the light, he instantly grew hospitable. Evidently the captain and the innkeeper were old acquaintances, if not occasional partners in trade. So Hal arranged a barter for what fresh horses were at the fellow's command; took lodgings for the night in the several outhouses, caused open fires to be made on the earthen floors therein, and ordered food and drink. He had the coach drawn into shelter, near one of the fires, and bedding placed in it, with other comforts from the inn.

He then informed Anne that she was to remain in her prison overnight; and he assigned to Francis a sleeping-place on a pile of straw, within sword reach of where he himself intended to guard the curtained opening of the coach. Anthony, on one of the fresh horses, should keep the usual watch for Barnet's party. Bottle, who had watched at Scardiff, was to sleep in the stable-loft, as was also Rumney, whose men were to occupy different outbuildings. No one was to remove his clothes, and, in case of alarm, all were to unite in hitching the horses, and to resume the flight.

The horses themselves were placed in stalls, but in as forward a state of readiness as was compatible with their easy resting. It was made clear that, should any of these movements be interrupted or followed by attack from a pursuing party, all the resistance necessary was to be offered.

The supper ordered was brought on wooden platters, and eaten in the light of the fires. Hal, as before, served Anne through the coach doorway, and she accepted the cakes and ale with neither reluctance nor thanks. But under her passiveness, Hal saw no abandonment of her purpose. He saw, rather, a design to gather clearness of mind and strength of body, for the invention and execution of some plan not only possible to her restraint, but likely to be more effectual than any she had tried when free.

When the company had supped, and the robbers could be heard snoring in the adjacent sheds, and Francis lay in the troubled sleep of excessive fatigue, and the regular breathing of Anne herself was audible through the coach curtain; when, in fine, every member of his strange caravan slept, save Anthony watching at the hill's southeastern brow, Master Marryott sat upon a log, and gazed into the sputtering fire on the ground, and mused. He marvelled to think how many and diverse and cumbrous elements he had assembled to his hand, and undertaken to keep in motion, for what seemed so small a cause.

To herd with robbers; to lavish the queen's money; to deceive a woman — the object of his love — so that he brought upon himself her hate meant for another; to carry off this woman by force, and put her to the utmost fatigue and risk; to wear out the bodies, and imperil the necks, of himself and so many others, — was it worth all this merely to create a fair opportunity — not a certainty — of escape for a Frenchified English Catholic, whose life was of no consequence to the country? Hal laughed to think how unimportant and uninteresting was the man in whose behalf all these labors and discomforts were being undergone by so many people, some of whom were so much more useful and ornamental to the world.

And yet he knew that the business *was* worth the effort; worth all the toil and risk that he himself took, and that he imposed upon other people. It was worth all this, perhaps not that a life might be saved, but that a debt might be paid, a promise made good, — his debt of gratitude to Sir Valentine, his promise to the queen. It was worth any cost, that a gentleman should fulfil his obligations, however incurred. To an Englishman of that time, moreover, it was worth a world of trouble, merely to please the queen.

But what most and deepest moved Hal forward, and made turning back impossible, was the demand in him for success on its own account, the intolerableness of failure in any deed that he might lay upon himself. Manly souls daily strain great resources for small causes, or for no cause worth considering, for the reason that they cannot endure to fail in what they have, however thoughtlessly, undertaken. The man of mettle will not relinquish; he will die, but he will not let go. It is because the thing most necessary to him is his own applause; he will not forfeit that, though he must pay with his life to retain it. Once his hand is to the plow, though he find too late that the field is barren, he will furrow that field through, or he will drop in his tracks; what concerns him is, not the reason or the reward, but the mere fact of success or failure in the self-assigned work. Men show this in their sports; indeed, the game that heroes play with circumstance and destiny, for the mere sake of striving to win, is to them a sport of the keenest. "Maybe it was not worth doing, but I told myself I would do it, and I did it!" Hal fancied the deep elation that must attend those words, could he truly say them three days hence.

About three hours after midnight he awoke his people, had the horses put to the coach, sent for Anthony by one of the robbers, — a renegade London apprentice, Tom Cobble by name, whose face he liked for its bold frankness, — and rode forth with his company toward Barnesley. They passed through this town in the early morning of Friday, March 6th, the third day of the flight. Though Anne showed the utmost indifference to her surroundings, Hal closed her curtain, as he had done at Rotherham, until the open country was again reached.

Soon after this, Mistress Hazlehurst changed her place to the forward part of the coach, and her position so as to face the backward part. She could thus be seen by any one riding at the side of the coach's rear, and glancing obliquely through the opening. It was, at present, Anthony Underhill that benefited by this new arrangement.

Five miles after Barnesley, Master Marryott ordered a halt for breakfast. As before, food was brought to the prisoners. The stop gave Captain Rumney an opportunity of peering in through the coach doorway.

When, at nine o'clock, the journey was resumed, Rumney, without a word, took the place behind Marryott, formerly kept by Anthony.

"By your leave, sir," said the Puritan, forced by this usurpation to drop behind the coach, "that is where I ride."

"Tut, man!" replied Rumney, with an insolent pretence of carelessness; "what matters it?"

"It matters to me that I ride where I have been commanded to," said the Puritan, with quiet stubbornness, heading his horse to take the place from which he expected the other to fall out.

"And it matters to me that I ride where I please to," retorted Rumney, with a little less concealment of the ugliness within him.

Anthony frowned darkly, and looked at Marryott, who had turned half around on his horse at the dispute. Rumney regarded Hal narrowly through half shut eyes, in which defiance lurked, ready to burst forth on provocation. Hal read his man, choked down his feelings, considered that an open break was not yet to be afforded, and to make the matter in which he yielded seem a trifle, said, quietly:

"My commands were too narrow, Anthony. So that you ride behind me, one side of the road will do as well as another. The fault was mine, Captain Rumney."

So Anthony fell back without protest or complaint. He cast his look earthward, that it might not seem to reproach Master Marryott. And a bitter moment was it to Master Marryott, for his having had to fail of supporting his own man against this rascal outlaw. A moment of keener chagrin followed, when Hal caught a swift glance of swaggering triumph — a crowing kind of half smile — that Rumney sent to Mistress Hazlehurst, with whom he was now in line of vision. It seemed to say, "You see, mistress, what soft stuff this captor of yours shall prove in my hands?" And in Anne's eyes, as Hal clearly beheld, was the light of a new hope, as if she perceived in this robber a possible instrument or champion.

But Master Marryott let none of his thoughts appear; he hardened his face to the impassibility of a mask, and seemed neither to suspect nor to fear anything; seemed, indeed, to feel himself above possibility of defeat or injury. He realized that here was a case where danger might be precipitated by any recognition of its existence.

During the next six hours, he saw, though appeared not to heed, that Anne kept her gaze fixed behind him, upon the robber captain. There was no appeal in her eyes, no promise, no overture to conspiracy; nothing but that intentional lack of definite expression, which makes such eyes the more fascinating, because the more mysterious. Even savages like Rumney are open to the witchery of the unfathomable in a pair of fine eyes. Hal wondered how long the inevitable could be held off. He avoided conversation with Rumney, did not even look back at him, lest pretext might be given for an outbreak. He was kept informed of the knave's exact whereabouts by the noise of the latter's horse, and, most of the time, by the direction of Mistress Hazlehurst's look. He had no fear of a sudden attack upon himself, for he knew that Anthony Underhill held the robber in as close a watch as Mistress Hazlehurst did.

In mid-afternoon, the caravan stopped within three miles of Halifax, for food and rest. Master Marryott stayed near the coach. Rumney, too, hovered close; but as yet a kind of loutish bashfulness toward a woman of Anne's haughtiness, rather than a fear of Master Marryott, — at least, so Hal supposed, — checked him from any attempt to address her. Marryott called Kit Bottle, and, while apparently viewing the surrounding country as if to plan their further route, talked with him in whispers:

"Thy friend Rumney," said Hal, "seems a cur as ready to jump at one's throat as to crawl at one's feet."

"'Twas lack of forethought, I'm afeard, to take up with the knave, where a woman was to be concerned," replied Kit. "It was about a red and white piece of frailty that he dealt scurvily with me in the Netherlands. Were there no she in the case, we might trust him; he hath too great shyness of law officers, on his own account, to move toward selling us."

"If he had a mind, now, to rescue this lady from us —" began Hal.

"'Twould be a sorry rescue for the lady!" put in Bottle.

Hal shuddered.

"And yet she would throw herself into his hands, to escape ours, that she might be free to work me harm," said he.

"An she think she would find freedom that way, she knows not Rumney. If thine only care were to be no more troubled of her, thou couldst do little better than let Rumney take her off thy hands."

"I would kill thee, Kit, if I knew not thou saidst that but to rally me! Yet I will not grant it true, either. She might contrive to tame this Rumney beast, and work us much harm. Well, smile an thou wilt! Thine age gives thee privileges with me, and I will confess 'tis her own safety most concerns me in this anxiety. Sink this Rumney in perdition! — why did I ever encumber us with him and his rascals?"

"Speaking of his rascals, now," said Kit, "I have noticed some of them rather minded to heed your wishes than Rumney's commands. There hath been wrangling in the gang."

"There is one, methinks," assented Hal, "that would rather take my orders than his leader's. 'Tis the round-headed, sharp-eyed fellow, Tom Cobble. He is a runagate 'prentice from London, and seemeth to have more respect for town manners than for Rumney's."

"And there is a yeoman's son, John Hatch, that rides near me," added Kit. "He hath some remnant of honesty in him, or I mistake. And one Ned Moreton, who is of gentle blood and mislikes to be overborne by such carrion as Rumney. And yon scare-faced, fat-paunched fellow, Noll Bunch they call him, hath been under-bailiff in a family that hath fled the country. I warrant he hath no taste for robbery; methinks he took to the road in sheer need of filling his stomach, and would give much to be free of his bad bargain. There be two or three more that might make choice of us, in a clash with their captain; but the rest are of the mangiest litter that was ever bred among two-legged creatures."

"Then win over quietly whom thou canst, Kit. But let us have no clash till we must."

Rumney and his men looked almost meek while passing through Halifax. And herein behold mankind's horror of singularity. In other towns these robbers had been under as much possibility of recognition and detention; but in those towns the result of their arrest would have been no worse than hanging, and was not hanging the usual, common, and natural ending of a thief? But in Halifax there was that unique "Gibbet Law," under which thieves were beheaded by a machine something like the guillotine which another country and a later century were yet to produce. There was in such a death an isolation, from which a properly bred thief, brought up to regard the hempen rope as his due destiny, might well shrink.

But the robbers could sleep with easy minds that night, for Master Marryott put Halifax eight miles behind ere he rested.

Similar arrangements to those of the preceding night were made at the inn chosen as a stopping-place. The coach, furnished for comfortable repose, stood near a fire, under roof. Hal, who thought that he had now mastered the art of living without sleep, set himself to keep guard again, by Francis, near the coach doorway. It was Anthony's night to share Rumney's couch of straw; Kit Bottle's to watch for Barnet's men.

Master Marryott, sitting by the fire, was assailed by fears lest the pursuivant had abandoned the false chase. If not, it was strange, when the slow progress with the coach was considered, that he had not come in sight. Hal reassured himself by accounting for this in more ways than one. Barnet must have been detained long in recruiting men to join in the pursuit. He may have been hindered by lack of money, also, for he had left London without thought of further journey than to Welwyn. He could press all necessary means into service, in the queen's name, as he went; but in doing this he must experience much delay that ready coin would have avoided. True, Barnet would have learned at Clown that the supposed Sir Valentine had named himself as a London player; but he would surely think this a lie, as Mistress Hazlehurst had thought it.

A slight noise — something like a man yawning aloud, or moaning in sleep — turned Marryott's musings into another channel. The sound had come from one of the other outhouses, probably that in which were Captain Rumney and Anthony Underhill. It put dark apprehensions into Hal's mind, because of its resemblance to the groan a man might give if he were stabbed to death in slumber.

Suppose, thought he, this Rumney were minded for treason and robbery. How could he better proceed, in order to avoid all stir, than to avail himself of the present separation of Hal's party; to slay Anthony first, while Bottle was away on the watch; and thus have Marryott and Kit each in position to be dealt with single-handed?

Hal now saw the error of having Anthony sleep out of his sight; for the Puritan was one who watched while he watched, and slept while he slept. The present situation ought not to be continued a moment longer. Yet how was Hal to summon Anthony? To awaken him by voice, one would have to raise such clamor as would alarm the robbers and perchance excite their leader's suspicions. A touch on the shoulder would accomplish the desired result quietly. Might Hal venture from his present post for the brief time necessary to his purpose?

Francis lay near the fire, his eyes closed, his respirations long and easy. The softer breathing of the prisoner in the coach was as deep and measured. Hal stole noiselessly out, and made for the shed in which the Puritan slept.

Anthony lay in his cloak, on a pile of hay, his back turned to that of Rumney. The highway robber's eyes were closed; whether he slept or not, Hal could not have told. But there was no doubt of the somnolent state of the Puritan. A steady gentle shaking of his shoulder caused him to open his eyes.

"Come with me," whispered Hal. The Puritan rose, without a word, and followed from the one shed to the other, and to the fire by the coach.

"'Tis best you sleep in my sight, beside the lad," said Marryott, turning toward the designated spot as he finished. In the same instant, he stared as if he saw a ghost, and then stifled an oath.

Francis was gone.

Hal looked about, but saw nothing human in range of the firelight. He hastened to the curtained opening of the coach. The same soft breathing — there could be no mistaking it — still came from within.

"She is here, at least," Hal said, quickly, to the somewhat mystified Anthony. "But he hath flown on some errand of her plotting, depend on't! He must have feigned sleep, and followed me out. He can't be far, as yet. 'Tis but a minute since. Watch you by the coach!"

With which order, Master Marryott seized a brand from the fire, and ran out again to the yard.

But he had scarce cast a swift glance around the place, ere he saw Francis coming out of the very shed from which Hal himself had led Anthony a few moments earlier.

"What is this?" cried Marryott, grasping the

boy's arm, and thrusting the firebrand almost into his face.

Francis stared vacantly for an instant, then gave a start, blinked, and looked at Hal as if for the first time conscious of what was going on.

"What's afoot, you knave?" said Hal, squeezing the page's arm. "What deviltry are you about, following me from your bed, hiding in the darkness while I pass, and going to yonder shed? You bore some message from your mistress to Master Rumney, I'll warrant! Confess, or 'twill go ill!"

"I know not where I've been, or what done," replied the boy, coolly. "I walk in my sleep, sir."

Hal searchingly inspected the lad's countenance, but it did not flinch. Pondering deeply, he then led the way back to his fire, and commanded the page to lie down. Francis readily obeyed.

Bidding the puzzled but unquestioning Puritan sleep beside the boy, Hal soon lost himself in his thoughts, — lost himself so far that it did not occur to him to step now and then to the door and look out into the night; else he might presently have seen a dark figure move stealthily from outhouse to outhouse as if in search of something. It would then have appeared that Captain Rumney, also, was given to walking in his sleep.

CHAPTER XV.

TREACHERY.

"God pless you, Aunchient Pistol! you scurvy, lousy knave, God pless you!"—
Henry V.

"HERE is the snow thou hast foretold," said Master Marryott to Anthony Underhill, as the cavalcade set out, three hours after midnight.

"And a plague of wind," put in Captain Rumney, with a good humor in which Marryott smelt some purpose of cultivating confidence.

The riders wrapped themselves in their cloaks, and muffled their necks to keep out the pelting flakes. The night being at its darkest, the snow was more "perceptible to feeling" than "to sight," save where it flew and eddied in the light of a torch carried by Bottle at the head of the line, and of a lanthorn that Hal had caused to be attached to the rear of the coach. Between these two dim centres of radiance, the horsemen shivered and grumbled unseen, and cursed their steeds, and wished red murrains and black plagues, and poxes of no designated color, upon the weather.

They passed through Keighley about dawn. Two miles further on, they stopped at an isolated house for breakfast. As Marryott opened the coach curtain (it had been closed against the whirling snow), to convey to the prisoners some cakes and milk, Mistress Hazlehurst motioned Francis to set the platter on a coach seat, and said to Hal:

"If you wish not to murder me, you will let me walk a little rather than eat. I seem to have lost the use of legs and arms, penned up in this cage these two days."

"Nay, 'tis but a day and a half," corrected Marryott. "But you may walk whiles we tarry here, an you choose. The snow is ankle-deep in the road, however."

"I care not if it be knee-deep."

"Will you promise to return to the coach at my word, if I let you out to walk?" Hal did not feel equal to putting her into the coach again by bodily force.

"God's light, yes! What choice have I?"

"And while you walk, I must walk beside you, and Francis at my other side."

"I have said, what choice have I?"

He offered his hand to assist her from the coach. But she leaped out unaided, and started forthwith in the direction whence the travellers had just come. Hal waited for Francis, and then strode after her, holding the page by a sleeve. Kit Bottle was busy looking to the refreshment of the horses. Captain Rumney was stalking up and down the road, his whole attention apparently concentrated upon a pot of ale he carried. Anthony Underhill had ridden back to a slightly elevated spot, to keep watch.

Master Marryott was soon at his prisoner's side. She could not, for snow and wind, long maintain the pace at which she had started from the coach. The weather reddened her cheeks, which took hue also from her crimson cloak and hood. Hal thought her very beautiful, — a thing of bloom and rich color in a bleak, white desert. It smote him keenly to remember that she deemed him her brother's slayer. He was half tempted to tell her the truth, now that she was his prisoner and could not go back to undeceive Roger Barnet. But would she believe him? And if she should, was it certain that she might not escape ere the next two days were up? Prudence counselled Hal to take no risks. So, in faintest hope of shaking her hatred a little, of creating at least a doubt in his favor, he fell back on the poor device of which he had already made one or two abortive trials.

"I swear to you, Mistress Hazlehurst," he began, somewhat awkwardly, "'twas not I that gave your brother his unhappy wound. There is something unexplained, touching that occurrence, that will be cleared to you in time."

A little to his surprise, she did not cut short all possible discussion by some sharp derisive or contemptuous answer. Though her tone showed no falling away from conviction, she yet evinced a passive willingness to talk of the matter.

"There hath been explanation enough for me," she answered. "I had the full story of my brother's servants, who saw all."

"The officers of justice could not have had a like story," said Hal, at random. "Else why came they never to Fleetwood house?"

"You well know. The quarrel was witnessed of none but your man and my brother's servants. They kept all quiet; your man, for your safety's sake; my brother's men, for — for the reason — My brother's men kept all quiet, too, till I came home."

"And why did your brother's men so? You broke off there."

"Oh, I care not if I say it! My brother's servants were not as near the encounter as your man was, and they saw ill; they were of a delusion that you struck in self-defence. And my brother, too, bade them hush the matter."

"'Twas as much as to admit that he was the offender."

"Well, what matters that? At best there was little zeal he might expect of his neighbors in visiting the law upon you. He was a man of too strong mettle; he was too hated in the county to hope for justice, even against a Catholic. Well you know that, Sir Valentine Fleetwood! But I would have had my rights of the law, or paid you in mine own way,[27] had not this other means of vengeance come to my hand! Self-defence or no self-defence, you shed my brother's blood, and I will be a cause of the shedding of yours!"

"But I say naught of self-defence. I say I am not he that, rightly or wrongly, shed your brother's blood!"

"God-'a'-mercy, sir, I marvel at you! 'Tis sheer impudence to deny what mine own family servants saw with their eyes and told me with their lips! Think you, because I am some miles and days from all witnesses of the quarrel, save your own man, my mind is to be clouded upon it?"

"I say only that there is a strange circumstance in all this business, that may not yet be opened to you. Well, I see that till time shall permit explanation, I must despair of seeming other to you than stained with your brother's blood. My word of honor, my oath, avail not —"

"Speak you of oaths and words of honor? There was some talk of oaths two days ago, before the constable of Clown!"

Hal sighed. He did not notice that, in drawing

him further into conversation, she had drawn him further from the coach, which was indeed now hidden behind a slight turn of the road.

"Well," quoth he, resignedly, "time shall clear me; and show, too, why I have had to put so admired a lady to so irksome a constraint."

"Say, rather, time shall give your prisoner revenge for all constraint. Think not you have put me to much distress! What says the play? Women can endure mewing up, so that you tie not their tongues!"

"I thank heaven you have not given me cause to tie your tongue!"

"Given you cause, — how?" she asked, looking full at him.

"Why, suppose, in the towns we passed, you had cried out from the coach to people, and I had found the closed curtain of no avail."

"What would you have done then?"

"Bound with a silken kerchief the shapeliest mouth in England! Ay, with these very hands of mine!"

"Ere that were done, I should have made stir enough to draw a concourse. Were I hard put to it, be sure I would attract questioners to whom you'd have to give account."

"Account were easy given. I should declare you were a mad woman committed to my charge."

"More perjury!"

"Nay, there is truly some madness in a woman's taking vengeance into her own small hands."

She answered nothing, and presently they returned to the coach. Captain Rumney stood pensively by his horse, his gaze averted, as if he thought of the past or the far away. He now looked mildly up, and mounted. The other robbers were already on their horses, Bottle at their head. Mistress Hazlehurst let Hal lift her into the coach. Francis followed. Marryott then whistled for Anthony, and got into the saddle.

"The snow falls thicker and thicker," remarked Captain Rumney, in a bland, sociable tone, while the caravan waited for the Puritan.

As soon as Anthony was in place, Hal motioned to Bottle, at whose word the robbers, with whip and rein, set their horses in motion. The harness strained, the coach creaked, the wheels turned reluctantly in the snow. The procession moved forward a short distance; then, suddenly, there was a splitting sound, a rear wheel fell inward, and the adjacent part of the coach dropped heavily to the ground. The vehicle, thereupon, was still, halting the horses with a violent jerk.

Anthony Underhill leaped from his saddle, and turned over the loose wheel. A single glance revealed that the axle had been, within a very short time past, cut nearly through with a saw.

Anthony looked at Master Marryott, who gazed at the axle with a singularly self-communing, close-mouthed expression. All was very clear to Master Marryott; a train of events had rushed through his mind in an eye's twinkling: Mistress Hazlehurst's subjugation of Captain Rumney by the use of her eyes; the nocturnal visit of her page to the robber in the single opportunity afforded by Hal's movements; the walk in which she had drawn Hal from the coach at a time when Anthony was on guard and Kit Bottle concerned with the horses. A few words would have sufficed for the message borne by Francis to Rumney, such as, "My mistress desires you to wreck the coach; she will make an opportunity." She had not asked Rumney to rescue her by force, for he might prove a worse captor than her present one. She had not asked him to injure the horses during the night, for the watch kept by Hal might prevent that, or the robber might be unwilling to sacrifice his own animals. What she sought was delay for the coming of Barnet; not an open revolt of the robbers, which might be so victorious as to put her at their mercy. And Rumney had obeyed her to the letter; had, doubtless, after receiving her message, searched the outhouses for a suitable tool; and probably carried at the present moment, beneath his leather jerkin, the hand-saw with which, during Hal's walk with Mistress Hazlehurst, he had severed the axle.

But, whatever lay concealed under his jerkin or his skull, Captain Rumney was now looking down at the wheel with a most surprised, puzzled, curious, how-in-God's-name-could-this-have-come-to-pass expression of face.

It was but the early morning of the fourth day of the flight. Could Hal but defer the inevitable break with his ally, for this day and another! Until the five days were up, an open breach with, or secret flight from, these robbers, meant the risk of either his mission or her safety. For such break or flight might leave her in their hands. This horrible issue could be provided against only by Hal's consigning her to protection in some town or some gentleman's house; but such provision he dared not make till his mission was accomplished, lest she defeat that mission by disclosures that would either cause his own seizure or raise doubts in Barnet as to his identity.

Decidedly, patience was the proper virtue here, and the best policy was that of temporizing.

"'Tis a curious smooth break," said Hal, with an indescribable something in his voice for the benefit of Anthony, and of Kit, who had ridden back to see what stayed the coach. "But I have seen wood break so, when decay hath eaten a straight way through it. Mistress, I rejoice to see you are not hurt by the sudden jar."

He spoke to her through the coach doorway.

Both she and Francis were sitting quite undisturbed. The jar had, in fact, not been sudden to them. As Hal knew, they had expected the breakdown. But his dissembling must be complete.

"Here's delay!" put in Captain Rumney, most sympathetically vexed.

"Yes," said Marryott, very dismally, as if bereft of hope. His wisest course lay in holding the plotters passive by making them think they had already accomplished enough. If Mistress Hazlehurst supposed that sufficient delay was now obtained, she would not further instigate Rumney. And without instigation Rumney was not likely to invite open warfare at a place only two miles from Keighley. In fact, he would not, of his own initiative, have chosen a spot so near a town, for causing the breakdown, which might result in tumult. He would have waited for a more solitary neighborhood. He was of no mind for needlessly chancing any kind of violent contact with the authorities. Mistress Hazlehurst, not divining his feelings on this point, had created the opportunity at this spot, and he had taken the risk. But he was well content that the supposed Sir Valentine accused him not. In roads more remote, accusation might be positively welcome; but not in close vicinity to a centre of law and order.

With a kind of vague, general sense of what Captain Rumney's mental attitude must be, Marryott felt that he need fear no interruption to the plan his mind now formed, in a moment's time, for an early resumption of the flight. But he did not communicate this plan to any but Anthony, who alone was necessary to its inauguration. Even Bottle was kept in the dark, in order that Rumney might not find, in being excepted from a council of leaders, a pretext for subsequent complaint.

As for his instructions to the Puritan, Hal gave them very quickly, in whispers, leaning down from his saddle to approach more nearly the other's ear.

Anthony, having listened without speech or sign, remounted his horse, rode to the house at which the breakfast had been obtained, and made a few brief inquiries of the man who came to the door.

The result of his questions was evidently not satisfactory; for he rode from the door, shaking his head in the negative to Master Marryott; and forthwith cantered off through the falling snow, toward Keighley.

Bottle, who had sat his horse in silent observation of these movements, as had Rumney also, now glanced at Hal as if to question the propriety of sending the Puritan away.

"Fear not," said Hal, reassuringly. "If he see thy friend Barnet ere he find what he seeks, he will drop all and come back a-flying. And then we shall meet Barnet, or dodge him, in what manner we must!"

It has been told that Marryott was always prepared, as a last resource, to use his forces in resistance to the pursuivant. A close meeting was to be avoided to the utmost, however; not only for its uncertainty of issue to the immediate participants, but for its likelihood of informing Barnet that the pursued man was not Sir Valentine. In the event of that disclosure, Hal saw safety for his mission in one desperate course; that was, to kill or disable the pursuivant and all his men. But such a feat of arms was barely within possibility, a fact which made Master Hal extremely unwilling that matters should come to an encounter. Therefore he groaned and fretted inwardly during the minutes of inaction that followed Anthony's departure. He sought relief from thoughts of a possible combat with his pursuers, in following out his plan for his forward movement; and saw with joy that the very method he had chosen for going on with his prisoner was the better adapted to his bearing her safely off from Rumney in case of a conflict with that gentleman.

"Have your men take their horses from the coach, Captain Rumney," Hal had said very soon after Anthony had departed. The words were spoken lightly, not as if they accorded with a plan, but as if they indeed had no other inspiration than was shown when Hal added, "'Tis no use now keeping them hitched to this moveless heap of lumber."

Prompt obedience had been given to an order so suggestive of greater delay. And now the robbers idly sat their horses, jesting, railing at one another, grumbling, and some of them wondering in dull discontent whither in the fiend's name they were bound. Anne and her page kept their places in the derelict vehicle, withholding their thoughts. Bottle and Rumney rode up and down, saying little. They were old soldiers, and used to waiting. Moreover, in the days of slow transit, patience was a habit, especially with those who travelled.

At last Anthony's figure reappeared, rising and falling in the whirling snow as his movements obeyed those of his horse. His manner showed that he did not bear any tidings of Barnet. He brought with him an old pillion and a collection of battered hunting-horns, the former behind his saddle, the latter all slung upon a single cord. It was to procure these things that he had gone back to Keighley, where there were saddlers, innkeepers, hostlers, smiths, and others from whom such articles were to be had. Hal's companions looked with curiosity at these acquisitions.

Marryott now ordered both Anthony and Kit to dismount. He then had the horse formerly ridden by Francis led back to the coach doorway. Here he caused Bottle to hold the animal, and Anthony to adjust the pillion behind the saddle thereon.

"Now, mistress," said Hal, when this was done, "pray let me aid you to the pillion."

From her seat in the coach she did not move, nor made she the smallest answer. She merely cast a look at Captain Rumney.

Hal saw the need of swift action; delay would give her mute appeal to the robber time to take effect. Summary proceedings would bewilder him.

"Tom Cobble, hold my horse," he said, and was afoot in an instant. In another, he was inside the coach, raising Mistress Hazlehurst bodily from her seat, and conveying her out of the doorway to the pillion, which was not too high or far to permit his placing her upon it. Taken quite by surprise, she found herself on horseback ere she thought to brace herself for physical resistance.

"The cord, Anthony," called Hal. The Puritan threw it to him, having already unfastened it from the hunting-horns. Before Mistress Hazlehurst had time to think of sliding from the pillion to the ground, Hal had her waist twice encircled by the cord, of which he retained both ends. He then, from the coach doorway, mounted the saddle in front of her, brought the rope's ends together before him, joined them in a knot, and let Kit Bottle lead the horse a few paces forward so that his prisoner might not impede matters by seizing hold of the coach.

"And now the boy, Anthony. Carry him on your

saddle-bow," said Marryott. The Puritan, reaching into the coach with both arms, laid hold of the page, and placed him on the saddle-bow; then, at a gesture, mounted behind him.

"Take one of the horns, Kit," was Hal's next command. "Give one to me, one to Anthony, one to Captain Rumney, and the other to Tom Cobble. John Hatch, lead the spare horse. And now all to your saddles. Kit, ride at the head. Anthony, you shall go at my right hand; Tom Cobble, at my left. Captain Rumney shall choose his place. And heed this, all of you: When I sound this horn, all ye that have like instruments, blow your loudest; the rest, halloo your lustiest; and every mother's son set his horse a-galloping till I call halt, taking heed to keep together. And now, forward!"

A minute later, the cavalcade was moving through the downcoming flakes, leaving the wrecked coach to bury itself in the snow.

Mistress Hazlehurst could not but see her captor's reason for the order of which a blast from his horn was to be the signal. Now that she was no longer concealed in the coach, it would be easier — the temptation would be greater — for her to make an outcry when passing habitations. The noise of the horns and of the hallooing would drown the words she might utter, and the galloping would rob her gesticulations of their intended effect. The conduct of the whole party would strike beholders as the sportive ebullition of a company of merry blades bent on astonishing the natives; and any cries or motions she might make would seem, in the flash of time while they might be witnessed, but of a piece with the behavior of her boisterous companions. There were roysterers of the gentler sex in those days, — witness Mary Frith, otherwise "Moll Cutpurse," who was indeed a very devil of a fellow.[28] Such roaring women were not of Mistress Hazlehurst's quality; but who would have time to discern her quality in the brief while of the company's mad transit through such small towns as lay before them?

It was less clear to her why her enemy should have placed her on the same horse with himself, when he might have bound her upon another, of which he could have retained hold of the bridle. But the case was thus: Though a possible contest with Rumney or Barnet might result in Hal's own personal escape, such a contest might, were she on another horse, enable her to free herself, and either make disclosures fatal to Hal's mission, or fall prisoner to the robber. But, she being on his horse, and unable to act independently of him, Hal's escape would leave her still his captive. That escape he must, then, contrive to make. He thus simplified his course in the event of an encounter; twined two threads into one; united two separate lines of possible befalling

"THE BRAZEN NOTES CLOVE THE AIR."

— his line and hers — so that they might be determined by a single, concentrated exertion of his own prowess.

Should matters so shape that her life be endangered by her position, Hal might, at the last moment, sever with his dagger the cord that bound her to him. She, being now deprived of weapons, could not do this.

As for Francis, stealthy and resolute as recent occurrences had shown him to be, there was nothing to fear from him while he bestrode the saddle-bow of Anthony Underhill.

It was eight o'clock when they started from the abandoned coach. A little after nine they passed through Skipton. The town was half invisible through the falling snow, which, as it came, was the sport of the same wind that made casements rattle and weather-cocks creak, and street-folk muffle themselves and pay small heed to passing riders.

To test his device and his men, Master Marryott, when half way through the town, sounded his horn and gave his horse the spur. The response, from all but Captain Rumney, was instant and hearty. The brazen notes clove the air, the men emitted a score of unearthly yells, the horses dashed forward; and the clamor, which caused the few snow-blinded outdoor folk to stare blinkingly, might well have awakened the ghosts of the ancient castle of the Cliffords.

But neither ghosts nor townspeople stayed the turbulent strangers.

When Hal ordered a cessation, outside the town, he found that the men were in the better humor for the little outlet to their pent-up deviltry; all with the exception of Rumney, who had galloped with the rest, but in silence.

Rumney had indeed been moody since the abandonment of the coach. He had kept his place behind Marryott, in full range of the eyes of the lady on the pillion, who, as she sat sidewise, could look back at him with ease. Her glances, eloquent of a kind of surprise at his inaction, gave him an ill opinion of himself which he soon burned to revenge upon some one. And his feelings were not sweetened by his men's good humor over an incident from which he had excluded himself.

Of the roads from Skipton, Marryott chose that which he thought would take him soonest into the North Riding. The cavalcade had gone perhaps four miles upon this road, when, suddenly, Captain Rumney called out:

"Halt, lads, and close in upon this quarry!"

His men checked their horses, some with surprise, some as if the order might have been expected. They drew their blades, too, — blades of every variety, — and turned their horses about.

Captain Bottle instantly urged his steed back

toward Hal, charging through the confusion of plunging horses in true cavalry fashion. Marryott himself wheeled half around to face Rumney. Anthony Underhill, with Francis on his saddle-bow, grimly menaced the robbers who had turned.

"What means this, Captain Rumney?" said Hal, quietly. Every sword in the company was now unsheathed.

"It means that I cry, stand and deliver!" replied the robber, finding all needful confidence and courage in the very utterance of the habitual challenge. He felt himself now in his own rôle, and feared nothing.

"Is it not foolish," answered Marryott, without raising his voice, "to risk your skin thus, for the sake of money that would be yours to-morrow in payment of service?"

"To the devil with your money, — though I'll have that, too, ere all's done! First deliver me the lady!"

"I am much more like to deliver you to the flames below!" replied Hal.

"Say you so! Upon him, boys!" cried Rumney, raising a pistol, which he had furtively got ready to fire.

Two things occurred at the same moment: Anthony Underhill got his sword engaged with that of the nearest robber who had moved to obey

Rumney's order; and Master Marryott struck Rumney's pistol aside with his rapier, so that it discharged itself harmlessly into the falling snow.

Hal's next movement was to turn Rumney's sword-point with his dagger, which he held in the same hand with his rein. Behind him, Mistress Hazlehurst clung to her pillion, in a state of mind that may be imagined. In front of Anthony Underhill, Francis, the page, made himself small, to avoid a possible wild thrust from the fellow that contested with the Puritan.

By this time Kit Bottle had reached Anthony's side.

"What, ye jolly bawcocks!" he cried to the robbers, his sword-point raised aloft, as if he awaited the result of his words ere choosing a victim for it. "Will ye follow this cheap rascal Rumney 'gainst gentlemen? He'll prove traitor to you all, an ye trust him long enough; as he did to me in the Low Countries! Mr. Edward Moreton, and honest John Hatch, and good Oliver Bunch, I call on you stand by true men!"

"And Tom Cobble!" shouted Hal, without looking back from his combat with Rumney, which, although it was now one of rapiers, they continued to wage on horseback. "You're my man, I wot! A raw rustical rogue like this, is not fit for London lads to follow!"

"What say ye, mates?" cried Tom Cobble. "I am for the gentleman!"

"And I!" quoth John Hatch, stoutly; Ned Moreton, airily; Oliver Bunch, timidly; and two or three others.

"A murrain on gentlemen!" roared a burly fellow, and a chorus of approving oaths and curses showed that a majority of Rumney's men remained faithful to their old leader.

"Good, my hearts!" cried their captain, his brow clearing of the cloud that had risen at the first defection. "There shall be the more pickings for you that are staunch! I'll kill every deserter!"

"Look to't you be not killed yourself!" quoth Master Marryott, leaning forward to keep the area of steel-play far from Mistress Hazelhurst.

Rumney had exchanged his emptied pistol for a dagger, and he imitated Hal in using it with the hand that held his rein. In rapier-and-dagger fights, the long weapon was used for thrusting, the short one for parrying. Such contests were not for horseback. When mounted enemies met, so armed, they would ordinarily dismount and fight afoot. But Marryott was determined not to separate himself from his prisoner, and Rumney chose to remain in readiness for pursuit in case his antagonist should resort to flight.

So this unique duel went on, — a single combat

with rapier and dagger, on horseback, one of the contestants sharing his horse with a lady on a pillion behind him! The combat remained single because Rumney's men had all they could do in defending themselves against the vigorous attack of Kit Bottle, Anthony Underhill, and the deserters from their own band.

These deserters, knowing that the defeat of the side they had taken would leave them at the mercy of the Rumney party, fought with that fury which comes of having no alternative but victory or death. There was not an idle or a shirking sword to be found on either side. Each man chose his particular antagonist, and when one combatant had worsted his opponent he found another or went to the aid of a comrade. In the narrow roadway, in blinding flakes, and with mingled cries of pain, rage, and elation, these riders plied their weapons one against another, until blood dripped in many places on the fallen snow that was tramped by the rearing horses.

The strange miniature battle, fought in a place out of sight of human habitation, and with no witnesses but the two prisoners so dangerously placed for viewing it, lasted for ten minutes. Then Master Marryott, whose adroitness, sureness, and swiftness had begun to appall and confuse Rumney, ran his rapier through the latter's sword-arm.

With a loud exclamation, the robber dropped the

arm to his side, and backed his horse out of reach with his left hand.

But Hal, with a fierce cry "Talk you of killing?" spurred his horse forward as if to finish with the rascal. This was a pretence, but it worked its purpose.

"Quarter," whimpered the robber captain, pale with fear.

"Then call off your hounds!" replied Hal, hotly, checking his horse.

"I will," answered the trembling Rumney, quickly. "Lads, a truce! Put up your swords, curse you!"

His men were not sorry to get this order, nor their opponents to hear it given. The fight had gone too evenly to please either side, and wounds — some of them perhaps destined to prove fatal — had been nearly equally distributed. Hal's adherents ceased fighting when their foes did, Kit Bottle being the last, and probably the only reluctant one, to desist.

"And now you will turn back, Master Rumney," said Marryott, in a hard, menacing tone, "and find another road to travel! Take with you the knaves that stood by you. The others, an they choose, shall remain my men, in my pay. Come, you rogues, march!"

Master Marryott backed to the side of the road, that Rumney's followers might pass. They did so, readily enough, those who were unhorsed being lifted to saddles by their comrades. Until the two parties were distinctly separated, and several paces were between them, every weapon and every eye on either side remained on the alert to meet treachery. All the deserters from Rumney stayed with Hal.

"'God bless you, Ancient Rumney,'" called out Kit Bottle, slightly altering a remembered speech from a favorite play, as the robber turned his horse's head toward Skipton. "'You scurvy, lousy knave, God bless you!'"

Rumney and his men rode for some distance without answer; Hal and his company, motionless, looking after them. Suddenly, when he was beyond easy overtaking, the robber leader turned in his saddle, and shouted back, vindictively:

"I scorn you, Kit Bottle! You are no better than an Irish footboy! And your master there is a woman-stealing dog, that I'll be quits with yet. He's no gentleman, neither, but a scurvy fencing-master in false feathers!"

"Shall I give chase and make him eat his words?" asked Kit of Master Marryott.

"Nay, the cur that whines for mercy, and receives it, and then snarls back at a safe distance, is too foul for thy hands, Kit! Let those fellows on the ground be put on horses and supported till we find a safe place for them. I'll not abandon any that stood by me. And then, onward! Madam, I trust you were not incommoded. Your page, I see, is safe."

Mistress Hazlehurst deigned no answer. Her feelings were wrapped in a cloak of outward composure.

The wounded men were soon made safe upon horses, and the northward journey was again in progress.

"I thank heaven we are rid of Captain Rumney!" said Hal to Kit Bottle, who now rode beside him, Anthony having taken the lead.

"I would thank heaven more heartily, an I were sure we *were* rid of him!" growled Kit, blinking at the snowflakes.

CHAPTER XVI.

FOXBY HALL.

"O most delicate fiend! Who is't can read a woman?" — *Cymbeline.*

THE forenoon on which this fray and separation occurred was that of Saturday, March seventh, the fourth day of the flight. Marryott's company now consisted of his two original followers, his two prisoners, Ned Moreton, Tom Cobble, Oliver Bunch, John Hatch, and a few more of the robbers. What wounds had been received were bound up as well as possible, with strips torn from clothing, and were so stoically endured as not to impede the forward journey. The able-bodied rode by the disabled, giving them needful support.

Marryott had travelled some two hundred miles from Fleetwood house in three and a half days, accomplishing an average of nearly sixty miles a day, despite all delays and the slow going of the coach. Now that the storm had come up, to make the roads well-nigh impassable, it would take a rider at least three and a half days to return from Hal's present place to Fleetwood house. Thus, even if the pursuivant should overtake the fugitives at any moment, seven days were already gained for Sir Valentine. Another day and a half would, under the storm-caused conditions of travel, procure him the full ten days.

Now, before the beginning of the storm, Roger Barnet, had he gone at the speed for which the men of his office were then proverbial ("like flying pursuivant" is Spenser's simile for swift-moving angels), would have overtaken a traveller hampered as Hal was. But it happened — so prone is circumstance to run to coincidence, as every man perceives daily in his own life — that Roger Barnet, too, had his special hindrances. That part of the chase which had culminated in his almost catching Hal at the hostelry near the Newark cross-road, had been delayed at the outset by the delivery of the queen's letters. And in the subsequent pursuit, when Hal's several impediments had given the pursuivant the best opportunities, Master Barnet had suffered most annoying checks.

Of these, there were those that Hal had conjectured; but, in addition, there was a bodily accident to no less a person than Master Barnet himself. In that very village of Clown, where Hal had been detained by the constable, an exhausted horse had fallen at the moment when the pursuivant was dismounting from it, and had so bruised the pursuivant's leg that he had been perforce laid up at the alehouse for some hours, unable to stand, or to sit his saddle. For his own reasons, of which a hint has been given earlier in this narrative, he had not allowed his men to continue the chase without him; but he had resumed it at the first moment when he could endure the pain of riding.

Of this interference of fortune in his behalf, Master Marryott knew nothing, as he and his riders toiled forward through the blown clouds of snow. He took it on faith that the pursuivant, obliged by duty and enabled by skill, was following through similar clouds somewhere behind. He would not, at this stage, give a moment's room to any thought opposed to this.

The travellers covered thirty miles or more, through unremitting snowfall and increasing wind; passing Rylston, Cumiston, Kettlewell, Carlton, Middleham, and Harmby, — names, some of which have lost their old importance, some of which have given place to others, some of which have quite vanished from the map, — stopping twice for food, drink, and to rest the horses. In the inhabited places, the riders were too much obscured by snow, the people outdoors were too few, for Mistress Hazlehurst to place any hope in an appeal for rescue. Nevertheless, to hearten his men up, and to leave the deeper trace for Barnet to follow, Marryott went through these places at a gallop, with great noise of voices and horns. Strange must have been the spectacle to gaping villagers drawn to casements by the advancing clamor, when this mad band of riders — one of them a woman — dashed into sight, as if borne by the wind like the snow clouds, rushed by with blast and shout, and disappeared into the white whirl as they had come!

All through the afternoon Mistress Hazlehurst was silent, close-wrapped in cloak and hood. She accepted with barely uttered thanks the ale and food that Master Marryott caused Kit Bottle to bring her from the rude inns near which they stopped. Hal showed his solicitude, at first, in brief and courteous inquiries regarding her comfort; then, as these were answered either not at all, or in the coldest monosyllables, in glances over his shoulder. Was her inertia, he asked himself, a sign that she had given up the battle? — or a sign that she was nourishing some new plan, sufficiently subtle to fit the new circumstances?

During the afternoon, Kit Bottle rode often among the men from Rumney's band, talking with them, and seeing how the wounded bore themselves.

As the riders passed in sight of Middleham castle, whose wind-beaten walls, with their picturesque background of Nature's setting, were now scarce visible behind the driven nebules of snow, Kit brought his horse close to Hal's, and said, in a low voice:

"Some of those fellows have ugly little cuts. They would fare better under roof, and on their backs, than on horse, in this weather."

"But where may they be left?" asked Hal. "What yeoman or hind would take them under shelter? And the inns where their robber-skins would be safe, look you, are those where Rumney is a favored guest. If he should come and find them, how many three-farthing pieces would their lives be worth, think you?"

"Thou speakest by the card there, God wot! But I have in mind a shelter where these honest knaves can lie safe, and where we all may snatch an hour or two of comfort. This Oliver Bunch hath turned himself inside out to me. The lands where he was under-steward, before the family fled to France for their necks' sake, are five or six mile ahead of us. The mansion, he tells me, is closed tight, and empty. Whether confiscation hath been made, I know not; but, be the place the crown's, or some one's else by gift or purchase, there it now stands for our use, without e'en bailiff or porter to say us nay. 'Tis called Foxby Hall."

"If it be so tight closed that others have not entered, for thievery or shelter, how can we get in?"

"With a key that this Bunch hath hid in a safe hole in the wall. It opens a side door. He hath kept his secret, for love of his old place of service, till this hour."

"He is a very worthy rascal, truly. Well, let us make the better haste to this house, that we may have the more time to tarry in it. Foxby Hall, say you? I like the name; it hath a sound of hospitable walls amidst the greenwood."

Speed was made, therefore; and about five o'clock, while the snow still fell unceasingly, the riders came to a place where, on one hand, the road was flanked by varied and well-wooded country, and where, on the other hand, there ran for some distance a wooden fence, beyond which there were at first fields, and then the stately trees of a park. The fence was finally succeeded by a stone wall, at a point where a similar wall ran back at right angle with the first. The wall along the road had in its middle a broken-down gate. Before this gate Oliver Bunch stopped; and, with a look at Kit Bottle, pointed through it.

When Hal drew up his horse, and looked into the grounds to which the gate afforded entrance, he saw, some way up a thinly-wooded slope, a turreted and gabled building. From its main front, which was parallel with the road, two wings projected forward. These three parts enclosed three sides of a square: the fourth side was bounded by a little terrace, which descended toward the road, and at whose foot ran a second wall, quite low, across part of the grounds.

The main front, which had two gables, was partly of stone, partly of wood and plaster. The wings, more recent, were of brick; they were flanked by turrets, and their ends were gabled. The windows of the main front were high, narrow, and pointed at the tops; those of the wings also were high, but they were wide and rectangular. There was a porched Gothic door in the middle of the main front; and one of the wings, in its inner side, had a smaller door. A basin for a fountain was in the centre of the square. Tall trees grew on the terrace.

"It hath an inviting look," said Master Marryott. "But 'tis far from the road. Were Barnet sighted, we could scarce get to horse and reach the gate ere he arrived."

"An't please your worship," put in Oliver Bunch, deferentially; "the house hath a way through the park, to a gate further on the road. 'Tis a shorter way to the north than the road itself is, sir, for it runs straight from the stables, while the road goes somewhat roundabout."

"Then seek your key, good Oliver Bunch; and heaven grant it be safe in its hiding-place!"

The fat household servant of former days slid from his horse with unwonted alacrity, and disappeared through the gate, gliding thence along the inner side of the wall. He soon returned with sparkling eyes, holding up the key.

"Lead Oliver's horse, Kit," said Hal. "Let him show us the way, afoot. Yon turret window hath a long view of the road. We can keep watch there for Barnet."

The worthy Bunch, gazing fondly at the deserted mansion amidst the trees, hastened up the gentle incline of land, followed by the riders. All looked with curious eyes upon the house as they ascended. The horse-path, after passing through an alley of neglected hedgerows, skirted the terrace, and led across one side of the square court to the Gothic main door.

Bidding the riders halt there, Bunch traversed the other side of the court, and vanished behind the angle of a wing. For some minutes the company waited in expectation, Hal watching Mistress Hazlehurst as her gaze slowly ranged the exterior of the house. At last an unchaining, unbarring, unbolting, and key-turning were heard from within the door. Then it swung heavily inward, with a creak, and Oliver Bunch appeared with a welcoming face.

"Anthony, you will look to the stabling of the horses," said Master Marryott. "Oliver Bunch, be so kind to show him where that may be done. Tom Cobble, take you charge of the boy, and follow me into the house. Master Moreton, have the able fellows help in the wounded. Captain Bottle, find you the turret window of yonder wing, and watch there till I send word. Come to this door, Anthony and Oliver, as soon as the horses be in shelter; I shall have commands, regarding their comfort and our own. Madam, I pray you dismount and enter!"

Hal had swiftly, on finishing his orders to the men, untied the cord that bound him to his prisoner, and had leaped to the ground, holding in one hand the loose ends.

She accepted his hand mechanically, in descending from the pillion, and then preceded him into the hall of the mansion.

This was a large, lofty apartment, with a timber roof, a great fireplace, walls hung with old tapestry and armor, and a stairway ascending along the rear. In a corner some trestles and boards remained as evidence of the last feast upon which the woven, many-colored hunting party in the arras had looked down.

Marryott sat beside Mistress Hazlehurst, on a bench by the empty fireplace, and watched Moreton and Hatch help the wounded men to a pile of rushes at one side of the hall. By the time that Anthony and Oliver had returned, Hal had made plans for the next few hours. He had travelled so rapidly since morning, that he thought he might make this mansion his stopping-place for as much of the night as he should take for rest. Beginning the nightly halt at five, instead of at eight, he might set forth again at twelve instead of at three; unless, of course, an alarm of pursuit should send him to the saddle in the meanwhile.

This plan would obviate the difficulty he had anticipated of finding a suitable night's lodging for his prisoner. As the next day would be the fifth and last of his flight, that difficulty would not recur after to-night. He saw, with elation, the end of his mission at hand; and at the same time, with a feeling of blankness and chill, the end of his fellowship with Mistress Hazlehurst. But meanwhile there was the immediate future, for which he thus arranged:

He learned from Oliver Bunch that there was an inn some distance beyond where the park path joined the highroad. To that inn he sent Anthony Underhill for provisions. Going and returning by the park way, which the travellers would use in a hasty flight, the Puritan would meet them in case of such flight during his absence.

Marryott then set his men to fetching logs and making fires: one in the great hall, for the benefit of the injured robbers; one in an upper chamber that he chose, upon Oliver's description, for Mistress Hazlehurst's use; and a third in the large room from which this chamber had its only entrance.

Guided by Oliver, Hal conducted his unresisting

prisoner up the stairs, thence through a corridor that made a rectangular turn, thence into the large room, and to the threshold of her chamber. He gave permission, unasked, that Francis might wait upon her, but stationed Tom Cobble in the large room with instructions to follow the page wherever the latter went outside her chamber, and to restrict his movements to the house itself. Having heard these orders and made no comment, Mistress Hazlehurst beckoned the page to follow, and disappeared into the chamber.

Hal had chosen as his own resting-place the large outer room. It was in the same wing with the turret to which he had sent Kit Bottle to keep watch. Perceiving that the great embayed window of the room gave as good a view of the southward road as the turret itself could give, Hal summoned Kit, and sent him to stay with the robbers in the hall below. The captain might sleep, if he chose; he had kept vigil the previous night. Hal would now watch from the window, until Anthony's return; then the Puritan should go on guard.

Tom Cobble sat, half asleep, on a chest at one side of the door to Mistress Hazlehurst's chamber. Marryott reclined on the window-seat, looking now through the casement at the snow-covered, rolling, grove-dotted country; now at the blazing, crackling logs in the fireplace opposite; now at the tapestry, which sometimes stirred in the wind that entered by cracks of door and window. The room was well furnished, as indeed most of the house was, for its occupants, whatever the cause of their flight from the country, had valued haste above property. They had not even taken all their trunks; for one of these stood in the room as a piece of furniture, in accordance with the custom of the time. This apartment had probably served as a ladies' room. It had a case of books; a table on which were some scattered playing-cards, and a draughts-board with the pieces in the position of an unfinished game; and another table, on which lay an open virginal, a viol, and smaller musical instruments. The chairs were heavy and solid. Overhead was visible the timber work of the roof.

Marryott went and examined the viol, and, returning to the window-seat, drew from it a few tremulous strains. As he was adjusting the strings, he heard a sound at the end of the apartment, looked up, and saw, to his surprise, that Mistress Hazlehurst was returning. Francis followed her. Her face showed the refreshing effect of the cold water with which Oliver had supplied her room. Hal watched her in silence.

Motioning Francis to sit by the fire, she crossed to the music-table, sat down before it, and touched the keys of the virginal. The response showed the work of weather and neglect upon the instrument;

but after twice or thrice running her fingers up and down the short keyboard, she elicited the notes of a soft and pensive melody.

After a while of silent listening, Marryott gently took up the melody upon his viol. For an instant he was fearful that she might break off at this, but she played on, at first as if not heeding his uninvited participation, and at last accommodating her own playing, where the effect required, to his.

From one tune they went to another, and then to a third and fourth. At first it was she that led in the transition; but, at length, having ventured with some trepidation to pass, of his own initiative, from one piece to another, he had the delight of being immediately accompanied by her. There was in her first note, it was true, an instant's dragging, as if she hesitated under the protest of certain feelings, but finally the yielding was complete, the accompaniment in perfect accord. Thereafter it was he that led, she that followed.

What might he infer from this? Aught beyond the mere outward appearance, the mere indifferent willingness to join in a musical performance for the sake of the aural pleasure? Or was there signified an inner, perhaps unconscious, yielding of the woman's nature to the man's? Was his domination over her, begun, and hitherto maintained, by physical force, at last obtaining the consent of her heart?

Marryott dared not think so; he recoiled in horror from the thought, when he saw himself, with her eyes, as her brother's supposed slayer. And then, still viewing himself with her eyes, he was fascinated by that very situation from which he had recoiled. It was, of course, as she must regard it, a tragic situation; in that circumstance lay both its horror and its fascination.

But did this situation exist? When he remembered that the mere attraction of the one woman for the one man, or the one man for the one woman, ofttimes annihilates all opposing considerations, he knew that this situation was not impossible. To be loved by this woman, even across the abyss of blood she saw between them! The idea possessed and repossessed him, though again and again he put it from him as horrible, or improbable, or both. Perhaps he spoke his thoughts in the notes he drew from his viol; perhaps she spoke thoughts of her own in the language of the virginal; perhaps they spoke unconsciously to each other's deepest hidden comprehension; neither could outwardly analyze an impression received from the other's playing, or certainly know whether that impression had been intended.

The day faded. The snow fell between the window and the trees of the park; fell as thick as ever, but more slowly and gently now, the wind being at less unrest. The firelight danced oddly on the tapestry, the shadows deepened in its brighter radiance. Not a word was uttered. Only the viol and the virginal spoke.

This strange concert was interrupted, at last, by the return of Anthony and Oliver, with a supply of cheese, spice-cakes, and apples, a bottle of wine, a large pot of ale, and a bag of feed for the horses. Marryott caused the wine and a part of the food to be brought to the room in which he sat. The ale and other provisions were served to the men in the hall. Anthony, after supping, and seeing the horses fed, was to keep the usual vigil on the road, as approaching horsemen might not be seen from the window after dark, and as the Puritan had slept the previous night.

"Will you sup in your chamber, or with me at this table?" Hal asked his prisoner.

Without speaking she pointed to the table on which Oliver Bunch had set the eatables. It was that on which the cards and draughts-board were. As the viands, with the glasses and plate that Bunch had furnished, occupied only the table's end next the fire, the draughts-board was not disturbed. Captor and captive sat opposite each other, as they had sat in the inn near the Newark cross-road. Tom and Francis, having lighted a candle-end brought by Oliver, stood to wait on them; but Hal, handing them a platter on which was a good portion of the supper, bade them go to another part of the room and wait on themselves. He gave them also a glass of the wine, reserving the rest, with a single glass, for his prisoner and himself.

The meal went in silence. Darkness fell over the outer world. The candle added little light to that of the fire; hence much of the room was shadowy. Only the table near the fire, where the two sat, was in the glow. Marryott would have spoken, but a spell had fallen upon him like that which had locked his lips on the first day of their travelling. Sometimes he sighed, and looked at her wistfully. When his eyes met hers, she would glance downward, but without disdain or dislike.

What was in her thoughts? What was her mind toward him? He sought answer in her face, but in vain. When it came to drinking from the same glass he used, she did so, in obedience to custom, with no sign of antipathy or scruple.

Supper over, Marryott idly turned to the cards lying near at hand. Three of them faced upward. He grasped these, and held them between thumb and forefinger in the light. It was strange. They were the knave of hearts, the queen of spades, the eight of clubs, — a fair man, a dark woman, a battle. Mistress Hazlehurst gave him a glance signifying that she noted the coincidence.

He reached for one of the cards that lay face downward, thinking it might foretell the issue of the battle. It was the nine of clubs, — more battle. He smiled amusedly, and looked at her; but her face told nothing. He turned to the draughts-board, which was portable, and carefully drew it nearer without displacing any of the pieces. There were four of each color left on the board. At first glance one could not see that either side had advantage. Hal observed, under his lashes, that Mistress Hazlehurst's look had fallen, with slight curiosity, upon the board. He made a move, with one of the white pieces, and waited. She continued gazing at the board. At length she placed a delicate finger on one of the black pieces, and moved. Hal soon replied. Thus was the game, left unfinished by players now self-exiled to foreign lands, and who little imagined at this moment by what a strangely matched pair it was taken up, carried on.

And, after all, it ended as a drawn game.

Mistress Hazlehurst, perceiving that one piece of each color was left on the board as a result of an exchange which she had thought would leave two blacks and one white, gave a little shrug of the shoulders; then rose, and walked toward her chamber.

Marryott swiftly seized the candle, and offered it to her, saying:

"We set forth again at midnight. I will knock at your door a little before."

She took the candle, and went from the room; but on her threshold she turned for a moment, and said, softly:

"Good night!"

Marryott stood in a glow of incredulous joy. Her tone, her gracious look, the mere fact of her uttering the civility, or of her volunteering a speech to him, could not but mean that she had softened. Had she come to doubt whether he was indeed her brother's slayer? Or had her heart come to incline toward him despite the supposed gulf of bloodshed that parted them? Either conjecture intoxicated him; the first as with an innocent bliss, the second as with a poignant ecstasy darkly tinged with horror and guilt.

Francis and Tom had fallen asleep where they had sat at supper. Anthony, as Marryott knew, had long since ridden out to keep his cold and lonely watch. Kit and the other men in the hall were asleep, for the sounds of their supper merriment had ceased to come up from below. The horses were in the stables, resting, in readiness for a swift departure. The fire crackled; the wind, having risen again, wailed around the turrets and gables of Foxby Hall, and the snow beat against the window. Marryott took a large book from the case, put it on a chest as a pillow, wrapped himself in his cloak, and lay down with his new and delicious dreams. From waking dreams, they soon became dreams indeed. For the first night in three, he slept.

CHAPTER XVII.

A WOMAN'S VICTORY.

"My heart hath melted at a lady's tears." — *King John*.

A SHRILL whistle roused Marryott from his sleep. He sprang to his feet. The fire was quite low now; some hours must have passed. The whistle was repeated; it came from outside the house, beneath the window. Marryott threw open the casement, letting in a dash of wind and snow, and leaned out. Below him, in the snowy darkness, was Anthony, on horseback.

"How now, Anthony?"

"A score of men have rid into Harmby, from the south. I saw them from this side of the town. I had gone so far back to keep warmth in my horse. 'Tis bitter cold. They stopped at the inn there, these men; whether to pass the night, or to get fresh horses, I wot not."

"Are they Barnet's men, think you?"

"There is no knowing. The darkness and snow make all men look alike at a distance. They might be the pursuivant's men, or they might be Captain Bottle's friends."

By "Captain Bottle's friends" the Puritan meant Rumney and his robbers.

"Harmby is but four miles away," said Marryott. "An they came on to-night, they would stop here to inquire of our passing. Or if they asked further on, and found we had not passed, they would soon hound us out. 'Tis well you brought the news forthwith, Anthony!"

"Why, as for that, 'twas eleven by Harmby clock when I turned my back on't. So it must be near starting-time now."

"Then go you to the hall and call the men, and bring the horses to the door. We shall ride by the road, if we can, to leave the trace there. But if these fellows by chance come up too soon, we shall use the way through the park."

"What of the wounded men, sir?"

"Those that cannot go with us may lie close in some outhouse loft here, with John Hatch to care for them. I'll give him money for their needs. Look to it all, Anthony. I'll meet you at the hall door."

The Puritan rode off, to round the corner of the wing. Marryott, not waiting to close the casement, awoke Tom Cobble and Francis, and sent them to join the men in the hall, the apprentice still in charge of the page. When these two had gone, Marryott knocked at Mistress Hazlehurst's door.

He waited. Nothing was heard but the wind, and the beating of flakes upon the window. He knocked again.

By roundabout ways came faint and indistinct scraps of the noise attendant upon Anthony's awakening the men.

"Mistress Hazlehurst!" called Marryott, softly. "It is time for us to go."

In the ensuing silence, a vague fear grew within him, — fear for his mission, fear for her. Could aught have befallen her?

"Madam!" he said, a little louder and faster. "I must bid you rise. We must set forth."

Marryott's heart was beating wildly. His was not a time of, nor this the moment for, false delicacy. He flung open the door, and strode into her chamber.

There was yet a little firelight left in the room. It shone upon the bed, of which the curtains were apart. Mistress Hazlehurst lay there, wrapped loosely in her cloak, the hood not up. Her eyes were wide open. Their depths reflected the red glow of the embers.

She sprang up, and stood beside the bed, her gaze meeting Marryott's. An instant later, she moved as if to step toward him, but seemed to lose her powers, and staggered.

He reached out to catch her, lest she should fall. But she avoided him, and hastened with swift but uncertain steps toward the door. Having neared it, she leaned against the post for support, and raised her hand to her forehead, uttering at the same time a low moan of pain.

"What is the matter?" asked Marryott, going quickly after her.

She moved, as by a desperate summoning of what small strength remained to her, into the outer room. She went as far as to the table near the fireplace. On this table she placed her hands, as if to prevent her sinking to the floor.

"What is the matter?" repeated Marryott, reaching her side in three steps, and putting his arms around her just in time to uphold her from falling.

"I know not," she whispered, as with a last remnant of departing breath. "I am dying, I think!"

And she let her head rest on his shoulder, as if for inability to hold it erect.

"Dying!" echoed Marryott, gazing with affrighted eyes into hers; whose lids thereupon fell, like those of a tired child.

She shivered in his arms, and murmured, feebly, "How cold it is!"

"Madam!" cried Marryott. "This is but a moment's faintness! It will pass! Call up your energies, I pray! I dare not delay. Already the men are waiting for us in the court below. We must to horse!"

"To my grave, 'twould be!" she answered, drowsily. Then a spasm of pain distorted her face. She became more heavy in Marryott's grasp.

"God's light! What am I to do?" he muttered. "Mistress, shake off this lethargy! Come to the window; the air will revive you!"

He moved to the open casement, bearing her in his arms. He feared to place her on the window-seat, lest the little animation she retained might pass from her.

She shuddered in the blast of wind.

"The cold kills me!" she said, huskily. "The snow hath a sting like needle-points!"

"Yet your face is warm!" He had placed his cheek against her forehead to ascertain this.

"It burns while my body freezes!" she replied.

"But your hands are not cold!" A tight clasp had made the discovery.

She did not move away her head, of which the white brow and dark hair were still pressed by his cheek, nor did she withdraw her hand. Neither did her body shrink from his embrace, though it trembled within it.

"I am ill unto death," was her answer. "I cannot move a step."

"But you are revived already. Your voice is not

so faint now. Madam, in a few moments you will have strength to ride."

"I should fall from the horse. My God, sir, can you be a gentleman, and subject a half dying woman to more of that fatigue which hath brought her to this pass — and on a night of such weather? If my voice has strength, 'tis the strength of desperation, which impels me to beg pity at your hands in mine hour of bitter illness!"

Thereupon, as if grown weaker, she sought additional support to that of his embrace, by clinging to him with her arms.

"But, madam, do you not perceive all is at stake upon my instant flight? A score of horsemen have entered Harmby; 'tis but four miles distant. They may be here any moment. Perchance they are the pursuivant and his men; perchance, Captain Rumney, with his band augmented! We must begone! God knows how it wounds my soul to put you to discomfort! But necessity cries 'on,' and ride forth we must!"

"Then ride forth without me. Let me die here alone."

"But I dare not leave you here. If Roger Barnet came and found you —" He did not complete the sentence. His thought was, that her account of him to Barnet might send men flying back for the real Sir Valentine. But, indeed, Marryott's continued flight, and her illness, would minimize the chances of Barnet's stopping where she was; or, if he did stop, of his waiting for much talk with her.

"An you take me with you," said she, "you may take but a cold corpse!"

The idea struck Marryott to the soul. To think of that beauty lying cold and lifeless, which now breathed warm and quivering in his arms!

"Mistress, you mistake! Your fears exceed your case! You will find yourself able to ride. I will wrap you well; I will let you ride in front of me, and I will support you. I must compel you, even as my cause compels me!"

"You would compel me to my death, to save your own life!"

"'Tis not my poor life I think of! There is that in my flight you wot not of."

"Then betake yourself to your flight, and leave me!" And, for the first time, she made some faint movement to push from his embrace.

"No, no!" he cried, tightening his grasp so that she ceased her opposing efforts. "For your own sake I dare not leave you. These riders may be Rumney and his men. If you should fall into their hands!"

"Leave me to their hands!" she cried, again exerting herself feebly to be free. "'Tis a wise course for you. If it be Rumney that hath followed, 'tis easy guessing what hath brought him. An he find me, he will cease troubling you."

"Madam, madam, would you be left to the will of that villain? Know you — can you suppose — ?"

"Yes, I know; and can imagine how such villains woo! But what choice have I? I cannot go with you. Would you drag me forth to meet my death? But that you cannot do, an you would. Here will I remain, and if you go you must leave me behind."

And, with an effort for which he was quite unprepared, she thrust him from her, and slipped from his somewhat relaxed embrace. The next instant she traversed, with wavering motions, the distance to the chest. Upon this she let herself fall, and straightened her body to a supine position.

When Marryott ran to her side, and tried to lift her, he found her so rigid that nothing short of violently applied force could place her upon horseback, or keep her there afterward.

A moment later a spasmodic shiver stirred her body, and she uttered so pitiful a groan that Marryott could no longer hold out against the conviction — which he had thus far resisted, as one hopes against hope — that she was indeed beyond all possibility of taking horse that night. Having, perforce, admitted to himself her condition, he ran and closed the casement, then returned to her.

"Madam, what am I to do?" he asked. "'Tis plain that a brief delay would find you no more able to go than you now are. For such illness as hath laid hold of you, after so long exposure, I well know one recovers not in an hour. If I tarried at all for you, it would needs be a long tarrying."

"Then tarry not," she moaned. "Go, and leave me."

"If I left men to protect you?"

"Ay, my page Francis! The boy would avail much against Rumney and the score of men you say are at Harmby!"

"If I left, also, the men who joined us from Rumney's band?"

"Why, those that are wounded would sure stay by me, for want of power to run away! And the other four might stay till they caught sight of their old leader. Then they would have choice of turning tail, or of crawling to him for pardon, or of dying, either in my defence or for his revenge."

"If I left Captain Bottle and Anthony Underhill with them?"

"Certes, if this score of men be the pursuivant's, 'tis better for you that your two faithful dogs die as your accomplices, and you go safe alone!"

"Madam, I deserve not this irony! I say to you again, 'tis not for mine own life that I would leave others to die on my account without me. 'Tis for

Sir — for the qu— for the cause to which I have bound myself, and of which you know not. My God, I would this were to-morrow's night! Then you would see how fearful I am for my life! But for another day, my life is not mine own!"

The woman to whom he spoke paid no heed to words whose significance she did not understand.

"Then why do you stay here?" she said. "Is it of my asking? Do I request aught of you? Go, and take your men with you. You may have need of them."

"That is true," thought Marryott, appreciating how much easier it was for the pursuivant to follow a trace left by three men than that left by one.

"Your two henchmen are stout fellows, I ween," she went on, speaking as with difficulty, "but scarce like to use much zeal in my behalf. I'll warrant that Puritan would not stir for me, were you not here to command him."

"'Tis true!" muttered Marryott, in a tumult of perplexity. "Against a score of desperate rascals, what six men under heaven would long risk their lives for a lady's sake, unless they were gentlemen, or by a gentleman led? And what gentleman leading them, and fighting with them, could hope to win unless he were armed, as I should be, by love for that lady? Well I know that gentlemen do not protect ladies by deputy, nor trust to underlings the safety of those they love!"

There was a moment's silence. She moved not; gave no start, or frown, or look of surprise, or other sign that she had noted this, his first spoken confession of love. Yet that very absence of all sign ought to have told him that she had heeded it, — that she had even been prepared for it.

"Bitter is my fortune," she replied, using a tone a trifle lower and more guarded than hitherto. "Of all who are at hand, only you, being a gentleman and moved by the spirit of chivalry, would protect a lady to the last, against odds. Only you, with the valor and strength that a chivalrous heart bestows, might hope to prevail against such odds. Only you, with the power of leadership over those men below, could give them either will or courage for the contest. Only your remaining, therefore, might save me from this villain. Your cause forbids your remaining. Go, then; save yourself, save your cause, and leave me to my fate!"

Her voice had fallen to a whisper. She now lay perfectly still, as if too exhausted even to deplore what might be in store for her.

"Oh, madam!" said Marryott, his voice betraying the distress he no longer tried to conceal. "What a choice is mine! Lest these men approaching be Rumney's, I dare not go from you; lest they be the pursuivant's, I dare not stay with you! Must I, then, leave you here, in this deserted house, in this wild night, to what terrible chances I dare not think of? Can you not ride forth? Is it not possible? Can you not find strength, somewhere deep-stored within you?"

Her only answer was a faint smile as at his incredulity to her state, or at his futile return to impossible hopes.

He had already forgotten, for the time, what strength she had found to make her body rigid.

"Fare thee well, then!" he cried, abruptly, and hastened, with steps almost as wild as hers had been, to the door leading to the passage.

A low sob arrested him at the threshold. He turned and looked at her; his heart, which seemed to have stopped as he was crossing the room to leave her, now began to beat madly.

She was not looking after him. She had not changed position. But, by the firelight, to which his sight was now accustomed, a welling up of moisture was visible in her eyes.

While he stood gazing at her, she gave another sob,—a convulsive note of despair, in which Marryott read a sense of her forlorn situation and possible fate; of being abandoned in dire illness, in an empty country-house, on this wildest of nights, to become, perchance, the prey of a vile, unscrupulous rascal.

By the time that Marryott, moving in long strides, had reached her side, her cheeks were wet with tears.

"Lady," he said, in a voice unsteady with emotion, as he flung himself on his knees beside her couch, and caught both her hands in his, "be not afraid! Though I forfeit my life, and fail in my cause, I will not go from you! May God above forgive me; and may those for whom I have these four days striven; and may my fathers, who never, for fear of man or love of woman, fell short of their given word! But I love thee! Ay, madam, 'tis a right I earn, that of holding thee thus in mine arms; thou know'st not what I pay for it! I love thee!"

He had resigned her hands, only that he might enfold her body; and she was so far from resisting his clasp that she had thrown her own arms, soft and warm, around his neck. She no longer wept, yet the tears still stood in her eyes; through them, however, as she met his impassioned gaze, glowed a light at once soft and powerful. Her nostrils heaved in quick but regular respirations. As his face neared hers, her lips seemed unconsciously to await the contact of his own. Nor did they fail of humid warmth when he pressed upon them a score of kisses.

"Oh, thou beautiful one!" he whispered, raising his face that he might find again in the depths of her eyes the rapture which, by the responsive intentness of her look, it was evident she found in his own eyes. "Never did I think I should prove so weak, or know such joy! Though I hazard my mission and my life, yet methinks for this moment I would barter my soul! For at this moment thou lov'st me, dost thou not? Else all kisses are false, all eyes are liars! Tell me, mistress! For thine own rest's sake, tell me; or be slain with mine importunings!"

"Wouldst thou have my lips," she whispered, and paused an instant for strength to finish, "confess by speech — what they have too well betrayed — otherwise?"

"I did not slay thy brother," he answered, still looking into her eyes. "That thou must believe! Yet thou wouldst love me, this one moment, even though the red gulf were indeed between us? Is't not so?"

She would not answer. When he again opened his lips to urge, she, by a movement of the arm, caused them to close against her own.

Then, as by a sudden change of impulse, she closed her eyes and thrust him from her with all the force of which her arms were capable.

CHAPTER XVIII.

THE HORSEMEN ARRIVE.

"'Faith, I will live so long as I may, that's the certain of it!" — *Henry V.*

THERE was a rapid, heavy tread in the passage without. Marryott hastily rose from his kneeling posture, turned, and took a step toward the door. Kit Bottle entered.

"All's ready for going, sir," said the captain.

"We shall not go," said Marryott, quietly, with as much composure as he could command. "We shall stay here the rest of the night; I know not how much longer."

"Stay here?" muttered Kit, staring at Marryott, with amazed eyes.

"Ay. Let Anthony take the horses back to stable. And —" Marryott felt that so unaccountable a change of plan required some further orders, as if there were a politic reason behind it; moreover, Kit's astonished look seemed to call for them. So, begotten of Hal's embarrassment in the gaze of his lieutenant, came a thought, and in its train a hope. "And then we'll make this house ready for a siege," he added. "Go below; send hither the boy Francis, and Tom Cobble, and let all the others await my commands in the hall."

Kit disappeared. He saw Marryott's plan as soon as it had taken shape. The word "siege" was key sufficient for the captain. Ten days were to be gained for Sir Valentine. Four were past. Four more would be required for a return to Fleetwood house in this weather and over snowbound roads. Two days thus remained to be consumed. If Foxby Hall could be held for two days against probable attempts of Roger Barnet to enter it, and without his discovering Hal's trick, the mission would be accomplished.

But after that, what of the lives of Master Marryott and his men? It was not yet time to face that question. The immediate problem was, to gain the two days.

Mistress Hazlehurst, who believed Marryott to be the real Fleetwood, and knew nothing of the matter of the ten days, saw in this prospective siege the certainty of the supposed knight's eventual capture; saw, that is to say, the accomplishment of the vengeful purpose for which she had beset his flight. She lay motionless on her improvised couch, her feelings locked within her.

"And now, mistress," said Marryott, turning to her, and speaking in a low voice, "what may be done for thy comfort? I have no skill to deal with ailments. It may be that one of the men below —"

"Nay," she answered, drowsily; "there is naught can do me any good but rest. My ailment is, that my body is wearied to the edge of death. The one cure is sleep."

"Shall I support thee to thy bed?"

"An thou wilt."

When he had borne her into her chamber, and laid her on the bed, she appeared to sink at once into that repose whence she might renew her waned vitality. He gazed for a moment upon her face, daring not to disturb her tranquillity with another caress. Hearing steps approaching in the passage beyond the outer room, he went softly from the chamber and met Francis and Tom.

"Your mistress sleeps," said he to the page. "Leave her door ajar, that you may hear if she be ailing or in want of aught. Go not for an instant out of hearing of her; and if there be need, let Tom bring word to me in the hall."

He then hurried down to where the men were assembled with Kit Bottle. The fire had been replenished, and some torches lighted. Marryott, seeing that Anthony and Bunch were still absent with the horses, awaited their return before addressing his company. In this interim, he strode up and down before the fire, forming in his mind the speech he would make. When the two came in, and had barred the door after them, Marryott said:

"My stout fellows, four miles yonder, or maybe less now, are a score of horsemen. Most like, they are either Master Rumney and a reinforced gang, or a pursuivant's troop from London with a warrant to arrest me. An it be Rumney, hounding us for revenge and other purposes, we can best offset his odds by fighting him from this house; and he must in the end give up and depart, lest the tumult bring sheriff's men upon him when the weather betters. But if it be the pursuivant, he will persist till he take me or starve me out, an I do not some way contrive to give him the slip. Now if he take you aiding me, 'tis like to bring ropes about your necks forthwith! So I give you, this moment, opportunity of leaving me; knowing well there is not one so vile among you to use this liberty in bearing information of me to shire officers, — which indeed they would find pretext for ignoring, in such weather for staying indoors. Stand forth, therefore, ye that wish to go hence; for once we fortify the house, none may leave it without my order, on pain of pistol-shot."

Whether from attachment to Marryott, or fear of falling into Rumney's hands, or a sense of present comfort and security in this stout mansion, every man stood motionless.

"Brave hearts, I thank you!" cried Marryott,

after sufficient pause. "And mayhap I can save you, though I be taken myself. But now for swift work! Captain Bottle, an there be any loose timber about, let Oliver show it you, and let the men bear it into the house. If there be none such, take what fire-logs there be, and cut timbers from the outhouses with what tools ye may come upon. With these, and with chests and such, ye will brace and bar the doors and all windows within reach of men upon the ground. As soon as Oliver has shown where timber may be found, let him point out all such openings to Captain Bottle. And meanwhile, till timber is here collected, I and the captain will begin the barricading with furniture. As the timbers are brought in, we shall use them, and when enough be fetched, every man shall join us in the fortifying."

"There be posts and beams, piled 'neath a pentice-roof by the stables; and fire-wood a-plenty," said Oliver Bunch.

"Good! And which door is best to carry it in through?"

"There is an old door from the kitchen wing to the stables; 'tis kept ever bolted and barred."

"Unbolt and unbar it, then! And make fast, instead, the outer stable doors, when ye have brought in the timber. Thus we may secure the horses,—which may now rest unsaddled; for here we must abide two days, at least. To it now, my staunch knaves! And leave all your weapons on these settles, and your powder and ball, that I may see how we are provided for this siege. I thank God for this storm, Kit; it must limit our besiegers to the enemies we wot of. No lazy rustics will poke nose into the business while such weather endures."

Leaving the wounded to rely solely upon repose, the men set about doing as they were ordered. Marryott and Kit took account of the weapons and ammunition. There were, besides the swords and daggers, a number of pistols, two arquebuses, a musket, and a petronel. Of these firearms, the pistols alone had wheel-locks, which indeed were still so costly that as yet they were to be found mainly in weapons for use on horseback, the longer arms, for service afoot, being fitted with the awkward and slow-working match-locks. There was good store of ammunition.[29]

Marryott and the captain thereupon threw off their doublets, and began barricading, starting at the main door, and using first the chests, trestles, and like material found in the adjacent rooms. When the long and thin pieces of timber began to come in upon the shoulders of the men, Hal caused them to be pointed at one end, that they might be used as braces, the blunt ends placed against doors and shutters, the sharp ends sunk into notches made in the floor. Pieces of various size and shape were utilized to bar, brace, or block up doors and windows in diverse ways. Narrow openings were left at some windows, through which, upon making corresponding openings in the glass, men might fire out at any one attempting to force entrance.

When the defences in the house were well begun, Hal sent Kit to superintend those of the stable, which, as has been shown, communicated directly with a wing of the mansion.

These occupations kept Marryott and his men busy for several hours. When they were completed, and Foxby Hall seemed closed tight against the ingress of a regiment, Hal, previously drained of strength by his long terms of sleeplessness, was ready to drop. But he dragged himself up-stairs to see how his prisoner fared.

Francis and Tom were asleep in the outer room. At Anne's half open door Marryott could hear from within the chamber the regular breathing of peaceful slumber. He went down to the hall again, and found the men, with the exception of Anthony, stretched upon the stale rushes. The Puritan was sitting by the fire.

"I shall sleep awhile, Anthony," said Hal. "I see no use in setting a watch, now that we need keep no more between us and these men than the walls of this house. If they come hither, their noise will wake us ere they can break in."

"Come hither they will, 'tis sure," said Kit Bottle, from his place on the floor, "if they be indeed Rumney's men or Barnet's. They will have heard tell of this empty house ere they come to it, and they will stop to examine. Or, if they pass first without stopping, and find no note of our going further north, they will come back with keen noses. When they hear horses snorting and pawing in the stables, — horses stabled at an empty house, look you! — they'll make quick work of smelling us out!"

"Well, 'faith, we are ready for them," said Hal, and sank to a reclining attitude near the fire.

"Ay, in good sooth," said Kit; "fortified, armed, and vict — No, by the devil's horns, victualled we are not!"

And the worthy soldier sprang to his feet, the picture of dismay.

"Go to!" cried Hal, rising almost as quickly. "Where are the provisions Anthony brought yestreen?"

"In those bellies and mine, and a murrain on such appetites!" was Kit's self-reproachful answer. "God's death, we're like to make up for a deal of Lent-breaking, these next two days!"

Hal became at once hungry, at the very prospect of a two days' complete fast. He wondered how his men would endure it; and he thought of the lady up-stairs. Already languishing from sheer fatigue, must she now famish also?

"We must get a supply of food!" said Marryott, decidedly.

"Where?" queried the captain.

"Where we got yesterday's. Some one must go, at once!"

"I will go," said Anthony. "I know the way."

"Rouse the innkeeper, at any cost," replied Hal, handing out a gold piece from the pocket of his hose.

"'Tis near dawn," returned the Puritan. "He will be up when I arrive there."

"Keep an eye open for our enemies."

"If I find them surrounding you, when I return," replied the Puritan, calmly, "I will make a dash for one of the doors. By watching from an upper window, you may know when to open it for me."

"And when you are within, it can be barred again," said Hal. "Best make for the same door by which you now go forth; 'twill save undoing more than one of our barricades."

"Let it be the lesser stable door, then," suggested Captain Bottle, "as he will go by horse. Moreover, if the enemy should force a way into the stables, there's yet the door betwixt the stables and the house, that we could close against them."

The world was paling into a snowy dawn, as Anthony rode forth from the stable a few minutes later.

Meanwhile, having aroused the useful Bunch, Hal had caused vessels to be filled with water from a well, and placed in a room off the hall. Kit then barred the stable door, but did not replace the braces and obstructions that had been removed to allow egress. He then volunteered to watch, in an up-stairs chamber of the kitchen wing, for Anthony's return. Assenting to this offer, Marryott returned to the hall, and lay down near Oliver, who was already asleep.

An hour later Hal was awakened by a call from Captain Bottle, who stood at the head of the stairs.

"Is Anthony coming back?" Marryott asked, scrambling to his feet.

"He is not in sight yet," was the reply. "And you'd best send Oliver to watch in my place. I can be of better use otherwise, now."

"What mean'st thou?"

"The horsemen are without. From yon room I saw them riding around the house and staring up at the windows."

"Which party is it?" said Hal, quickly, repressing his excitement.

"Rumney's."

Hal's brow darkened a little. He would rather it had been Barnet's, for then he should have been free of all doubt whether the pursuivant had indeed clung to the false chase.

At that instant a loud thud was heard on the front door, as if a piece of timber were being used as a battering-ram.

"You are right; I will send Oliver to watch," said Marryott.

He did so, with full instructions; and then roused all the able-bodied men. He distributed the firearms and ammunition; assigned each man to the guardianship of some particular door and its neighboring windows; gave orders for an alarm, and a concentration of force, at any point where the enemy might win entrance; left Kit in charge of the hall, at whose door there was present threat of attack, and hastened up-stairs to a gallery where an oriel window projected over that door. He looked down into the quadrangle. It was now broad daylight; snow was still falling.

Whether from a desire to avail himself of the bad weather for an attempt to plunder this deserted house, or from a suspicion that Oliver Bunch might have been both able and willing to open the mansion to the travellers, or from other reasons for thinking that they might be here, Captain Rumney had indeed led his troop into the grounds, made a preliminary circuit of the mansion, heard the horses in the stables, found all doors fast, detected signs of barricades in the windows, dismounted his company in the court, and caused a number of his men to assault the door with the fallen bough of a tree.

CHAPTER XIX.

THE HORSEMEN DEPART.

"Beauty provoketh thieves sooner than gold." — *As You Like It.*

When Marryott looked down from the oriel, he saw the horses huddled in a corner of the quadrangle, Rumney standing by the fountain, and several men about to swing the long piece of timber against the door a second time. Afar, at the gate by the road, as Hal could descry through the leafless trees, a mounted man kept watch. Master Rumney preferred to avoid witnesses, in his violation of the peace this Sunday morning.

Marryott flung open the casement, and leaned out, a pistol in each hand.

"Back!" he cried to the men with the branch. "Back, or two of you shall die!"

The men stopped short, looked up at him, and stood hesitating.

"Batter down the door!" shouted Rumney to the men. "I'll look to this cock!"

And he raised a pistol and fired at Hal. The ball sang past him and found lodgment in the wall of the gallery. The men sprang forward with the treebranch. True to his threat, Hal let off both his pistols. Two men fell,—one struck in the shoulder, the other in the thigh. One howled, the other stared up at Hal in a kind of silent amazement.

With a wrathful curse, Rumney fired a second pistol at Marryott. But Hal, having now to reload his weapons, had disappeared in good time. Moreover, Rumney's aim was bad, for the fact that his better arm, wounded the previous day, was now bound up and useless. Handing his pistols to two men, for reloading, and grasping from one of these men a weapon already loaded, the robber fiercely ordered his rascals to resume the assault upon the door. They obeyed. The door quivered at their blow; but its bars and braces held. As the men were rushing forward for a third stroke with their improvised ram, flame and smoke suddenly belched forth from the windows nearest the door, and two more fellows sank to the snow. Kit Bottle and one of Hal's wounded followers had fired through holes they had made in the glass.

Rumney's men rushed panic-stricken from the quadrangle, seeking protection beyond the angle of the kitchen wing. Their leader followed them. The men with the horses led off the frightened animals to the same place. The court was now clear. Marryott returned to the hall.

"At this rate, we shall soon see Captain Rumney's heels, or his corpse," said Hal, to Kit Bottle.

"I know not," was the reply. "We have but taught him the folly of haste and open attack. He will try craft next. Now is the time to watch every hole by which even a mouse might crawl into this house. 'Tis well that stout fellow, Hatch, has guard of the stable door. I would the Puritan were back! I'm some troubled for the safety of his saintly skin. He is a likable dog, for all his sour virtuousness. God-'a'-mercy, how his conscience will bite at this breakage of the Sabbath!"

Marryott went up to the room where Tom and Francis were. The sound of firing had aroused them, and they were in great curiosity. Mistress Hazlehurst, Francis said, still slept. Marryott gave the two lads a brief account of matters, for the information of the lady if she awoke. He then rejoined Kit in the hall.

The morning wore on. Silence continued, without and within the house. No further sign came of Rumney's presence in the vicinity. Marryott began to discuss with Bottle the probabilities of the robbers having fled, appalled at the utterly bootless loss of four men. "Rumney is a deviceful rascal," was the burden of Kit's replies.

Hal made the rounds of the house. Neither Moreton nor Hatch, nor Oliver at his upper window, had sound or sight of the enemy to report. No one was to be seen from the windows. The mounted watchman at the gate had disappeared. But, as Bottle said, when Marryott returned again to the hall, these facts did not answer the question of Rumney's proximity. There were outbuildings, detached from the house; in these the rascals might have taken refuge while biding the formation of a plan. The watchman might have concealed himself behind the gatehouse.

While Hal and his lieutenant were sitting in talk, near the fire, there arose a sound of hasty steps in an upper corridor, and Oliver Bunch appeared at the stair-head.

"Master Underhill is coming!" he announced, in a loud, excited whisper.

"Follow us!" replied Hal, starting off with Kit at once. The three traversed some rooms, a passage, and part of the kitchen wing, and arrived in the half dark stables.

"Open the small door!" called Marryott, in a low tone, to John Hatch. "And stand all, with sword and pistol, to bar the way 'gainst any but Underhill!"

Hatch undid the door, and flung it wide; then drew his weapons, and stood beside Marryott and Kit, just within the entrance. Behind these three crouched Oliver Bunch, trembling, but with sword and pistol in hand.

Through the blown flakes in the park, Anthony could be seen riding madly for the door. His cloak stood out behind him. From his left shoulder swung a bag, which evidently contained the acquisitions of his journey to the inn. In his right hand he held his naked sword. The manner of his riding, the direction of his look, showed that he saw possible enemies who might attempt to cut him off.

Marryott took a step forth from the stable, and followed Anthony's look. It was directed toward a long shed, whose open side, being from the house, was invisible to Hal, but visible to the Puritan. As the young gentleman fixed his glance on that shed, there ran out from it nine or ten men, afoot, whose manifest purpose was indeed to intercept Anthony. Hal recognized them as of Rumney's band, but their leader was not with them. Anthony spurred his horse for a final dash.

The foremost robber fired a pistol. Anthony's horse swayed, toppled over, lay quivering on its side. The Puritan fell free of the animal, having swung his leg over its back in the nick of time. Ere he could rise, his enemies were close upon him.

Marryott and Kit fired their pistols into the pack; then dropped these smoking weapons inside the stable door, and rushed out with ready swords to save the Puritan. Two robbers had sunk down as if tripped up by a rope, and two behind these fell over them in the onward rush. The fellows menacing Anthony, warned of the coming of Hal and Kit by the latter's loud-bellowed curses, turned so as not to be taken in the rear by them. This gave the Puritan time to rise to his feet. While his two rescuers engaged the nearest knaves, Anthony, to save the provisions, skirted the crowd and made for the door. But he was headed off by other rascals. John Hatch now ran forward to his aid, leaving Oliver Bunch alone to hold the doorway.

Two robbers, seeing this opportunity of gaining an entrance, charged the door. The trembling Bunch emptied his pistol into the breast of one, and made a feeble sword-thrust at the other. But the sword was dashed from his shaking hand. Oliver saw his antagonist's blade flash toward him, and dropped to the ground, uncertain whether he was killed or not. The robber, not to lose time, and joined by one of the knaves that had previously fallen unhurt, sprang over the servant's body, and ran through the stables, toward the door to the kitchen wing.

Kit Bottle killed his man in time to meet the attack of the second fellow that had fallen unhurt. Marryott was still engaging his first opponent, a black-bearded rascal of great strength and agility.

Hal had at last detected the weak place in the other's guard, and was about to profit by it, when suddenly a fearful shriek, far-off but piercing, made his heart jump. It was borne from a window of the further wing of the mansion; was, as he recognized with a chill of the senses, from Mistress Hazlehurst.

He instantly leaped back from his antagonist, turned, and ran for the open door. Half way through the stables, he came upon one of the two robbers that had gained entrance. The fellow wheeled about, at sound of footsteps behind. With a single thrust, Hal cleared the way of him, and bounded on. At the door to the kitchen wing, the other robber was encountered in similar manner, and was as speedily removed. Gaining the main part of the mansion, Hal heard additional screams and cries for help, which now reached his ears by indoor ways. Like a madman, he dashed through the intervening rooms, cleared the hall, rushed up the stairs, traversed the corridor, sprang across the outer room, which was empty, and entered her chamber.

In the centre of the apartment lay one of Rumney's men, apparently done for. Near him were Francis, with a bleeding gash across his forehead, and Tom Cobble, his jerkin reddened by a fresh wound in the body. At the open window, a man was holding ready the top of a ladder, whose foot must have rested on the ground outside; while

"RUMNEY . . . BACKED QUICKLY TO THE WINDOW, AND MOUNTED THE LEDGE."

another man was tying the wrists of Mistress Hazlehurst, who was standing in a half fainting position in the single available arm of Rumney.

The visible top of the ladder explained all. With a small force, leaving his other men at the shed, Rumney had caused this ladder — found in one of the outbuildings — to be stealthily placed at the chamber window, and had made good his ascent so quietly that even Tom and Francis, in the outer room, knew not of his presence until apprised by the shriek that had summoned Marryott.

Whether Rumney had known that this was Anne's chamber might be inquired into later. The present business was to rescue her from his grasp, and Hal rushed blindly forward to the work, his sword still dripping with the blood it had taken in the stables.

A smile of joy on Anne's face, driving the terror from her eyes, welcomed him to the task. But ere he could thrust at her captor, the latter had swiftly turned, so as to be shielded by her body. Rumney then, bearing her in one arm, as if she were of small weight, backed quickly to the window, and mounted the ledge. Hal rushed after.

The man who had been tying her wrists dropped to his knees, caught Hal's legs in both arms, and brought him heavily to the floor; then clambered over him on all fours, and grasped his sword-wrist with a powerful hand. Hal cast a glance of dismay at Anne, who looked down at him with astonished and terrified eyes. Rumney, shouting two words as to some one holding the bottom of the ladder, bestrode the window, and set foot on one of the rounds. Doubtless, having no able arm free to grasp the ladder with, he was to be supported by the man who should follow him down.

"God's light, she is lost!" cried Hal, in tones of despair.

Just then there came, from the direction of the road, a peculiar sound, half cry, half whistle. It gave Captain Rumney a start; made him turn pale and stand still, with one foot on the ladder. It caused the man at the ladder's top to look anxiously at Rumney, and the robber upon Hal to rise and stride toward the window. By the time Hal was on his feet, the call was repeated a little nearer. Rumney hesitated no longer. With a muffled oath, he released Mistress Hazlehurst, and slid, rather than stepped, down the ladder. Hal's man seized Anne, dragged her back from the window ledge to clear the way for himself, and thereby — probably without intention — saved her from losing her balance and falling out of the window. This rascal was speedily followed down the ladder by the one who had held its top; and the chamber was thus suddenly freed of robbers, excepting the inert one on the floor.

Marryott's first act was to cut the bonds from Anne's wrists. Motioning away his proffered further assistance, she regained the bed, and lay down exhausted, breathing rapidly from the excitement of the recent peril. Hal thereupon looked out of the window, and saw Rumney and three men running toward the rear of the wing, behind which they soon disappeared. What meant this sudden flight?

Marryott would have questioned Anne, but she received his first inquiries with shakes of the head, and with an expressed desire to be left alone. He then examined the wounds of Francis and Tom, which were painful, but apparently not serious. He assisted these two to the outer room, and dragged out the body of the robber, who, it proved, had fallen victim to the long knife of Tom Cobble. He now groaned, and opened his eyes. Finding that he possessed his senses, and promising to send water to him, Hal interrogated him as to why Rumney had selected that particular window for his stolen entrance. The knave replied, weakly, that when the robbers first rode around the house, they saw the lady standing at that window.

This, if true, was news to both Francis and Tom; but they had been asleep until roused by the shooting below. It was also a circumstance hard to reconcile with Anne's manifest illness, and it made Hal thoughtful.

Returning to the lower part of the house, whither more than one consideration called him, Hal was surprised to encounter Kit Bottle in the hall. The captain's face was wet with perspiration and blood.

"What?" cried Hal. "Is all well at the stable door?"

"Ay, the rascals heard their cry of danger, and took to their heels for the shed where their horses were. Rumney and some others joined them from behind the house, and forthwith it was switch and spur with all that were left of them. They're off now, like the wind."

"And Anthony?"

"He and our men are safe inside; they're barricading the stable door. There be some few scratches and knocks among us; nothing more."

"What made the rascals fly so suddenly? A cry of danger, say you? What danger?"

"A cry of danger raised by their watchman in the road. He joined them as they fled. Let us go up and look."

The two ascended to the oriel whence Hal had fired down on Rumney's first assault. Kit's gaze instantly sought the road. At the distant gate stood a large group of horsemen, who appeared to have just come up, and to be scanning with interest the front of Foxby Hall. Several of them wore cuirasses and steel head-pieces. In a moment, one of these turned his horse toward the mansion; the others followed.

"'Tis plain now," said Kit. "Rumney's watchman liked not the looks of this party; perhaps he recognized that fellow at their head, and took him to be after the Rumney gang."

"And who is the fellow at their head?" asked Hal, with a strange thrill, — for he divined already the answer.

"'Tis Roger Barnet," said Kit, gruffly.

CHAPTER XX.

ROGER BARNET SITS DOWN TO SMOKE SOME TOBACCO.

"At least we'll die with harness on our back."— *Macbeth*.

THE avenue by which the pursuivant and his men were approaching the house would lead them first near the wing in which was Mistress Hazlehurst's chamber. Marryott remembered the ladder still outside her window.

"Devil's name!" he cried. "They may enter as Rumney did! Follow me, Kit!"

He led the way to her chamber. In the outer room, the wounded robber begged for the water that Marryott had promised. But Hal first pointed out to Kit the top of the ladder, and then proceeded with him to draw it up into the chamber. This was an act of some difficulty, by reason of the ladder's length and weight. When its top struck the roof of the apartment, it had to be turned to a horizontal position, and then moved diagonally across the floor, so that its foremost end should pass through the doorway to the outer room. While Hal guided this end, Bottle remained at the window, tugging at the ladder's rear.

It thus befell that Bottle alone was at the window when the pursuivant's troop — men far different in appearance and equipment from Rumney's band — rode into sight.

At one and the same instant, Bottle desisted from his exertions and stared down at the horsemen, and Roger Barnet halted his party with a curt gesture and gazed with hard coolness up at Kit.

"I see thou know'st me, Hodge," growled Bottle, at last. At this, Marryott stood still, far within the chamber, and listened for the answer.

It came, without emotion, in a voice that suggested iron, as some voices are said to suggest silver or gold.

"I thought 'twas you, the night Sir Valentine Fleetwood ran away," said Barnet. "And 'twas more certain, when louts by the way mentioned an ugly big rascal, red-faced of drink, and of never keeping fish-days."

"I trust I may still be eating meat on fish-days, when thou'rt eaten of worms!" replied Kit.

"Thou'lt fast a long fast, fish-days and other days, when I carry thee to London!" said Barnet. "Hudsdon, take ten men; place five behind this house, five north of it. Look you, Bottle, tell Sir Valentine Fleetwood I would speak with him in the queen's name."

"What if Sir Valentine Fleetwood be not here?"

"Thy presence tells me he is."

"And I also tell you that he is!" cried another voice, that of Mistress Hazlehurst, who had risen from her bed and rushed to the window. "He is here, Master Pursuivant! He is in this very room! He has made a prisoner of me!"

"'Tis well, mistress!" replied Barnet. "We'll soon make a prisoner of him."

With that, and after designating men to guard this side of the house, he rode with others toward the front, Hudsdon having already led away the ten to watch the rear and the further side.

Kit turned and looked at Marryott, but the latter had eyes for Mistress Hazlehurst only. The energy of her movement from the bed to the window, the vigor of her voice, gave the lie to her illness.

"'Twas well feigned!" said Hal, quietly, after regarding her for a short while in silence.

There was a little sorrow in his tone, but no reproach. His thought was the same as hers, which she uttered while squarely meeting his gaze.

"I had an enemy's right to use what means I could, having once declared myself, and the more so as I was your prisoner."

"'Tis most true," assented Hal. He would have much liked to explain that what saddened him was, not that she had counterfeited illness, but that she had counterfeited a willing response to his embraces. Why should she have thought it necessary to carry the pretence so far? A choked, blinded feeling came upon him. But he dared not succumb to it. Kit Bottle was looking on, awaiting orders, and the injured robber was crying for water. From the deceived, humiliated lover, Marryott became perforce the alert commander of besieged fugitives.

"This lady must be watched," he said to Kit. "Till I send Anthony to take your place see that she does not, by passing them this ladder, or by hanging curtains or such stuff from the window, give Barnet's men the means of climbing into the house. Nay, mistress, our watchman will not disturb your privacy. From the outer room he can look through the door to your window. Seest thou, Kit? —the ladder lying flat through the doorway will forbid her closing the door. If there come sign of her at the window, or meddling with ladder or door, then thou must invade her chamber, and do as may seem best. You are warned, madam!"

With a courteous bow he left her. Bottle established himself outside her door, squatting upon the ladder, his eye following its side-pieces across her room to the window.

In the hall, Marryott found Anthony Underhill

listening passively to the door-knocks of Roger Barnet, which were accompanied by calls upon Sir Valentine Fleetwood to open in the queen's name. The Puritan assured Hal that the stable was now as strongly fortified as it had been ere his departure in quest of provisions. Marryott, thereupon, sent him to take Kit's place at Mistress Hazlehurst's door, and then despatched Oliver Bunch (who had with some surprise discovered himself to be still alive) with water for the wounded robber, and with instructions to care for the latter's injuries and for those of Tom and Francis.

Hal then made again the round of the house. Moreton, Hatch, and the least wounded of yesterday's deserters from Rumney, were at their original posts, to which Anthony had taken it on himself to order their return. Each man reported that his door had been tried from without, but that no violent attempt had been made to force entrance.

Coming back to the hall, Marryott saw Kit Bottle mounted on a trestle, and surveying the quadrangle through a clear place in a window.

"He has had his men dismount and the horses led away," said Kit, alluding, of course, to Roger Barnet. "He has set two guards, I think, at the front end of each wing, and two in the court. He is sitting on the edge of the fountain. He seems a little lame o' the leg."

"What think you is his intent?" asked Marryott, not risking to Barnet a possible glimpse of his face, for fear of an untimely undeceiving.

"'Tis for time to show. He will either attack or wait. But 'tis less like he will attack."

"Why?"

"Because he is a prudent dog and a patient. Those gaping bodies on the snow tell how Rumney's gang fared 'gainst men firing from inside these stout walls. Barnet thinks he has the hare mewed up, and 'tis as cheap to wait for't to venture out as 'tis to risk flesh and blood in trying to come at it. And, moreover, a fight might give the man he seeks a chance to die by sword or pistol, whereas 'tis a point of honor with Barnet to take his prisoner well and whole to London. He is a feeder of headsman's blocks and hangman's nooses! Ay, he has chosen to wait; 'tis certain now."

"How know'st thou?"

"He is filling his tobacco-pipe, and motioning one of his men for use of a slow-match. When Roger sits down to smoke, he hath made up his mind for a season of waiting. And there is no man can out-wait Roger Barnet when he is sucking his Nicotian. He is then truly patience on a monument, as Master Shakespeare's comedy says."

"If he wait till to-morrow night, my work for others will be done! 'Twill be six days since we left Welwyn, and 'twill take four and over, in this weather, for any man to ride back thither."

"And then 'tis a matter of our own necks, I ween! Let me tell thee this, lad: While Roger Barnet thinks the man he wants is in this house, he will wait to starve him out, though he wait till doomsday. And if he learns 'tis not his man that he hath been chasing, he will infer that the other man is by that time 'scaped, and he will wait still for the man that has tricked him. He will carry some victim back to London for this, be sure on't!"

Kit had come down from the trestle, and was standing with Hal at the fireplace.

"Well, after to-morrow," said Marryott, "we may use our wits, or our valor and skill, to break through the circle he has drawn around us."

"'Twill take sharp wits to slip through Roger Barnet's vigilance, now he has closed around us. As for valor and skill, what shall boot our small force 'gainst his, who are stout men all, well armed, and most of them clad above the waist in steel? Tut, lad, don't think old Kit is disturbed upon it! I'll die as well as another, and better than most! I tell thee these things merely in fireside talk, as I should speak of the weather."

"How if we shoot Barnet, from one of the windows?"

"'Twould not help. Firstly, as the preacher at

Paul's Cross says, we might miss him, or his cuirass and morion might save him. He might take offence, and act as if we forced a fight upon his patience; might set fire to the timber part of this house and burn us out betimes. Secondly, if we killed Barnet, his man Hudsdon might do the burning. Hudsdon, look you, is, in his particular humor, a man of as good mettle as Barnet. These be no Rumneys!"

"But if we so diminished Barnet's troop, by shooting them one by one from the windows, then we might sally forth, fire or no fire, with fair chance of cutting our way through."

"Ay, were it not that, for every man we slew, Barnet would send to Harmby or elsewhere for two men to fill the vacant post. As 'tis, the foul weather, and the pride of doing his own work unhelped, will stay him from demanding aid of the country; but an we force him to it, ere he give us the upper hand he will use to the full his power of pressing men, and requiring local officers, in the queen's name."

"Why, then, is there no course, no chance?"

"None but what time may bring, and time we shall gain by letting Roger wait. He will stay where he is, in hope of starvation driving out his man weak and easy to be taken, or of our knaves rebelling from hungry stomachs and delivering up their leader.

But we'll see to it the men be staunch; and some time must pass before our bellies take to grinding one side 'gainst the other!"

"'Tis well Anthony brought —" began Marryott, but was interrupted by the entrance of Oliver Bunch at the top of the stairs.

"An't please your honor," said Oliver, "the lady desired I should ask when she might have breakfast, for that she is faint with hunger."

"Why, so am I; and the rest of us, I doubt not," said Marryott. "We shall eat forthwith. Where are the provisions Anthony brought, Kit?"

"I thought to have told you sooner," replied the captain, in a strangely resigned manner; "in the fray outside the stable door, Rumney's knaves got Anthony's bag of victuals from him, and when they ran off they forgot to leave it behind!"

There was a considerable silence, during which Kit Bottle looked darkly into the fire, and Marryott muttered several times under his breath, "A murrain on't!" Then, adopting the captain's mien of uncomplaint, Hal said to Oliver:

"Tell the lady we have no food and can get none. Later, I may contrive to obtain some for her, from the enemy that surrounds us."

"Why," said Kit Bottle, as Oliver disappeared, "an thou dost that, thou'lt betray our empty state to Roger Barnet."

"What matter?" said Hal. "We can hold out two days, that's certain. And after that,—Barnet will but know he need smoke the less tobacco till our starving out, that's all!"

CHAPTER XXI.

ROGER BARNET CONTINUES TO SMOKE TOBACCO.

"The best man best knows patience." — *Thierry and Theodoret.*

THE day dragged on, — grayest of gray Sundays. The snowfall ceased, but the sky remained ashen, and the wind still moaned intermittently, though with subdued and failing voice. In the great, silent house, faint creaks had the startling effect of detonations, and the flapping of tapestry in the wind seemed fraught with mysterious omen.

Marryott, in the course of his next round of the mansion, told the men of the loss of the provisions. Some of them had already known of it. No complaint was uttered. The men replied with a half respectful, half familiar jest, or with good-humored expression of willingness to fast awhile. Fortunately, the supply of water was such as to obviate any near dread of the tortures of thirst.

When he went to the room adjoining Mistress Hazlehurst's chamber, Marryott found Tom, Francis, and the robber, all three quiescent under the ministrations of Oliver Bunch. Anthony Underhill, seated on a trunk that he had placed on the end of the prostrate ladder, was observing the Sabbath by singing to himself a psalm. Scarce audible as was his voice, it still had something of that whine which the early English Puritans, like the devoutest of the French Huguenots, put into their vocal worship, and from which some think the nasal twang of the Puritans' New England descendants is derived.

Mistress Hazlehurst either was, or wished to seem, asleep; for when Marryott knocked softly upon her half open door, that he might more courteously explain to her the lack of food, she gave no answer.

He, thereupon, sent Kit Bottle to the oriel window to sound Roger Barnet's mind toward supplying the prisoner, who was indeed to be considered the pursuivant's ally, with food.

Kit put the necessary question, taking care to show no more of his person than was needful, and to keep his eyes upon the firearms of the pursuivant and the two guards in the court.

But Roger Barnet, who still sat smoking with a kind of hard, surly impassibility, made no movement as to his pistols. Neither did he show a thought of ordering his men to fire. He evinced a certain grim satisfaction at the evidence that the besieged had no provisions. He then expressed a suspicion that Kit was using the lady's name in order to obtain food for his own party, and said that if Sir Valentine Fleetwood desired the lady not to hunger, Sir Valentine might set her free. He, Barnet, would provide her with an escort to some neighboring inn or gentleman's house.

But Marryott, who was listening unseen at Kit's elbow, dared not yet risk her describing himself as Sir Valentine Fleetwood to the pursuivant; and so he prompted Kit to reply that the lady was too ill to go at present from the house. To which Roger, between vast puffs of smoke, tranquilly replied that he feared the lady must for the present go hungry.

Afire with wrath at this stolid churlishness, Hal caused Kit to remind Barnet that the lady had come into her present case through aiding the pursuivant himself. Roger answered that he had not requested the lady's assistance. At Marryott's further whispered orders, Kit informed Barnet that, but for her work, the latter should not at that moment have had Sir Valentine surrounded. Roger replied that he had only Kit's word for that; moreover, what mattered it? He was not responsible for the lady's ill fortune, even if she were creditable with his good fortune. In short, and by God's light, he would not let any food enter that house unless he and his men went in with it!

"When your bellies will no more away with their

emptiness, open the door and let us in," he added, phlegmatically, and replaced his pipe in his mouth as if the last word had been said.

"Nay, thou swinish rogue," said Kit, "we're better taught than to leave doors open in March weather!" He then bombarded his old-time comrade of Walsingham's day with hard names. Barnet showed no resentment, but continued to smoke stolidly. At last, when his reviler had well-nigh exhausted the vocabulary of Thersites, Roger began to finger abstractedly the butt of one of his pistols; at which gentle intimation, Kit suddenly disappeared from the window.

"There is no help for it," said he to Marryott. "She must starve with the rest of us unless you set her free."

"That I must not do till Tuesday morning," said Hal, with an inward sigh. He went from the gallery, and told Francis, for Mistress Hazlehurst's information should she inquire, of the failure of his attempt to obtain food for her. She still slept, or feigned sleep.

Marryott then newly assigned the posts to be guarded, dividing the company into two watches, one headed by himself, the other by Bottle. The latter took the first period of duty. The men who were thus for a time relieved were prompt to assuage their thirst, though water was a beverage unusual to them; then they stretched themselves on the rushes in the hall to sleep. Hal also slept.

At evening, being awakened by Kit, he and his quota of men arose to do sentinel duty during the first half of the night.

"Is Barnet still yonder?" he asked Kit, before leaving the hall.

"No; he has set Hudsdon in's place. Roger has divided his troop into watches. He and some of his men have made their beds in the outhouses. Hudsdon and the rest have planted torches in a line around the house. There's not an ell's distance of the mansion's outside, from ground to second story, that cannot be seen by the torch-light. The men are posted beyond the line, out of our sight; only here and there you may catch now and then the light of a slow-match that some fellow blows. If we made a sortie from the house into their torch-light, they would mow us down with muskets and arquebuses from the dark."

Marryott sat out his watch in a partly torpid state of mind. The deception that Mistress Hazlehurst had practised upon him, though he acknowledged an avowed enemy's and unwilling prisoner's right to practise it, had struck down his heart, benumbed it, robbed it of hope and of its zest for life. He thought of nothing but present trifles — the writhing of the flames in the fireplace, the snoring of the sleepers on the hall floor — and his chances of accomplishing his mission. All things, he felt, could be endured, — all but failure in the task he had so far carried toward success. Regarding his life, which indeed seemed to be doomed, he was apathetic.

During the second half of the night, Marryott slumbered, Bottle watched. Dawn found Roger Barnet again at the fountain's edge, again smoking. But, as Kit observed while furtively inspecting him through a window, he puffed a little more vehemently, was somewhat petulant in his motions, more often changed position. Bottle, from having known him of old, and from his slight lameness, took it that he was in some pain.

His injured leg was, indeed, a seat of great torment; but of this, being stoical as well as taciturn, the frowning man of iron gave no other sign than the tokens of irritation noticed by Kit.

"I'm afeard Roger will be, later, of a mind to hasten matters," said the captain. "Peradventure his tobacco is falling low."

"I pray 'twill last till the morrow," said Marryott.

This morning (Monday) the sky was clear, but it was a cold sun that shone down upon the world of snow around beleaguered Foxby Hall. Marryott was on the watch till noon. Then, Kit having taken his place, and before lying down to sleep, he went to see if Mistress Hazlehurst had aught to request. He felt that, though his position as her captor was one of necessity, it nevertheless required of him a patient attention to all complaints and reproaches she might make.

But she made none. To his inquiry, spoken after a gentle knock upon her door, she answered that she desired of him nothing under heaven but to be left alone. If she must starve, she would choose to starve not before spectators. He informed her that he intended to give her, on the morrow, her freedom, as the royal pursuivant had offered her an escort and might be trusted to treat a lady with respect. To this she made no reply. Hal thereupon went away.

When he was awakened to resume guard duty, at evening, he learned from Kit that the afternoon had been without occurrence. Roger Barnet had continued to show signs of an ailing body, and hence of an ailing temper, but had not deviated from his policy of waiting. The men in the house were very hungry; they had ceased jesting about their enforced fast, and had betaken themselves to dumb endurance. Hal was made aware by his own pangs of the stomach, his own feverish weakness of the body, how they must be suffering, though only two days of abstinence had passed.

The precautions of the besiegers this evening were like those of the preceding night. Marryott looked more than once, through narrow openings in the windows, at the torches lighting up redly the snow that stretched away from the walls of the mansion.

Some time after dark, while Marryott was pacing the hall, Kit Bottle suddenly awoke, and after gazing around a few moments, said, quietly:

"Methinks, lad, 'tis eight o'clock, or after."

"'Tis so, I think," replied Hal, softly.

"Then 'tis full six days since we rode from Sir Valentine Fleetwood's gate."

"Ay, just six days."

"Then thy work is done, boy!"

"'Tis done, old Kit; and thanks to thee and Anthony, with your true hearts, strong bodies, and shrewd heads!"

"Thou'rt a valiant and expert gentleman, Hal; beshrew me else!"

Whereupon the old soldier turned upon his side, and slept again, and Hal looked dreamily into the fire.

Their words had been no louder than whispers. Nor was Hal's feeling aught like the bursting elation, the triumph that would shout, the joy that intoxicates. It was but a gentle transition from suspense to relief, from anxiety to ease of mind; a mild but permeating glow of satisfaction; a sweet consciousness of having done a hard task, a consciousness best expressed by a single sigh of content, a faint smile of self-applause.

At midnight, giving place again to Kit, Marryott sank into a troubled sleep, in which he dreamed of juicy beef, succulent ham, every kind of plump fowl, well basted, and the best wines of France, Spain, Italy, and the Rhine. He woke to tortures of the stomach, and the news that Roger Barnet was still smoking, but peevishly walking, despite his lameness of leg, to and fro in the courtyard.

"I tell thee, Hal," said Bottle, after imparting this information, "we may look to see things afoot soon! If Roger is a devil of pertinacity when he is upon the chase, and a devil of patience when he waits, he is a devil of activity when his body ails overmuch!"

"We shall be the sooner forced, then, to set our lives upon a cast!"

"Ay, and better work losing them, than stretching them out to the anguish of our bellies! This fasting is an odious business. The men are chewing the firewood and their leather jerkins."

"Have they complained?" asked Hal.

"Not a dog among 'em! These be choice rascals all! They bear hunger with no more words than dumb beasts. They'll starve with thee, or die with thee, to the last knave of them!"

Marryott looked silently at Bottle; and saw in his

face the very dog-like fidelity he described in the others. He knew what uncomplaining, unpretending steadfastness there was in Anthony Underhill, too.

"Brave hearts!" murmured Hal, and the next instant he had taken a resolution.

"Is Roger Barnet a keeper of his word?" he asked.

"When he hath not overmuch to lose by it," replied Kit, wondering at the question.

"If, on condition of his letting mine innocent followers go free, I proposed to shorten his task by giving myself up, and he agreed thereto, would he keep that agreement?"

"But, God's death, Hal, thou'lt propose no such thing!"

"Thou'lt propose it for me; till all is done I must not show my face. And thou'lt not name me as Sir Valentine Fleetwood, but speak of me merely as the gentleman you serve. So when Barnet discovers I am not the knight, he will find himself still bound by his word to the condition."

"But old Kit will never be go-between to buy his life with thy giving thyself up!"

"'Troth, thou wilt! For, look you, since I must in any case be taken, why need also my men suffer? Wilt rob me of my one consolation, the saving of my faithful followers? Wilt send me entirely sad of heart to London? Wilt not let me cheer myself with knowledge of having done this little deed befitting a gentleman? Have I not full right to get my self-approval by this act? Wouldst thou hinder my using the one right by which I may somewhat comfort myself? Thou wilt do as I bid thee, old Kit; else I swear on this crossed hilt I will go forth at once, and surrender myself the more unhappily for that I may not save my men!"

"Nay, Hal, softly! If the thing lies so to thy heart, 'tis not old Kit shall go against thy wish. But I have the right of giving myself up with thee. Save the rest an thou wilt, I shall not be sorry. But let Kit Bottle attend thee still, to the end of it!"

"Now thou talkest arrant foolishness, Kit! For look you, if thou'rt free, canst thou not serve me to the better effect? Consider how many miles and days it is to London. Once I am this fellow's prisoner, and seem to have no will or spirit left, may not my guards grow heedless? An thou art free, riding after me to London, who can say what chance may not occur for rescue and escape? Let me but save thee and these true fellows by giving myself up; then may we look for means of saving myself on the journey to London." Hal said this but to induce Kit to accept freedom with the others if it could be obtained, and it seemed to make the desired impression.

"Why, there is something in that," said Kit, thoughtfully. "But we have been wasting talk. Roger Barnet, now that thy taking is but matter of time, will not make terms. He is no man for concessions or half-way meetings."

"But he hath much to gain by my offer: the time saved, the certainty of taking his man alive and without loss to his own party, the greater ease of carrying one prisoner than many to London. He should be glad of pretext to be rid of the underlings."

"Truly said, in sooth. But the nature of the man is against making treaty with an opponent, e'en though to his own advantage."

Marryott thought for a moment. Then he said:

"Let him not seem to make treaty with his opponent. Let the treaty be with my seeming betrayers. This will better accord with his nature, methinks. My men shall offer to give me up to him, in purchase of their own freedom. So will he regard my men as choosing to become his allies, and he will think that through them he gets the better of their master; he will have justification for letting them go free."

"By my troth, thou'rt a knower of men, Hal! Roger would be ashamed to profit by a treaty with his enemy, but not by treachery of that enemy's following. There'll be some relish in fooling him thus!"

"Then set straightways about it. Speak to him from the oriel, stealthily, as befits the seeming treason."

"I hate even to seem traitor to thee, Hal; but 'tis for thy purposes, and to make a gull of Roger Barnet."

With which the captain mounted the stairs leading to the gallery, leaving Marryott waiting by the fire.

Kit had the skill of gesture and grimace, to convey across the quadrangle to his one-time comrade that secret things were to be told, and that a truce, if granted, would not on his part be violated. Barnet, who could rely upon the steel he wore and the pistols he carried, as well as on Kit's pantomimic word of honor, strode boldly over to a place beneath the window. With an appearance of great caution, Kit asked him, on behalf of himself and his comrades, not of the gentleman they served, what would be done with them if they were taken. Roger lightly answered that he would see them hanged. This led naturally to the broaching of Kit's terms.

The ensuing conversation was of some length, and carried on mostly by Kit, who skilfully put before the pursuivant's mind the advantages to be gained by accepting the offer. Now, as Barnet's warrant called for Kit's supposed employer only, as Barnet had been so many days from London, as the lameness of his leg tried his patience, as the mansion looked impregnable, and as he was loath to resort to local assistance in storming it, it really seemed folly for him to reject an important bird in hand for the doubtful satisfaction of bagging a number of insignificant birds who might prove only a burden to him. He held out, however, until he could bring himself to relinquish the cherished hope of conducting his old friend Bottle to the gallows.

It was at last agreed that Kit and his comrades should deliver over their commander, disarmed and with wrists bound, at the main door, within half an hour.

As soon as Marryott was informed of this, he summoned all the men (save Kit, to whom was assigned the guardianship of Mistress Hazlehurst's chamber for the while), and told them of the agreement. They stared at him and at one another with little show of feeling, and in silence, excepting Anthony, who muttered:

"I had as lief I had been left out of the purchase."

"Go to Mistress Hazlehurst's door, Anthony," said Marryott, "and send hither Captain Bottle, that he may tie my hands and deliver me forth. And conduct the lady hither, that she may go forth at the same time. I think she will not delay, for you will tell her she is to have her freedom."

He then divided his money among the men, that they might shift for themselves after his surrender;

obtained the promise of the able-bodied to care for the wounded; and finally ordered them to remove the defences of the door. Hal had previously furnished Kit's purse; Anthony had his own supply of coin.

When Mistress Hazlehurst came down the stairs, a little pale and haggard from her fast, but no less beautiful of eye and outline, and with no less clearness of skin, Marryott stood already bound, Kit at his side, the men waiting silently in the background. She noticed that Hal's hands were behind his back, but could not make sure whether they were tied. Slightly puzzled at the scene, she looked back at Anthony as for an explanation.

Kit Bottle motioned one of the men to open the door; he then indicated to Mistress Hazlehurst, by a gesture, that she might pass out. She did so, in some wonder. Francis, whose head was bandaged, followed her. Anthony stopped at the other side of Marryott than that on which Kit Bottle was.

Beyond the porch outside, and facing the door, stood Roger Barnet; several men were in line on either hand of the way. The pursuivant looked at Anne as if she were not the one he expected. He made way for her to pass, however; but as soon as she had done so, she turned and looked curiously back at the open door.

Forth came the supposed Sir Valentine Fleetwood,

walking listlessly, his hands still behind his back, Kit and Anthony grasping him by either shoulder.

"Take your man, master pursuivant," said Bottle, huskily. He and the Puritan then stopped, and seemed to thrust their prisoner slightly forward for Barnet's acceptance; but they still held his shoulders.

Barnet, whose left hand clasped a document, took a step toward the prisoner, who perforce remained motionless. Then the pursuivant paused, and stared at Hal with a mixture of bewilderment and slow-gathering dismay. The armed men craned their necks to see the object of their long pursuit.

"Why," said Barnet, his voice faltering for once, "this is not the man!"

Mistress Hazlehurst became acutely attentive.

"'Tis the gentleman we have served these last six days," replied Kit Bottle, with great composure.

"God's life!" cried Barnet, having recovered full vocal energy, "there is a scurvy trick here, to give Sir Valentine Fleetwood chance of leaving this house while I'm befooled! But 'twill not serve! All sides are watched! Into the house, you four; search every corner, and drag out the fox!"

The men to whom Barnet spoke hastened to obey, leaving four of their comrades with their leader.

"They'll find naught, Roger," said Kit. "I swear

this gentleman is he we have been travelling with from Welwyn."

"He says truly, pursuivant!" cried Mistress Hazlehurst, stepping forward to Barnet's side. "'Tis Sir Valentine Fleetwood, of a surety; for I, too, have travelled with him these six days."

"I don't gainsay you have travelled with him, lady," said Barnet. "But if you take him for Sir Valentine Fleetwood, either you know not Sir Valentine as well as I do, or your eyes play you tricks!"

"Nay," put in Marryott, quietly, "blame not others' eyes, man, till your own eyes never see false!" With which he thrust out his left elbow, stiffened his neck, and took on what other outward peculiarities he had caught from Sir Valentine.

"By the foul fiend," said Barnet, in a tone that befitted his dark, wrathful look, "there has been some kind of vile player's work here! 'Twas a false beard, that night!"

"Ay!" spoke up one of his men. "I have wondered where to place the gentleman. Your word player sets me right. He is an actor I have seen at the Globe, and in the ale-houses. I forget his name."

"Is it Marryott?" asked Barnet, remembering what he had learned in Clown.

"Ay, that's it! I drew him many a pot of beer when I was a tapster."

"Then by the devil's horns," quoth Barnet, irefully, "he hath played his last part when he hath played upon me, with his false beard and like devices! If, indeed, you have led me off, Master Marryott, and Sir Valentine Fleetwood hath fled over seas, by God, it shall go hard but you die in's place for aiding a traitor! I take you in the queen's name, Sir Player. Nay, question not my right; I have blank warrants for emergent use; your name is soon writ; and back to London you shall ride, with your feet tied 'neath the horse's belly! Mistress, this is part your doing; for you told me 'twas Sir Valentine passed you i' the road that night. You have had all your labor for the wrong man, and given the right one time to 'scape both you and me!"

But his words might have fallen upon the ears of a statue. Anne had realized in a flash all that words could tell her, and this much more: that the captured man loved her, and was a prisoner through her use of his love; and that, even though she had had the resolution to feign illness,—

Thought failed her, and she stood leaning on the shoulder of her page, pallor and inertia betokening the utter consternation of her heart.

CHAPTER XXII.

SPEECH WITHOUT WORDS.

"Her eye discourses; I will answer it." — *Romeo and Juliet.*

LATE in the afternoon of that day — Tuesday, March 10th — there rode into Skipton from the north, and took lodging for the night at the principal inn, a party of horsemen, commanded by a stout, hard-browed, black-bearded man, and conducting a pale, tired young gentleman whose hands were tied behind him and whose ankles were fastened with a rope that passed beneath the body of his led horse.

When the troop had come to a halt, and accommodations had been bespoken, the leader caused two of his men to release the prisoner's legs, but not his hands, and then marched with him, preceded and followed by guards, to an upper room overlooking the stableyard. Here four armed men were left with the prisoner, to whom presently supper was brought. Though without weapons, his wrists were still kept tied; his food had to be conveyed to his mouth by one of his guards. He might sleep on the bed when he chose; but asleep or awake he must remain thus guarded and bound.

Five minutes after the arrival of this troop at the inn, a smaller party appeared from the same direction. Its chief figure was a weary-looking young lady, deeply buried in her thoughts, and attended by a youthful page whose head was bandaged, a bold-faced old fellow, and a lean and sad-visaged man in sombre garments. This company, finding the first inn now full, sought and obtained lodging at a smaller one, not far away.

On the journey thither, these two groups of riders had been more than once in sight of each other. Both Marryott and Barnet had observed that Captain Bottle and the Puritan were serving Mistress Hazlehurst as escort, — a circumstance that seemed to the pursuivant quite natural, since the lady was no friend of Marryott's and the two men were, in Barnet's belief, Marryott's betrayers. Barnet himself had offered to let her ride under his protection on the southward journey; but she had refused, and had watched in silence, with Kit and Anthony, the departure of the prisoner from Foxby Hall. Whatever arrangement she had made with the two men must have been made after that departure.

Hal explained matters to himself by the supposition that Kit Bottle and Anthony, whom she, too, must regard as his betrayers, had offered her their escort, that they might with less suspicion follow close upon the heels of his captors toward London. He knew that she was ill supplied in purse for the homeward journey, and he guessed that she had obtained of Anthony a loan of money to pay the escort and inn charges. In this guess, he was right; but it was scarce possible that he should have divined what other understanding had passed between the lady and his two adherents.

He was glad, in the dull way in which thought and feeling now worked within him, that she had found so good an escort. When she had declined Barnet's offer, he had feared she might unwittingly expose herself to new danger, though he had believed that Kit and Anthony, knowing his own wishes, would protect her, in spite of herself, to some gentleman's house where she might procure both money and servants.

As for the robbers who had shared his siege at Foxby Hall, Hal knew, by their absence from Mistress Hazlehurst's party, that they had been left to choose their own ways. The money he had given them would enable them to transport themselves to distant parts of the kingdom ere Rumney was likely to traverse again the neighborhood of Foxby Hall.

Hal slept lightly but calmly. His slumber was but half slumber, even as his waking state was a kind of lethargic dream. He recked not of past, present, or future.

At dawn breakfast was brought to him and readily eaten. So indifferent had he become, so little feeling was active in him, so little emotion was there to affect his physical state, that not even his appetite was altered; his body led a healthy, normal existence, save for the fatigue from which it was already recovering, but his mind and heart languished half inert.

After breakfast the southward road was resumed, with no deviation from the order of the previous day. Anne's party rode out from the other inn as Barnet's was passing. Was this mere accident, thought Hal, or was it by precaution of Kit Bottle?

The way was choked with snow. In some places this had drifted so as to bury the fences, where it happened — as was rare — that the road was flanked by such enclosures. In other spots, the earth was swept bare. The drifting still continued, for, though the day was clear, another high wind had arisen. It blew the fine, biting crystals into the riders' faces, reddened their cheeks and eyelids, and seemed to add to the discomfort of Roger Barnet.

For the sufferings of the pursuivant, due to the use of the wounded leg when it demanded rest, were now plainly telling upon him. His face was haggard; under his breath, he was fretful; such manifestations, on the part of a man so obstinate against the show of pain, meant that he was in physical agony.

At Halifax, he ordered a rest for dinner. The day being very cold, Marryott was led to a room in the inn's topmost story, where he dined with four guards precisely as he had supped at Skipton. Before entering the town, he had lost sight of Mistress Hazlehurst's party; indeed, it was not often, on the journey, that he availed himself of some bend of the road to turn his head and look back.

When he had finished his dinner, Marryott let his glance stray idly through the window. He had a view of a side lane that ran, apparently, from a street beneath his room. The lane ended at its junction with another street. Up and down that other street, so as to cross the end of the lane at brief intervals, a riderless horse was being led by a boy whose head was wrapped around with handkerchiefs. Was not the boy Francis? And why was he exercising a saddled horse in such a place so far from this inn, not perceptibly near any other? The question dwelt in Hal's mind for a moment; then fled, at Barnet's summons to horse.

Not till he had covered several miles out of Halifax did Marryott catch his next glimpse of Anne and her three attendants. They were then at a good distance behind; but gradually during the afternoon they decreased the distance, — a natural enough thing to do, for the proximity of Barnet's martial-looking troop was a protection. That evening both parties lodged at Barnesley. The state of the roads, and of Barnet's leg, had forbidden faster progress. It was not quite dark when Hal was led into the chamber where he was to sup and sleep. He sat down on a joint-stool by the window.

Ten minutes passed. Awaiting his supper, he was still looking listlessly out of the window at the darkening evening. Was not that Anthony Underhill yonder, leading a riderless horse to and fro upon the green that was visible through a gap in the row of houses opposite the inn? It was odd that he should haply be repeating in Hal's view at supper-time the action that Francis had performed in Hal's sight at dinner-time. The arrival of pickled herrings and ale drew Marryott's eyes from the window, and his mind from the spectacle.

The next morning, on arising to depart, Marryott by chance beheld, this time with a touch of wondering amusement, another repetition of the same performance, with the single difference that now the leader of the horse was Kit Bottle.

When some hours of the forenoon journey had been spent, Marryott, looking back, saw with a little surprise that Anne's party was close behind his own. Barnet rode at his side, leading his horse; half of the escort rode two and two in front, the other half in the rear. These rear horsemen intervened between Hal and Anne; but as he ascended the side of a hollow he could look over the heads behind him to her as she descended the farther side.

Her glance met his; and in it was a kind of message, which she seemed to have long awaited the moment for delivering. With all possible eloquence of eyes and face, she appeared to express apology, a request for pardon, a wish to serve him! Ere he could assure himself by keener inspection whether he had read aright the look that had thrilled him out of his lethargy, he had reached the crest of the ascent, and the men behind him had closed his view.

Poignantly alive now in mind and heart, he tormented himself for several miles with conjectures whether her expression had been intentional on her part or correctly translated on his. This he could best ascertain by sending her, at the first opportunity, a look in reply.

When he was next in line of sight with her, he glanced back his answer. It consisted merely of a faint smile, soft and kindly, by which he hoped to say that he understood, forgave, and loved.

To his unutterable joy, she instantly responded with a smile that was the echo of his own.

This conversation, carried on so silently and at such distance, but so decisive and full of import, was of course so conducted that Marryott's captors suspected nothing of it. A certain curiosity as to whether his supposed betrayers were following him toward London was natural on the part of one in his situation, and it accounted, in Barnet's mind, for his looking back.

At Clown, dining in the very ale-house chamber whence Mistress Hazlehurst had looked at his detention by the constable's men, Marryott saw, some way down the lane from which the coach had been drawn, a riderless horse led back and forth by Francis. It flashed upon him at last that the continual recurrence of this scene must be more than mere coincidence.

In the afternoon, Marryott had but one opportunity to exchange looks with Anne. This was where the road turned sharply in such direction that, by glancing sidewise and across the back of Barnet's horse, he could see her through a sparse copse that filled the angle. Her expression now suggested alertness and craft, as if for his imitation; and she pointed with her forefinger to the horse ridden by Francis at her side. The trees cut off his view ere the gesture was complete; but he understood; it meant, "You will find a horse ready, if you can break from your guards!"

CHAPTER XXIII.

THE LONDON ROAD.

"How many miles to London town?"—Old Song.

AND now Master Marryott was himself again, with the will to break away if he could, and the eye for the opportunity if it should occur. It was plain that she had ceased to view him with antagonism or indifference. And her interest in him — an interest so strong as to overcome or exclude resentment toward him as the agent of Sir Valentine Fleetwood's escape from her as well as from the government — surely sprang from some more powerful feeling than mere regret for a man placed by her in a peril she had designed for another. To have caused her to order or sanction the holding of the horse in readiness, her interest must have fully taken up her mind. Perhaps to this fact was due her evident relinquishment of revenge upon Sir Valentine, as much as to that knight's present inaccessibility, and to the stupefying blow her vengeful impulse had received in the disclosure that her far and toilsome quest in its service had but led her from the right object to the wrong one.

Whence had this interest arisen? Doubtless from her musing on the love he had shown in staying to protect her that night at Foxby Hall; on the annoyances and delays to which she had subjected him during his long flight, and on his uniform gentleness to her in his necessary severity toward her.

Could he indeed break from his guards and escape, that he might satisfy himself on these questions, and profit in his love by that interest!

But Roger Barnet's vigilance, like his iron grip on Marryott's bridle when they rode, and on Marryott's arm when they alighted, seemed to increase with his increasing distress of body.

This night they ate and slept at Nottingham. Barnet occupied a second bed in Marryott's chamber. More than once Hal was awakened from sleep — a sleep in which his dreams carried out the wildest plans of escape — by the pursuivant's groans of pain. At dawn Roger's face was that of a man who had neither slept nor known a moment's ease. It was with a desperate stiffening of muscles and clenching of teeth that he forced himself to rise for the continuance of his journey.

Marryott had taken pains to view out the whereabouts of the led horse the previous evening, when, as usual, it had appeared in sight of his window. He marvelled not that his friends never failed to find a spot on which his gaze might alight. Kit Bottle, as he knew, had ways of learning, from inn menials of either sex, what room was taken for the prisoner. This morning the horse was at a place some distance from where it had been yesternight. Bottle was leading it; and the picture had a new figure, in the shape of a horse a little farther off. This second horse had a rider, — Anne Hazlehurst!

What would he not give now for means of escape? But there, hemming him in, were his four silent, stalwart guards; and beyond them, with cold eyes now red-rimmed from a restless night but fixed implacably on him, was the equally silent Barnet.

The wind had blown itself to other regions; the day was as fair as it was serene; it was milder, too, than days had been of late. But Hal's captors made poor travelling. Barnet had to halt often, as he could now scarce endure the pain caused by the movement of his horse. He stopped for dinner when he had ridden no farther than to Melton Mowbray and when it was no later than eleven o'clock.

Marryott took what scant comfort of mind he could, in this slowness of the journey toward London. Yet slow as it was, it was all too fast. London was but little more than a hundred miles away, now. Only a hundred miles of opportunity for that miracle of accident, or ingenuity and skill, by which he might save himself for the joys awaiting him in Anne Hazlehurst's love! Life had begun to taste ineffably sweet. The world was marvellously beautiful on such a day. But when he faced the terrible likelihood of a speedy hurling hence to "that undiscovered country," where there could not be a fairer sky to look upon, or purer air to breathe, and where there was no Anne Hazlehurst, the beauty of the day mocked him.

And the sight of the horse, too, mocked him, as it passively waited to bear him far from the reclaiming pursuit of death the moment he might slip from death's arms closing tighter around him. His heart cried "Avaunt, death! I am not for thee! Love and beauty await me; they, and this glad earth even now waking to joy at the first breath of spring! I am for this world, with its music and its wine, its laughter and its poetry, its green fields and its many-colored cities, its pleasures of good-fellowship, its smiles of the woman beloved! Unhand me, death; go your ways, black monster; I am life's own!" He had moments wherein he was half mad, not with the fear of death, but with the love of life; yet his madness had so much method in it that he gave no outward sign of it, lest his alertness for some means of escape might be suspected.

Back in the saddle, after dinner, to decrease by another afternoon's riding those hundred miles to

London town, Marryott observed in Barnet's face the fierce resolution which a man gathers for a last fight against physical anguish. So these two rode side by side, the captor concealing tortures of the body, the prisoner veiling tortures of the mind. At two o'clock they clattered into Oakham. When they arrived before the gate of a large inn, Roger Barnet suddenly called a halt, and said, in tones whose gruffness was somewhat broken by a note of bodily suffering:

"We'll tarry the day out here, and start fresh on the morrow. The foul fiend is in my leg!"

He thereupon sent Hudsdon to order rooms made ready, so that the prisoner might, as usual, be conducted from the horse to his chamber without stoppage. Barnet did not yet ride into the inn yard, for he noticed a crowd and a bustle therein, and preferred not to enter until it should be certain he would not have to go elsewhere for lodging. Here, as in other towns, the pursuivant kept his men close around the prisoner, as much to conceal the latter's bound wrists and legs from lookers-on as for any other purpose. Thus few people, if any, observed that here was a prisoner, and so no crowd collected.

As Hal sat his horse, awaiting Hudsdon's return, he bethought him that this day was Friday, March 13th, — the tenth day since his departure from Fleetwood house. The time he had undertaken to obtain for Sir Valentine would be past that evening, — and Welwyn was still seventy miles away!

This geographical fact, connected as it was with the certainty that he had more than accomplished his adventure, called up another and less pleasing fact, of which indeed he needed little reminder, — the fact that not a hundred miles now remained of the road to London.

His reflections were cut short by the reappearance of Hudsdon, who spoke to Barnet in whispers. The party then rode around to a side door of the inn, doubtless to avoid taking the prisoner through the crowd in the great yard. The hostess had already opened this door. Barnet and four men alighted from their horses, enabled Hal to dismount, and led him, at the heels of a chamberlain, through passages and up-stairs to a room. He had noticed, as he entered, that hostlers had already come from the inn gate to take the horses to stable by the usual route.

Hal's first glance, on entering his chamber, was for the window. To his dismay, it opened, not so as to give a view of street or of places exterior to the inn, but so as to command a part of the square inn yard, which was enclosed on three sides by the inn itself, on the fourth by a wall and gate. What hid a portion of this yard, which was far below, was the downward-sloping roof of the long upper gallery or balcony that traversed the three inner sides of the house. Situated as he now was, he could have no sight of the waiting horse.

"What do you see to make you stare so?" asked the watchful Barnet.

"Naught but the crowd in the inn yard," replied Hal, with barely the heart to dissemble. "'Tis more than common, methinks."

"Yes. Heard you not what Hudsdon said? There is to be a play in the yard; the town will not give the guildhall for plays on a Friday in Lent." [30]

"A play? Who are the players?"

"The lord chamberlain's men that are now travelling. They are wont to play at the Globe,— why, that is where you played, is't not so?"

But Hal heeded not the question. The lord chamberlain's men! Shakespeare, Sly, his friends, who a moment since had seemed worlds and ages away!

And, that very instant, a familiar voice rang out above the noise of the crowd below.

CHAPTER XXIV.

HOW A NEW INCIDENT WAS ADDED TO AN OLD PLAY.

"If he come not, then the play is marred." — *A Midsummer Night's Dream.*

THE cause of Marryott's not having seen the person whose voice he now heard, or the little board platform raised to serve as a stage, was that this platform was directly below his window, and hence hidden by the balconies with which the lower stories, unlike that in which he was, were provided.

The crowding of guards around Marryott, the distraction Barnet owed to his pain, had deterred the two from noticing, when outside the gate, the playbills attached to the posts. The play announced was "The Battle of Alcazar," by Mr. George Peele. There was still a special favor for anti-Spanish plays. Fresh in memory was that English victory over Spain whence arose the impulse of expansion destined, after three centuries of glory, to repeat itself in a new Anglo-Saxondom from a victory over the same race, when the guns of Dewey and Sampson should echo back in multiplied volume the roar of

Drake's and Howard's. History has nowhere repeated itself more picturesquely.

But after the play had been selected and announced, there had arrived at the inn, with a small regiment of servants, and a good part of his household furniture for his better accommodation, young Lord Tyrrington and his newly wedded lady. A squire in my lord's service had preceded him and bespoken the entire second story of one of the wings. My lady, on taking up her quarters, had learned with delight that London actors were to give a play in the yard. She had expressed to her husband, on whom she still looked with the soft eyes of a bride of a fortnight, the wish that the piece might be a love-play. Her spouse, as yet deeply enraptured with her and with love, had sent straightways for the master of the players. The result of the interview was the oral announcement which Marryott now heard from lips whose facility was well known to him.

Prefaced by delicately hinted compliments to the noble couple, and by gross open flattery of the worthy, excellent, and good people of Oakham, the announcement was to the effect that, instead of performing "The Battle of Alcazar," the lord chamberlain's servants would enact Master William Shakespeare's most admired and lamentable tragedy of the love of "Romeo and Juliet." Whereupon there was loud and prolonged applause, and the musicians, on the inn-balcony above the rear of the stage, struck up a tune for the beguilement of the crowd until the actors should be ready to begin.

"'Twas Will Sly," said Marryott, half to himself.

"You know him, I ween," said Roger Barnet, who had listened to the announcement with close attention, and who seemed to have softened a little under the stress of some concealed inclination.

"Marry, the days and nights we have tossed the pot together!" replied Hal.

"I ween you have been gossip and comrade to all of them," went on Roger, with guarded interest. "You know Burbage, and Shakespeare, and the rest?"

"I may say I know Burbage and the rest, and I have lived under the same roof with Master Shakespeare. I am acquaint with his outer life, which is, perforce, much like other men's, and with his talk, which varies so gently between sincerity and subtle irony, that one can never be sure; but to know the man himself were to know a world."

"I like his plays better than all others," said Roger. "And of all his plays, this 'Romeo and Juliet' best. I have read Arthur Brooke's poem of the tale, and William Paynter's story in 'The Palace of Pleasure;' but they are pale dullness to this tragedy. It hath rare love-making in it!"

The steeliness of Barnet's eye had melted to a soft lustre; a warmth had come over his face. Marryott looked at him in amazement. That this hard rascal, this complacent spy and implacable man-hunter, — even in that day when rough soldiers were greedy for wit and beauty and fine thought, — should have read poems and novels, and should possess a taste for rare love-making, was indeed one of those marvels which prove how many-sided (not inconsistent) is the individual human.

"If we could hear it better than we're like to do," suggested Marryott, "'twould a little distract us from our ills of mind and body, — for I take it from your twitchings that you suffer some."

The pursuivant was careful against showing how welcome this suggestion was; for he had felt that it would better emanate from the prisoner, in whom a desire to see the play was quite proper, than from an officer who ought to hold in supreme indifference all but duty.

"Why," said he, "I wot of no reason why you may not be allowed to see this play, under guard. Dawkins, go to the landlady and require for me a room in one of yonder wings, well toward the front of the yard, that we may see the stage from it. God forbid I should deprive a doomed man of two hours' forgetfulness!"

When, some minutes later, the change of rooms

had been effected, Marryott found himself looking down from a gabled window, which, being over one side of the yard, gave a complete oblique view of the stage at the yard's rear. He sat on a low stool, his hands pinioned behind him, Roger Barnet at his side. Four armed men stood close around, leaning forward for all possible view over the heads of the two.

The musicians, now visible in the gallery over the back of the stage, were still playing. The second story balcony across the yard from Hal's window was occupied by the lord and lady and their numerous attendants, a group whose rich attire presented all hues, and every kind, of silk, velvet, and costly cloth. My lady, close to the railing, and leaning expectantly over it, wore on her head a caul of golden thread; and one of her maids held a peaked Minever cap ready to be donned in case of cold. My lord, sitting at her side, bent so near that the silk rose at the end of his love-lock often brushed the cheek of her in whose honor it was still worn, despite their being now married. His lordship might have taken a seat upon the stage, but he preferred to remain where he could mark the significant love speeches to his lady's attention by gentle pressure of his hand on hers.

Three or four rustic gallants sat on the stage, and talked ostentatiously, with a great deal of very knowing laughter, each one keeping a side glance upon the noble lady in the balcony, to see what impression he was making; for each was convinced that her softly eager looks toward the stage were cast in admiration of himself.

The stage was of rough boards upon an underwork of upright barrels and trestles. At its back there hung from the balcony a curtain behind which a few makeshift steps descended to the door of an inn parlor now used by the actors as a tiring-room. The balcony thereabove was not devoted exclusively to the musicians; like all the other galleries around the yard, and to which chambers of the inn opened, this one held crowds of spectators, — inn guests and town's people. But of this one, that part immediately over the stage had, since the change of play, been cleared of people, and now remained so, with poles placed on either side as barriers. This part was reserved as Juliet's balcony; an inn chamber gave access to it from the rear. The height of the stage was such, that the floor of the balcony would be level with Romeo's eyes; but that mattered nothing to the imagination of an Elizabethan audience.

Even the steps leading to the balconies were crowded; the yard itself, paved with cobble stones, was more densely so, and with rougher and noisier people. Here were the lowest classes represented, but not those alone; here was a rawer wit than among the groundlings of the Globe Theatre; here was a smaller measure of acuteness than there, and here was a loutishness that was there absent.

The inn gates were now closed, but for a narrow opening, where stood two of the players' men to receive the money of what spectators might yet arrive.

The hour when the play ought to have begun had passed. But the crowd was the more tolerant of a burden upon its patience, for the fact that "Romeo and Juliet" had been substituted for the other play. Shakespeare's love-tragedy, which at first production had made the greatest success in the brief history of English drama, was the most popular play of its time; and to a county town of the insignificance of Oakham, it was still a novelty, bright with the lustre of its London triumph.

But at length the pleasure of anticipation lost power to sweeten the delay of realization. The crowd murmured. The musicians, who had fallen to playing "I am the Duke of Norfolk," for there being nothing else left unplayed, became the targets of derisive yells; the unseen players, behind the curtain, were called upon to hasten. My lady had changed her position several times, and my lord was beginning to wonder why the devil —

And then the curtain was pushed a little aside, and Master Sly stepped forth again, now dressed for the part he was on this occasion to enact, — that of Mercutio. The crowd gave a shout of welcome, the musicians came to an abrupt but grateful stop. "The prologue," remarked several of the knowing, and then indignantly bade others hush, who were making the same remark.

But Master Sly's air was not suggestive of an ordinary prologue. It was hesitating, embarrassed, a little dubious of consequences. He began, rather to my lord than to the audience as a whole, a halting, bungling speech, of which the purport was that, by reason of the sudden illness of an actor who played a part necessary to the movement of the tragedy, and as no unoccupied player in the company knew the part, either "Romeo and Juliet" must be for the occasion abandoned, or its performance marred by the reading of the part, "which marring must needs be the greater," said Mr. Sly, "for that it is a part of exceeding activity, and hath some furious fighting with the rapier."

Here was a damper, whose potent effect became at once manifest in blank looks on faces noble and faces common. My lord and his lady were as much disappointed as the rudest artisan or the pertest grammar-school truant. The assemblage was yet in that chilled silence which precedes murmurs of displeasure, and Mr. Sly was drawing breath to submit the alternative of another play or the marred performance, when from a gable window high above all galleries a voice rang out :

"Go to, Will Sly! I'll wager 'tis the part of Tybalt; and that Gil Crowe's illness comes of the same old cause!"

Master Sly stared aloft at the distant speaker. So did every auditor to whom the window was visible; and those in the balconies under it leaned over the railings and twisted their necks to look upward.

"Why,—'tis thee, Harry Marryott,—i' the name of God!" cried Sly, after a moment of blinking,—for Hal's gable was sun-bathed, and blue sky was above it. "What dost here, Hal? What surprise is this you give us?"

"No matter!" answered Hal. "I said truly, did I not?"

"Surely thou didst, and a mur—! Why, boy, thou canst play Tybalt! You studied it in London!"

"And played it once, when Master Crowe was—ill!"

"Why, here's good fortune! My lord, 'tis one of our actors, who hath been a time absent from us. You will enjoy to see him in the fighting. Haste thee down, Master Marryott!"

A clapping of hands behind the entrance-curtain told Hal that the other players had heard, and that they welcomed; some, indeed, were peeping out from the edges of the curtain.

Lord Tyrrington looked across the yard, and up to the gable window, and called out, "Well met, sir!" with a kindly face; and his lady, delighted at the turn of affairs, smiled sweetly. Whereat the crowd cheered lustily, and all eyes were fixed on Hal with approval and pleasure.

"Alas!" cried Hal. "I may not stir from here. I am a prisoner to this officer of the queen."

The smiles slowly faded from the countless faces below. Roger Barnet, who had been taken by surprise at Hal's first salutation to Sly, and whom the swift ensuing colloquy had caught at a loss, frowned, and wished he had interfered earlier.

"Nay," called Sly, "it can be for no grave offence. The —"

"'Tis a charge of aiding treason," replied Hal, to cut matters short.

Sly stood a little appalled. A deeper silence and a new interest took possession of the gazing crowd.

"Why, even so," said Sly, at last, "the officer may —"

The officer now thought it time to speak for himself. "My prisoner is my prisoner," he said, in a somewhat surly and defiant tone, "taken in the queen's name, with proper warrant; and in the queen's name I hold him here in close guard."

Will Sly, after a perplexed look at the pursuivant

by Hal's side, turned his eyes in a tentative, questioning way to the young lord. The crowd followed his glance. My lord felt the pressure of the general wish upon him. His lady whispered something to him, in a kind of pouting, appealing way, with a disapproving side glance at Roger Barnet. My lady herself was only a knight's daughter. To her, a lord was a person of unlimited influence. When a wife imagines that her husband is all-powerful, he does not like to disabuse her mind. When he is deeply in love with her, and she asks him for a pleasure which he has himself offered, he will go far to obtain it. Moreover, here was a multitude looking to him, the great Lord Tyrrington, as to its champion against a vile, sport-spoiling hound of the government.

"How now, officer?" cried my lord, in a tone of lofty rebuke. "The queen's name — God save her gracious Majesty! — comes as loyally, methinks, from lips that do not make it a common byword of their trade. Warrant, say you? Your warrant, sirrah, requires not that you guard her Majesty's prisoner rather in one part of this inn than in another part. Let him be guarded upon yonder stage. 'Tis as safe a place, with proper watching, as the chamber you are in."

"My lord —" doggedly began Barnet, who had noted Sly's form of address. But ere he could proceed, there arose from the yard, and was taken up by the galleries, a clamor so mandatory, so threatening to a possible thwarter of the general will, that the pursuivant, who in his day had seen a mob or two at work, became passive. Moreover, he had been as cast down as any one at the prospect of his favorite play's being supplanted or spoiled; and deep within him was a keen curiosity to see his prisoner act on the stage. Standing at the window, therefore, Roger made a curt gesture of yielding to the unanimous will.

"My lord," said he, when the cheers of satisfaction had hushed, "sith it be your desire, and haply the pleasure of my lady, and the wish of these good people, I no more say nay. Your lordship will of a surety grant me, and require of these players, that I may dispose guards to my own liking, and for the queen's service, during the time of my prisoner's use in the play."

My lord was quick to approve of this condition. "Your prisoner, mayhap," he added, "will give his word not to attempt escape."

"Ay, my lord," cried Hal, at once, "if this officer rely on that word alone, and dispense with guards about me."

Marryott knew, of course, and Barnet promptly affirmed by word, that the latter would prefer to rely on his guards. Hal showed no offence at this;

had he thought his word would be accepted he would not have offered it.

"Then," said he, when Barnet had expressed himself, "I will not give my word."

The pursuivant was content. He attributed Hal's attitude to a mere idle punctilio which would not accept moral bonds without a reciprocal withdrawal of physical ones, even though freedom from moral bonds was useless. Barnet was accustomed, in his observations of gentlemen, to such bootless niceties in matters of honor.

The musicians were put to it for another quarter of an hour, and Barnet conducted the prisoner down-stairs and to the tiring-room. He placed a guard at each entrance to that room, stationed others in the yard so that one breasted each side of the small stage, set two upon the steps between stage and tiring-room, and established himself on a three-legged stool on the stage. He seemed to have conveniently forgotten that Tybalt, even during the acts wherein he appears, is less time on the stage than off. He had put the faithful Hudsdon, however, at the door from the tiring-room to the steps behind the stage. Indeed, Hal's freedom was little more than it had been in the chamber, save that, Tybalt being a swordsman's part, his hands were now unbound.

Barnet had assured himself that the rapiers used

by the actors were blunted so as not to pierce. He knew, too, that he had won the crowd by his concession to their wish, and that he should have all the spectators, including the lord's people and the inn-folk, as active barriers against any dash the prisoner might rashly venture for liberty.

Hal's friends had crowded around him in the tiring-room, which was lighted with candles against the gloom caused by the curtain at the back of the stage. Even Burbage had pressed his hand, and uttered a hope that there might be nothing in this treason matter. "Fortune send thee safe out of it, whatever it be!" was Master Shakespeare's wish. "If thou camest to grief, Hal," said the Juliet, the same pert stripling that had played Ophelia eleven days before, "I should weep like a real girl!" Gil Crowe alone had nothing to say, for he was stretched half clad, in the corner where he had fallen, in the deepest drunken slumber.

Master Shakespeare wore the white beard and religious cowl of the Friar; a habit that had wakened in Hal's mind a thought to be quenched the next moment by Barnet's injunction to the guards of the tiring-room:

"And lose not sight of him an instant while he is here, lest during an eye-wink he slip into some player's disguise of face and body, and pass one of you unknown."

His comrades, especially Master Shakespeare and Will Sly, would have inquired more closely into the circumstances of Hal's detention, but the young man was so pleasantly exhilarated by the reunion with his friends, so carried out of himself at the prospect of playing this part, that he put direful matters aside as not to be talked of. With his dulled rapier in hand, and without having to change costume, he stood surrounded by the players, at the tiring-room door, waiting to go on the stage.

The music ceased again; the speaker of the prologue stepped out, and, while the audience came gradually to a hush, delivered his lines from the centre of the platform. A boy fastened to the curtain at the back a scroll reading, "A Street in Verona." The two Capulet serving-men came on, and their rude double-meanings made the crowd guffaw; then the two Montague men, then Benvolio, then Tybalt precipitating the brawl, then the crowd of adherents of both houses; and the ensuing fray, unduly confined by the smallness of the platform, came near involving Roger Barnet and the gallants sitting at the sides.

Noting more heedfully how dense was the crowd that pressed from the yard's farthest boundaries to the stage, and recognizing the guards about the latter, Hal had a sickening feeling of being mured around with a wall no less impassable for that it was human.

His mind reverted to the last time he had acted on a stage; to the face he had seen then. Where was she at this moment? Was the horse waiting? Unmanned for an instant, he felt his eyes moisten.

When he made exit, after the Prince had quelled the tumult, he stood silent in the dark tiring-room, sad at heart.

Meanwhile, Roger Barnet and the audience were enjoying the performance. The pursuivant, nearer to the great Burbage than he had ever before been during a play, drank in Romeo's every word. In due time, the stage being for a moment vacant, a boy supplanted the first card with one reading, "A Room in Capulet's House." The scene of the Nurse with Juliet and her mother drew some very conscious blushes from my lady in the gallery, the too reminiscent Nurse's part losing nothing of mellowness from its being played by a portly man.. The street card reappeared, and brought on Mercutio to deepen the audience's entrancement. Another substitution introduced the masquerade, during which the Tybalt, covered with an orange-tawny cloak and wearing a black mask, was held in particular note by Barnet, Hudsdon having followed him to the stage and pointed him out in his visored appearance.

During the second act, with its balcony scene, its wisdom so impressively spoken by Master Shakespeare in the Friar's part, its wit contest between

Romeo and Mercutio, Roger Barnet was in the seventh heaven. Throughout this act, Hal, seated listlessly in the tiring-room, was under the eyes of Hudsdon and other guards. The first scene of the third act, heralded by the useful street scroll, brought his great and last great occasion.

"It may be my last stage-playing in this world," he thought, and resolved it should be worthy the remembrance of his comrades.

"'By my heel, I care not,'" quoth Sly as Mercutio, and Tybalt, taking the cue, strode out with his followers, to force the deadly quarrel.

The brief exchange of defiance with Mercutio, the vain attempt of peacemaking Benvolio to lead the foes from public gaze, made keen the audience's expectation. Romeo entered; refused to be drawn by Tybalt's fierce words into fight; tried to placate the other's hot anger. Mercutio invited the quarrel to himself, drew rapier, and belabored Tybalt with wit. Tybalt, with a ready "I am for you," flashed out his blade in turn. There was fine clashing of steel, excellent fencing. Romeo rushed in to stop the duel, calling on Benvolio to beat down the weapons. Is it wonder that the audience was a-quiver with interest, under complete illusion? For here was a truly fiery Tybalt; here was Mercutio, the most fascinating character in Shakespeare; here as Romeo was Burbage himself, accounted the greatest actor in the world. Is it wonder that Roger Barnet, sitting not a man's length away, hung breathlessly, and with wide eyes, upon the scene?

"Hold, Tybalt! good Mercutio!" cried Romeo.

But Mercutio had received his thrust, and Tybalt turned to flee with his followers. Barnet heard him cry out something as he ran; got an impression of legs disappearing behind the rear curtain; and, with the greater part of the audience, kept his eyes on the group whence the youth had fled.

For Mercutio was panting in Romeo's arms; declaring himself hurt, and calling feebly a plague on both the houses; replying to Romeo's encouraging words with: "No, 'tis not so deep as a well, nor so wide as a church-door; but 'tis enough, 'twill serve: ask for me to-morrow, and you shall find me a grave man. I am peppered, I warrant, for this world. A plague o' both your houses!" And so till Benvolio led him off gasping with his dying breath, "Your houses!"

And now it was Romeo's task to hold the multitude's illusion with deploring speeches; and to work up anew its breathless sympathy, at the news of Mercutio's death and that the furious Tybalt was coming back again.

"'Alive, in triumph! and Mercutio slain!'" cried Burbage.

"'Away to heaven, respective lenity.
And fire-eyed fury be my conduct now.'"

And Romeo, trembling with the emotion of the situation, stood with sword ready to receive the slayer of his friend, lips ready to begin, "Now, Tybalt, take the villain back again —"

The audience stood in a suspense not less than Romeo's, every gaze intent upon the place where Tybalt should come forth.

But from that place, no one appeared.

Why did Tybalt delay? What was the matter?

It was an embarrassing moment for Mr. Burbage. He whispered something to the Benvolio, who thereupon went to the curtain at the rear and pushed it aside. He disclosed a number of those actors known as servitors, waiting to come on as citizens, and behind these the Prince with Montague and Capulet and their ladies.

"Where's Marryott?" called Benvolio to these. "'Tis his cue. The stage waits for Tybalt."

Those about the doorway looked into the tiring-room. "He is not here," replied several.

"He is not come from the stage yet," said Hudsdon. "I have kept my eye for him."

"Why," said Benvolio to the fellows who had played Tybalt's followers, "came he not off with you?"

"I remember not," said one. "'Tis certain he ought to have."

"'Tis certain he did not," said one of the guards on the steps.

Hudsdon made his way through the group on the steps, strode upon the stage, and, going to the centre thereof, to Mr. Burbage's utter amazement, said to Roger Barnet:

"There's deviltry afoot! The prisoner came not yonder, yet he is not here!"

"What say'st thou?" replied Roger, turning dark, and springing to his feet. "Thou'st been cozened, Hudsdon! He fled yonder; I saw him!" And he pointed toward the tiring-room.

"Nay," said one of the gallants on the stage, "he fled over the balcony, into the house." The speaker indicated the balcony used by Juliet, which, as has been said, was no higher above the back of the stage than were the eyes of a man standing. "That I'll swear. He grasped the balustrade, and drew himself up, and bent around, and put knee to the balcony's edge; and then 'twas short work over the balustrade and across the balcony."

"Ay, 'tis so!" cried out many voices from near the stage, and from the occupied part of the balcony itself.

"Why, then, Hudsdon, take three men, and search the house," cried Roger, for whom Mr. Burbage had indignantly made way by retiring to the back of the stage. Then the pursuivant turned to his informants: "An ye had eyes for so much, had none of you the wit to call out whither he went?"

"I thought it was part of the play," lisped the gallant. "I thought he ran away lest he be taken for killing the witty gentleman."

"Why, so he did," quoth Barnet, "but he ought not to have run to the balcony!"

"Marry, look you," said the other, "he cried 'Away!' and started for the curtain; then he said, 'Nay, I'll to the balcony!' and so to the balcony he went. I thought 'twas in the play."

"I knew the play," called out a gentleman in the balcony, "but I thought the action had mayhap been changed. We all thought so, who saw him pass this way."

"Devil take prating!" muttered Barnet. "Dawkins, go you with three men and seek in the street hereabout for him, or word of him. You three, to the stables, and out with the horses! A murrain on plays and play-acting!—I don't mean that, neither, Master Shakespeare" (for the poet had hastened to the stage to see what the matter was), "but I've been a blind ass this day, and I would I had your art to tell my feelings!"

And he limped after Hudsdon, to assist in the search of the house.

This was a large inn, and required long searching. As for the men ordered to seek in the adjacent streets, they were a good while hindered in making their way through the crowd in the yard. Those who went to take out the horses were similarly impeded.

Meanwhile, for a time there was clamor and confusion among the spectators. Some of the dull witted, who had lost interest in the play after the novelty of the opening scenes, followed the four men to the street. The most, thinking the prisoner might be found in the house, chose to remain where they were, deciding not to sacrifice a certain pleasure for the uncertain one of joining a hunt for an escaped prisoner. So there were calls for the play to go on. It was therefore taken up at the point where Marryott had failed to appear, Master Shakespeare assuming Tybalt's part for the one short speech, and the swift death, that remained to it. Thenceforward there was no stoppage. My lord and his lady listened with rapt attention, and when at last the two lovers lay clasped in death many of the audience had forgotten the episode that had interrupted the third act.

But Roger Barnet had other occupation than to watch the resumed play. It was not given him to end as agreeably an afternoon so pleasantly begun; yet matter to distract his thoughts from his lame leg was not lacking. The search of the inn yielding nothing, the scouring of the immediate neighborhood being fruitless, the pursuivant sent his men throughout the town for a clue. One came back with news that a man of the prisoner's description had been seen taking the Stamford road. Another returned with word that the lady who had followed from Foxby Hall had tarried a short while at another inn; and a third brought information that this lady and her escort of three had later left the town by the road to London. She had not, indeed, had Barnet's reason for staying in Oakham, and it was quite natural that she should have continued her homeward journey. Her departure seemed not connected in any way with the prisoner's flight.

Meanwhile the horses had been waiting ready in the street during the time necessary for these inquiries.

"To saddle, then," said Barnet to Hudsdon, "every hound of us! I'll on to Fleetwood house, you to the Stamford road. 'Tis the fiend's work that your man hath two hours' start. I wonder how far he is."

Just about that time, as the players were sitting down to supper, Master Shakespeare said:

"I pray Fortune the new action Hal put in my tragedy shall prove indeed the winning of his freedom!"

CHAPTER XXV.

SIR HARRY AND LADY MARRYOTT.

"This wild-goose chase is done; we have won o' both sides." — *The Wild-Goose Chase.*

MARRYOTT, in the midst of the fight with Mercutio, had in a flash two thoughts, one springing from the contact of his glance with the balcony, the other following instantly upon the first. The first was, that a man might gain the balcony by one swift effort of agility and strength; the second was, that when momentous action holds the attention of spectators to one part of a stage, a person elsewhere on the stage may move unobserved before their eyes, if his movement be swift, silent, and in harmony with what has preceded, — a fact well known to people of stage experience. No incident in the drama more focuses attention than the dying scene of Mercutio; spectators have no eyes for Tybalt, of whom they retain but a vague impression of hasty flight.

The thing was scarce thought, when the time had come to act it. To make all seem right to those he must pass near, and inspired by necessity, he indeed spoke, for their ears alone, the words, "Away! Nay,

I'll to the balcony;" at the same time casting his sword against the curtain, so that it fell less loudly to the stage. He seized two balusters, swiftly raised himself, and then — not proceeding exactly as the rustic beau had described — lodged a foot in the angle of a brace supporting the balcony, set his other foot on the balcony's edge, and rose ready to swing his body over the rail. To do this, and to glide across the balcony and through the way left open for Juliet, was the matter of a second. He was conscious, as he crossed the balcony, of slightly surprised looks from the musicians at one side, and from a few spectators at the other; but as he plunged into the room, he heard behind him only the lamenting voice of Romeo. Most of the spectators, and those chiefly concerned in his doings, had not observed his flight; like the dupes of a juggler, in watching one thing they had missed another; and those who perforce had seen his exit thought all was as it should be.

Across the room he ran, to a door leading into a passage. He traversed this to the end, where a window gave upon the street. Through the window ere he had time to think of possible broken bones, he hung from the ledge, and dropped. The fall was from the second story only. He slipped sidewise on alighting, jarred his elbow, and bruised his leg. But he was up in a moment. The street was deserted, — everybody in the neighborhood was at the play.

He looked in both directions, but saw no horse. Then he started on a run, to make a circuit of the inn. If the horse was not in sight on one side, it must be so on another. Fortune could not so cruelly will it that when at last he had made the dash, performed the miracle, his friends should, for the first time, fail him. He directed his steps so as first to pass the inn gate, and be gone from it ere Barnet's men should have time to sally out. This he accomplished, but without glimpse of the horse. He turned into a street on the third side of the inn; traversed it to its junction with a lane leading toward the side where he had landed from the window; darted into this lane with the fast-beating heart of a dying hope, passed half-way through it, glanced with dreading eyes down a narrow passage conducting from it, and saw, in a street beyond, the waiting horse.

How he covered the length of the passage, and vaulted into the saddle, he never could recall. His first remembered impression, after sight of the horse, was of being surrounded by Anne, Kit, and Anthony, all mounted; and seeing Francis glide away afoot in quest of a horse for his own riding. There was more gravity than joy in the faces of the three; the sight of him alive and free of his guards was too marvellous for outward rejoicing. Such joy is like passions, of which Raleigh wrote, that they —

"... are likened best to floods and streams:
The shallow murmur, but the deep are dumb."

Anthony avoided Hal's glance by looking down; Kit Bottle cleared his throat; from Anne's eyes there was the least gush of tears, and her voice trembled as she spoke:

"God be thanked! I dared not hope for this!"

"Nor I," he replied. "Whither do we ride?"

"You, to the Lincolnshire coast, with Anthony. He knows secret ways of embarkation to France."

"But you?—you waited with the horse, that you might ride with me, is't not so?"

"No; that I might see all done, with mine own eyes, and you escaped. Anthony has money for your needs to France. I will ride home, with Captain Bottle and Francis. Tarry not another moment. You are to ride first alone. Anthony will leave this town with us, and then make by cross-ways to join you soon on the Stamford road. This paper tells where one shall wait for the other, for Anthony may ride the faster, knowing better the ways. I have writ it so, for greater surety and less delay. Go now; here's money, of Anthony's lending. Nay, for God's sake, tarry not!"

"But thou? When shall I see or hear?"

"Anthony will tell you how to send word. Tarry not, I entreat!"

"Thou'st been too good to me!"

"Nay, 'tis not goodness alone —"

And she finished with a look straight and deep into his eyes. He seized her hand, and kissed it fervently.

"And thou'lt wait?" he whispered.

"Forever, if need! — but let it not be so long."

With his free hand, he grasped Kit Bottle's, and wrung from the old soldier a husky "God bless thee, boy!" Then he spurred forward in the direction silently pointed out by Anthony. At a bend of the street, he turned in his saddle, and cast a look back. His friends were motionless upon their horses, gazing after him with saddened, softened faces. A slight movement of Mistress Hazlehurst's gloved hand, and his horse had carried him from the scene; but he bore that scene ever in his heart's eye, day and night, to the coast, which, thanks to his good start and tireless riding, he reached uncaught; over sea to France, where Anthony soon brought him into sight of Sir Valentine Fleetwood, who had arrived at Dieppe not a day sooner than Hal had disembarked at Boulogne; in Paris, where Hal got an honorable post in a great man's household through the influence of Sir Valentine's wife, — for it turned out that the knight, unknown to Queen Elizabeth, had a wife, after all, a French lady whose virtue and beauty easily explained her husband's willingness to save his life at another's risk.

She was of great wealth, and, it happened, of equal gratitude; whence it fell out that, when Master Marryott returned to England, after the accession of King James, he came as owner of an estate previously purchased in his name by Anthony Underhill; an estate sold by the crown, under confiscation,— no other estate, in fact, than that pertaining to Foxby Hall, in Yorkshire.

Now it had come out that Mistress Hazlehurst's brother, before getting himself killed by Sir Valentine Fleetwood, had overladen his estate with debt, and, in conspiracy with his sister's man of business, had made way with her portion also. When the courts of law had finally established beyond doubt that she was penniless, Master Marryott was about returning to his own country, fully informed, by Anne's correspondence, of the state of her affairs. So there was afforded the unique spectacle of a lady who had remained unmarried while she was supposably an heiress, obtaining a husband the moment she was shown to be a beggar.

"I think, love," said Sir Harry (he was knighted under King James, on no better pretext than having, with his own servants, rid the northern counties of a famous robber called Rumney the Highway, whom Marryott's man Bottle slew in single combat), "I think I will write my memoirs, as everybody in

France does." He sat idly touching a viol in an upper window-seat of Foxby Hall, one summer evening, while Lady Marryott as idly fingered a virginal near him.

"How now, Hal? Hast done aught wonderful in thy time? 'Faith, thou shouldst have told me!"

"Rail an thou wilt, sweet! But there is much for wonder in the matter that brought us together,— not in any doing of mine, forsooth, but in Fortune's doing. For look you, had I not indeed tarried here that night you counterfeited illness in this room, you might perforce have talked with Roger Barnet ere the six days were done, and he have sent back to Sir Valentine, who left not Fleetwood house till the last hour. Thus, perchance, Sir Valentine had not escaped to France; had he not done so, I had not fared well there, and met his lady, whose gratitude took the shape of filling my purse. I had not then come back as owner of Foxby Hall at the very time my love was disowned of Fortune. But for the sad quarrel 'twixt your brother and Sir Valentine, and for my having taken up the queen's thankless errand, I had not met you in the road that night; but for the continuance of my pretence to be Sir Valentine, thou hadst not followed me to the end we wot of."

The queen's death had unsealed his lips,— though only to his wife, who was one woman that could keep a secret, — regarding her Majesty's commission.

"Why, then," said Anne, "but for the queen's lingering love of the knight, and but for her dread of seeming weak to her councillors, — for that I will take oath was her reason, — we should not be here together this moment. Ne'ertheless, 'twas a cruel queen, merely to save her pride a brief unpleasantness, to send a young gentleman to risk his life!"

"Marry, Anne, I have heard of ladies who were not queens, sending great lords further, for less! But look you, I took the errand for no reward, being minded like to Master Spenser's knight:

> "'Upon a great adventure he was bond,
> That greatest Gloriana to him gave
> (That greatest glorious Queen of Faerie land),
> To win him worship, and her grace to have.'

"Nay, I know thou'lt say, much virtue in her grace! But bethink you, if I looked for no other direct reward, and got none, neither did I look for the indirect rewards Fortune took it on herself to pay me withal. If I sought only the queen's grace, and mayhap received small share of that, was I not put in the way of winning thy grace, my sweet, and of all else I have?"

"Nay, perhaps Fortune had found other ways to bring these things to thee. Look out of the window,

Harry, and bid Kit Bottle not make little Will run so fast. Thine old bully is the child's undoing!"

"Nay, the lad is safe with Kit; though indeed the old rascal spoils him some. What was he doing yesterday, but teaching him to counterfeit Anthony Underhill's psalm-singing? A steward of Anthony's years deserves more courtesy."

"If the boy grow up as brave a gentleman as thou, Hal, I shall be content. There be honors waiting for him in the world, I trow."

"Why, he hath some honor already, methinks, in being Will Shakespeare's godson. 'Sooth, the players will not know him for the same lad when we go again to London, he hath shot up so tall. But thou wert speaking of that night, when thy feigned tears conquered me in this room —"

"Nay, thou wert speaking of it, love."

"Thou hast never told me; never have I dared ask: was — all — counterfeit that night?"

"Why, — my lord, — the illness, indeed, was counterfeit; but the kisses — though perhaps I had withheld them, save for my purpose — were real enough, God wot, once my lips were loosed! And I marvel I could still cling to my revenge, yet yield myself to thine arms so willingly! Nay, Hal, there's no need to act the scene anew! Out on thee, madcap, thou'st crushed my kirtle —!"

THE END.

NOTES.

NOTES.

NOTE 1. (Page 12.)

Mr. Fleay seems satisfied that 1601 was the year of the production of Shakespeare's first "Hamlet." But he believes it was "hurriedly prepared during the journey to Scotland," where the players had arrived by October, when they were at Aberdeen. "In their travels this year they visited the Universities of Oxford and Cambridge, where they performed 'Julius Cæsar' and 'Hamlet.'" That "Hamlet" was the second of these two plays produced, seems evident from the allusion of "Corambis" ("Polonius") to his having played "Julius Cæsar" at the University. But this speech might have been added to the first version after its original production, and before the publication in 1603 of the garbled first quarto; for two plays whose London productions are assigned by Fleay to 1601 ("Satiromastix" and "The Malcontent") contain allusions to "Hamlet." If the lord chamberlain's company did not act again in London in 1601 after its departure on its travels, how account for these allusions, unless "Hamlet" had been acted in London before the company's departure? Dr. Furnivall would forestall this question by saying that "the 'Hamlet' allusions in and before 1602 are to an old play." But it seems as fair to conjecture a slightly earlier production of the new play, in accounting for these allusions, as a general revival of interest in an old play; and the fact that the allusions are not true to speeches actually occurring in Shakespeare's first "Hamlet" will not weigh with those who consider the methods of satire and burlesque. The lines in the play that seemingly attribute the company's travelling to the popularity of the "little eyases" (the Chapel Royal children acting at the Blackfriars Theatre) are rather such as would have been designed for a London audience on the eve of the company's departure, as a pretext for an exile due to royal disfavor, than for University audiences, to whom the players would less willingly confess a waning of London popularity; or than for a London audience after the company's return, when the allusion, though still of interest, would be the less likely to serve a purpose. The conclusion here driven at is, that Sir Henry Marryott's narrative is not to be impugned because he places the first "Hamlet" performance before the company's departure from London, while the investigators place it after. Heaven forfend that, even on a single unimportant question, the present writer should rush in where angels fear to tread, to the arena of Shakespearean controversy, to whose confusion even such a master as Mr. Saintsbury refrains from adding!

NOTE 2. (Page 14.)

The occasion for the lord chamberlain's players to travel was one of the numerous minor episodes of the

Essex conspiracy. That plot to seize Whitehall, and dictate a change of government to the queen, was hatched at Drury House by the Earl of Essex and his friends, in January. Early in February Essex was ordered to appear before the council, and he received an anonymous letter of warning. It was decided that the rising should occur Sunday, February 8th. On Thursday, February 5th, Essex's friends went to the Globe Theatre to see Shakespeare's "Richard II." performed, — a play affording them a kind of example for their intended action. (In the trials in March, Meyrick was indicted for "having procured the out-dated tragedy of 'Richard II.' to be publicly acted at his own charge, for the entertainment of the conspirators.") Of the shareholding members of the company of players, the one who had arranged this performance was Augustine Phillips. The rising in London, when it occurred, was abortive, and Essex was taken to the Tower, those of his adherents who surrendered, or were caught, being distributed among different London prisons. On February 18th, the confessions of several of Essex's friends were taken. The next day, Essex and Southampton, Shakespeare's friend, were brought before a commission of twenty-five peers and nine judges, in Westminster Hall. Things were done expeditiously in that reign: at 7 P. M., the same day, sentence of death was pronounced upon Essex, and he was taken back to the Tower. Six days later, February 25th, he was beheaded. Southampton was kept a long time in prison. Four of Essex's associates were executed. One of several remarkable features of this little affair was that the band of conspirators included Catholics and Puritans, as well as men of the established church. To return to the players: Mr. Fleay says it is "clear that the subjects chosen for historical plays by Marlowe and Shakespeare were unpopular at court, but approved of by the Essex faction, and that at last the company incurred the serious displeasure of the queen. So they did not perform at court at Christmas, 1601." In the previous Christmas season, they had given three performances at court. In Elizabeth's reign, this company acted at court twenty-eight plays, twenty of which were by Shakespeare, eight by other men. This shows that the age which could produce a Shakespeare could appreciate him, — as somebody has said, or ought to have said.

Note 3. (Page 18.)

"Boys were regularly apprenticed to the profession in those days," says the anonymous author of "Lights of the Old English Stage." "Each principal was entitled to have a boy or apprentice, who played the young and the female characters, and for whose services he received a certain sum." This certain sum was, of course, paid out, like the rent and other common expenses of the theatre, before money taken in was divided among the different shareholders. All the principals were shareholders. The Globe Theatre was owned by the Burbages. Hence Richard Burbage would first receive rent, as owner of the playhouse, and would later receive his part of the profits as a shareholder. As to these apprentices, one finds mention of "coadjutors," "servitors," and "hired men," not to speak of "tire-boys," "stage-boys," etc. Those boys that played female parts must have played them effectively, notwithstanding the unwillingness of Shakespeare's Egyptian queen to see, on the Roman stage, "some squeaking Cleopatra boy my greatness." Else would Shakespeare have dared to write, for acting, such parts as Juliet and Beatrice, and, above all, such as Rosalind and Viola, in which a boy, dressed as a boy, should yet have to seem a girl disguised? The anonymous writer already quoted says of these boys: "Thus trained under great masters, it is not to be wondered at that they grew up to be such consummate masters of their art." It is well known that women did not appear on the stage in England before 1662, forty-six years after Shakespeare's death.

NOTE 4. (Page 19.)

If anybody supposes that Burbage would not be thought a great or a finished actor, were he now alive and acting just as he did in his own day, let that person read the various poems written at his death and descriptive of the effect produced by him on his audiences. His Romeo " begot tears." His Brutus and Marcius " charmed the faculty of ears and eyes." " Every thought and mood might thoroughly from " his " face be understood." " And his whole action he could change with ease, from ancient Lear to youthful Pericles." In the part of the " grieved Moor," " beyond the rest he moved the heart." " His pace " suited with " his speech," and " his every action " was "grace." His tongue was "enchanting" and "wondrous." Bishop Corbet tells in verse how his host at Leicester, in describing the battle of Bosworth field, used the name of Burbage when he meant King Richard. Or let the skeptic read what Flecknoe says: "He was a delightful Proteus, so wholly transforming himself into his part, and putting off himself with his clothes, as he never (not so much as in the tyring-house) assumed himself again until the play was done. . . . His auditors" were "never more delighted than when he spoke, nor more sorry than when he held his peace; yet even then he was an excellent actor still, never failing in his part when he had done speaking; but with his looks and gesture, maintaining it still unto the height." His death, in 1618, so overshadowed that of the queen of James I., as a public calamity, that after weeping for him, the people had no grief left for her Majesty.

Note 5. (Page 20.)

As to false beards worn on the stage at that time, recall Nick Bottom's readiness to discharge the part of "Pyramus" in "either your straw-color beard, your orange-tawny beard, your purple-in-grain beard, or your French crown-color beard, your perfect yellow;" and, later, his injunction to his fellow actors to get good strings to their beards; regarding which injunction, George Steevens says: "As no false beard could be worn without a ligature to fasten it on, Bottom's caution must mean more than the mere security of his comrades' beards. The good strings he recommends were probably ornamental. This may merely show how little a former-day Shakespearean commentator might know of the acting stage. A bad "ligature" might give way and make the actor ridiculous by the sudden shedding of his beard. Such an accident was one against which Bottom, being of an active jaw, might be particularly precautious. In a full beard, ascending at the sides of the face to meet the hair of the head, the ligature could be completely concealed. But often glue was used, to fasten on false beards. "Some tinker's trull, with a beard glued on," says a character in Beaumont and Fletcher's "The Wild-Goose Chase." Sir Walter Raleigh wore a false beard in his betrayed attempt to escape down the Thames, night of August 9, 1618. Real beards of the time were of every form,—pointed, fan-shaped, spade-shaped, T-shaped, often dyed.

Note 6. (Page 32.)

"Fencing was taught as a regular science," says George Steevens, in a note to "The Merry Wives of Windsor." "Three degrees were usually taken in this art, a master's, a provost's, and a scholar's. For each of these a prize was played. The weapons they used were the axe, the pipe, rapier and target, rapier and cloak, two-swords, the two-hand sword, the bastard-sword, the dagger and staff, the sword and buckler, the rapier and dagger, etc. The places where they exercised were, commonly, theatres, halls, or other enclosures." A party of young gallants at a tavern, says Thornbury, would often send for a fencing-master to come and breathe them. The great dictator in fencing, duelling, etc., in London, about 1600, was Vincentio Savolio, whose book on the "Use of the Rapier and Dagger" and on "Honor and Honorable Quarrels" was printed in London in 1595. The Dictionary of National Biography says he was born in Padua, and, after obtaining a reputation as a fencer, came to England and was taken into the service of the Earl of Essex. "In 'As You Like It,' Touchstone's description of the various forms of a lie is obviously based on Savolio's chapter 'Of the Manner and Diversitie of Lies.'" Though a great swordsman, Savolio seems to have been anything but a brawler, or an abettor of fighting. In his book he deprecates quarrels upon insufficient causes.

Note 7. (Page 45.)

Nobody needs to be reminded that the original of Justice Shallow is supposed to have been Sir Thomas Lucy, the knight of Charlecote Hall, whose deer the legend has it Shakespeare stole; as steal them he probably did, if deer there were to steal, and if Shakespeare was not totally different from other boys with the opportunities for dangerous frolic afforded by a rustic environment and a middle-class condition of life. On this subject one might pleasurably re-read Washington Irving's account (in "The Sketch Book") of his visit to Charlecote Hall. Regarding the proneness of provincial great men to boast of their wickedness in the metropolis, Falstaff hits off the type, as it is not yet entirely dead, when he says of Shallow: "This same starved justice hath done nothing but prate to me of the wildness of his youth, and the feats he hath done about Turnbull Street: and every third word a lie, duer paid to the hearer than the Turk's tribute." The rest of the speech, wherein it is shown what figure Master Shallow really made in Turnbull Street, is not here quotable; but it is none the less readable.

NOTE 8. (Page 46.)

One might fill pages with the mere names of the different classifications of Elizabethan rogues, and of the several members of each kind of gang. We have not at all advanced in thievery since Elizabeth's day. The "confidence game" played by New York "crooks" on visitors from the interior, this present year, was played under another name, in Shakespeare's time. The "come-on" of present-day New York is but the lineal descendant of the "cony" of Sixteenth Century London. Of thieves, impostors, and beggars, a few of the varieties were: Rufflers, upright men, hookers, wild rogues, priggers of prancers (horse-thieves), pallyards, fraters, prigs, curtals, Irish rogues, ragmen, jackmen, abram men, mad Toms of Bedlam, whipjacks, cranks, dommerers, glimmerers, travelling tinkers, and counterfeit soldiers, besides the real soldiers who turned to crime. "Laws were made against disbanded soldiers who took to robbing and murder," says Thornbury; "and the pursuit by hue and cry, on horse and foot, was rendered imperative in every township." There were ferreters, falconers, shifters, rank riders,—the list is endless. The generic name for gambling cheats was rooks, and these were divided into puffs, setters, gilts, pads, biters, droppers, filers. Gull-gropers were gamblers who hunted fools in the ordinaries (eating-houses); each gang was composed of four men, — leader, eagle, wood-pecker, gull-groper (this name serving for the variety as well as for the species). A gambling gang with another method of operation was made up of the setter or decoy duck, the verser and barnacle, the accomplice, the rutter or bully. Some gamesters used women as decoys. Of dice tricks, there were those known as topping, slurring, stabbing, palming, knapping, besides various others. In addition to having all these — and many more — varieties of rogues to support, the nation was overrun with gipsies, who thieved in a world of ways. The whole population of England in 1604 is said to have been only about 5,000,000; that of London was little more than 150,000. And yet, the known rogues being deducted, and the secret rogues, there seem to have been some honest people left.

Note 9. (Page 48.)

The Marryott memoirs (chief source of this narrative), in recounting the talk at the Mermaid, naturally do not pause to describe the tavern. The slight description here given has had to be pieced together, of scraps found in various places, one being a magazine article containing what purport to be actual details, but which have the look of coming from some bygone work of fiction. Stow, in his "Survay of London" (1598), has nothing to say of the Mermaid; he twice mentions the "fair inns" in Bread

Street. I fancy that if there were anywhere the authentic materials for a full description of the house, such zealous lighters-up of the past as Besant (who in his "London" describes the Falcon but not the Mermaid), F. F. Ordish ("Shakespeare's London," a charming little book, inside and out), Loftie (in his excellent history of London), Hubert Hall (who in his "Society in the Elizabethan Age" describes the Tabard in Southwark but not the Mermaid), Walter Thornbury (whose two volumes on the England of Shakespeare are rich especially on tavern life, mainly as reflected in plays and pamphlets of the time), Edwin Goadby (whose compact little book on the same subject is crowded with matter), and the host of others, including the most recent biographers of Shakespeare, would have found it out. A thing we certainly know of the Mermaid, in addition to its location and its three entrances, is that the wine and the wit there elicited from Francis Beaumont to Ben Jonson these famous "Lines sent from the country with two unfinished comedies, which deferred their merry meetings at the Mermaid:"

"In this warm shine
I lie and dream of your full Mermaid wine.
. . . .
Methinks the little wit I had is lost,
Since I saw you, for wit is like a rest
Held up at tennis, which men do the best
With the best gamesters. What things have we seen
Done at the Mermaid! Heard words that have been
So nimble, and so full of subtle flame,
As if that every one from whence they came
Had meant to put his whole wit in a jest,

> And had resolved to live a fool the rest
> Of his dull life; than when there hath been thrown
> Wit able enough to justify the town
> For three days past, wit that might warrant be
> For the whole city to talk foolishly,
> Till that were cancelled; and when that was gone,
> We left an air behind us, which alone
> Was able to make the two next companies
> Right witty, though but downright fools more wise."

Note 10. (Page 48.)

For the better observance of the Lenten statutes, in every ward of London a jury was sworn, and charged by the aldermen, "for the true inquisition of killing, selling, dressing, or eating of flesh this present Lent, contrary to the laws and statutes of this realm and her Majesty's proclamation and express commandment." In accordance with this the jury "made diligent search divers and sundry times in all inns, tabling-houses, taverns, cook-houses, and victualling-houses within their ward," and thereupon either "resolved that they" had "not hitherto found any to offend against these laws," or they presented the names of those who had "so continued to offend, to the officer." Mr. Hubert Hall says: "The non-observance of these fast-days was no slight matter. Not only did the fisheries suffer in consequence, but the benefits of an occasional variation of the interminable diet of salt beef and bad beer must have been incalculable. The obligation of the crown toward one class of its subjects may not have been economically imperative, but a patriarchical government was bound to consult the welfare of each." When Philip Sidney was at Oxford, his uncle solicited for him "a license to eat flesh during Lent," he being "somewhat subject to sickness."

NOTE 11. (Page 50.)

According to Mr. Fleay, "Every Man out of His Humor," produced at the Globe Theatre in 1599, was the first of Ben Jonson's personal satires against his contemporaries. Jonson had to remove these satires to the Blackfriars, that same year; when began the "war of the theatres," a war conducted, through plays laden with personalities, by the writers and actors of one theatre against the writers and actors of another. This "war" seems to have endured till after the time of our narrative, and to have died a natural death. Its most celebrated productions were Jonson's "The Poetaster" and Thomas Dekker's reply thereto, "Satiromastix." Jonson's "comical satires" were acted at the Blackfriars by the Chapel Royal boys, the "little eyases" derided in "Hamlet." Mr. Fleay finds that Jonson's satires were directed against Shakespeare as well as against Dekker and Marston. Certain allusions and characters, in Shakespeare's plays produced apparently about this time, have been taken as his contributions to this war. With another rival company, also of boys, — those of St. Paul's cathedral, — the lord chamberlain's players were friendly. Mr. Saintsbury says that Jonson, Dekker, Chapman, and Marston "were mixed up, as regards one another, in an extricable but not uninteresting series of broils and friendships, to some part of which Shakespeare himself was, it is clear, by no means a stranger." But he observes that the direct connection of these quarrels, "even with the literary work which is usually linked to them, will be better established when critics have left being uncertain whether A was B, or B, C." I have heard it suggested, in fun, that the war may have been a device to stimulate public interest in the theatres. The Elizabethan age had its visitations of the plague, and was therefore, by the not too cruel dispensers of good and evil, spared the advertising malady of our nineteenth and twentieth centuries. Should anything like this war of the theatres occur to-day, it would not take a Scotland Yard or Mulberry Street detective to smell out ulterior motives at the back of it. The Elizabethans, besides their other advantages, enjoyed that of living too soon to know or even foresee the crafty self-advertiser or the "clever press agent;" else had there surely been an additional verse in their Litany, followed by a most fervent "Good Lord, deliver us!"

NOTE 12. (Page 51.)

"But that a gentleman should turn player hath puzzled me." To make an actor of a young gentleman, might, indeed, become a "Star Chamber matter." Among other "misdemeanors not reducible to heads," given in a Bodleian Library MS., entitled "A Short View of Criminal Cases Punishable and Heretofore Punished in the Court of the Star Chamber in the Times of Queen Elizabeth, King James, and His Late Majesty King Charles," is this: "Taking up a gentleman's son to be a stage player." See John S. Burn's notices of the "Star Chamber."

NOTE 13. (Page 56.)

All the world knows that in 1623, seven years after Shakespeare's death, the first collected edition of his plays appeared, under the supervision of, and from manuscripts provided by, Masters Heminge and Condell. "We have but collected them," say they in their dedication inserted in the subsequent folio (1632), "and done an office to the dead, to procure his orphans, guardians; without ambition either of self-profit or fame: only to keep the memory of so worthy a friend and fellow alive, as was our Shakespeare." In the first folio are printed "The names of the principal actors in all these plays." "William Shakspeare," heading the list, is followed in order by "Richard Burbadge," "John Hemings," and "Augustine Philips;" further down come "William Slye" and "Henry Condell." Harry Marryott's association with the company was too brief, his position too far from that of a "principal actor," for his name to be included in the list.

NOTE 14. (Page 59.)

Shakespeare's London residence in October, 1598, was in the parish of St. Helen's, Bishopsgate (Fleay, Ordish, and others). Countless biographers make him a resident of the Southwark side of the river, as, "He lived near the Bear Garden, Southwark, in 1596. In 1609 he occupied a good house within the liberty of the Clink." "His house was somewhere in Clink Street. As he grew more prosperous, he purchased a dwelling on the opposite shore near the Wardrobe, but he does not seem to have occupied it." But it turns out that William Shakespeare had two brothers, either or both of whom dwelt in Southwark, a fact that confuses the apparent evidence of his own residence there. His house in Blackfriars, "near the Wardrobe," descended by will to his daughter, Susannah Hall. His purchase of New Place, at Stratford, was made in 1597; but, though he may have at once installed his family there, he certainly remained for some years afterward a Londoner.

NOTE 15. (Page 63.)

Turnbull Street was a notorious nest of women of ill fame, and of men equally low in character. Falstaff's mention of it has been quoted in a previous note. In Beaumont and Fletcher's burlesque, "The Knight of the Burning Pestle," the speech of a prisoner, alluding to his fair companion, contains this bit of humor:

> "I am an errant knight that followed arms
> With spear and shield; and in my tender years
> I stricken was with Cupid's fiery shaft,
> And fell in love with this my lady dear,
> And stole her from her friends in Turnbull Street."

It was also known as Turnmill Street. "Turnemill Street," says Stow, "which stretcheth up to the west of Clerkenwell" (from the "lane called Cow Cross, of a cross sometime standing there").

Note 16. (Page 69.)

Concerning Queen Elizabeth's temper, there is, besides a wealth of other evidence, this from the "Character of Queen Elizabeth," by Edmund Bohun, Esq., published in Nichols's "Progresses and Public Processions of Queen Elizabeth:" "She was subject to be vehemently transported with anger, and when she was so, she would show it by her voice, her countenance, and her hands. She would chide her familiar servants so loud, that they that stood afar off might sometimes hear her voice. And it was reported that for small offences she would strike her maids of honor with her hand; but then her anger was short and very innocent. And when her friends acknowledged their offences, she, with an appeased mind, easily forgave them many things."

Note 17. (Page 78.)

The famous story of the ring is perhaps too well known to be repeated here. The queen had once given the Earl of Essex a ring, which, if ever sent to her as a token of his distress, "might entitle him to her protection." While under sentence of death, the earl, looking out of his prison window one morning, engaged a boy to carry the ring to Lady Scroope, the Countess of Nottingham's sister, an attendant on the queen, and to beg that she would present it to her Majesty. "The boy, by mistake," continues Birch's version of the story, "carried it to the Lady Nottingham, who showed it to her husband, the admiral, an enemy of Lord Essex. The admiral forbid her to carry it, or return any answer to the message, but insisted on her keeping the ring." When, two years later, this countess was on her death-bed, she sent for the queen, told her all, and begged forgiveness. "But her Majesty answered, 'God may forgive you, but I never can,' and left the room with great emotion. Her mind was so struck with the story, that she never went into bed, nor took any sustenance from that instant, for Camden is of opinion that her chief reason for suffering the earl to be executed was his supposed obstinacy in not applying to her for mercy."

NOTE 18. (Page 80.)

Of one of Queen Elizabeth's most characteristic traits, Miss Aikin says: "It has been already remarked that she was habitually, or systematically, an enemy to matrimony in general; and the higher any persons stood in her good graces, and the more intimate their intercourse with her, the greater was her resentment at detecting in them any aspirations after this state; for a kind of jealousy was in these cases superadded to her malignity; and it offended her pride that those who were honored with her favor should find room in their thoughts to covet another kind of happiness, of which she was not the dispenser." When Leicester married the widowed Countess of Essex, the queen had him confined in a small fort in Greenwich Park, and would probably have sent him to the Tower, but that the Earl of Sussex dissuaded. Later, when Essex married Sir Philip Sidney's widow,

Walsingham's daughter, Elizabeth showed rage and chagrin in a degree only less than in the case of Leicester. One of her attendants wrote, " Yet she doth use it more temperately than was thought for, and, God be thanked, doth not strike at all she threats." Both these marriages were conducted secretly, and without previous request for the permission her Majesty would have refused. So was that of Southampton, in 1598, by which that nobleman so incurred the queen's displeasure that, when she heard that Essex, commanding the troops in Ireland, had appointed him general of the horse, she reprimanded and ordered Essex to recall his commission. It was her unhappy fate that all her favorites, save Hatton, should marry.

Note 19. (Page 82.)

" She was jealous of her reputation with the old and cool-headed lords about her," writes Leigh Hunt, of Elizabeth at the time of the Essex conspiracy. That she had grown loath to betray the weaknesses which in earlier years she had made no attempt to conceal, is to be inferred also from the lessening degrees of wrath she evinced as her favorites, one after another, married; and from Bohun's statement, regarding her anger, that " she learned from Xenophon's book of the Institution of Cyrus, the method of curbing and correcting this unruly passion." A wonderfully human and pathetic figure : the vain woman whose glass belied the gross flattery of her courtiers, yet who could delude herself into believing them sincere ; the " greatest Gloriana " whose worshippers declared her favor their breath of life, yet risked it for the smiles of mere gentlewomen ; the stateswoman, wise enough to see her kingdom's future safety in the death of her beautiful rival, courageous enough to sanction that death, weak enough to shift the blame on poor Davison; the queen, who could say on horseback, to her " loving people," " I know I have but the body of a weak and feeble woman, but I have the heart of a king, and of a king of England, too, and think foul scorn that Parma, or Spain, or any prince of Europe, should dare to invade the borders of my realms;" and yet had to study in a classic author, how to keep from slapping the faces of her maids!

NOTE 20. (Page 85.)

The pursuivants who, in this and the next reign, executed warrants of arrest, are not to be confused with the pursuivants of the Heralds' College. "Send for his master with a pursuivant, presently," orders Suffolk, concerning an apprentice's master accused of treason, in " Henry VI., Part II." It is of these pursuivants that Hume writes as follows, concerning persons who sued great lords for debt in Elizabeth's reign: "It was usual to send for people by pursuivants, a kind of harpies, who then attended the orders of the council and high commission; and they were brought up to London, and constrained by imprisonment, not only to withdraw their lawful suits, but also to pay the pursuivants great sums of money." The pursuivant, with his warrants, proclamations, and his constant " In the queen's name," is a familiar figure in Elizabethan literature. In Sir Valentine Fleetwood's case, the council would have been perhaps equally or more in custom had it entrusted the prisoner's conveyance to London to some gentleman of equal rank to his.

NOTE 21. (Page 86.)

In telling Marryott that she was "not wont to go so strong in purse," the queen spoke figuratively, rather than meant that she had for once assumed the functions of purse-bearer, or that a purse habitually carried by her was now uncommonly well provided. True, either of these may have been the case. Shakespeare must have modelled the minor habits of his queens somewhat upon those of Elizabeth; and he makes Cleopatra give a messenger gold, presumably with her own hand. But Elizabeth's allusion was to her poverty, and in keeping with her extreme economy, concerning which Hume says: "But that in reality there was little or no avarice in the queen's temper, appears from this circumstance, that she never amassed any treasure, and even refused subsidies from the Parliament, when she had no present occasion for them. Yet we must not conclude that her economy proceeded from a tender concern for her people; she loaded them with monopolies and exclusive patents. The real source of her frugal conduct was derived from her desire of independency, and her care to preserve her dignity, which would have been endangered had she reduced herself to the necessity of having frequent recourse to Parliamentary supplies. The splendor of a court was, during this age, a great part of the public charge; and as Elizabeth was a single woman, and expensive in no kind of magnificence except clothes, this circumstance enabled her to perform great things by her narrow revenue. She is said to have paid four millions of debt, left on the crown by her father, brother, and sister, — an incredible sum for that age."

Note 22. (Page 87.)

Elizabeth's forenoons, according to Bohun, were usually thus passed: "First in the morning, she spent some time at her devotions; then she betook herself to the despatch of her civil affairs, reading letters, ordering answers, considering what should be brought before the council, and consulting with her ministers. When she had thus wearied herself, she would walk in a shady garden, or pleasant gallery, without any other attendance than that of a few learned men. Then she took her coach, and passed in sight of her people to the neighboring groves and fields; and sometimes would hunt or hawk. There was scarce a day but she employed some part of it in reading and study."

Note 23. (Page 92.)

"'The circuit of the wall of London on the land side'" (writes Stow in 1598), "to wit, from the Tower of London in the east unto Aldgate, is 82 perches; from Aldgate to Bishopsgate, 86 perches; from Bishopsgate in the north, to the postern of Cripplegate, 162 perches; from Cripplegate to Aldersgate, 75 perches; from Aldersgate to

Newgate, 66 perches; from Newgate in the west, to Ludgate, 42 perches; in all, 513 perches of assize. From Ludgate to the Fleet Dike west, about 60 perches; from Fleet Bridge south, to the river Thames, about 70 perches; and so the total of these perches amounteth to 643, . . . which make up two English miles, and more by 608 feet." The gates here mentioned, as Besant says, " still stood, and were closed at sunset, until 1760. Then they were all pulled down, and the materials sold." Even in Stow's time, the city had much outgrown its walls; of its outer part, the highways leading to the country had post-and-chain bars, which were closed at night.

NOTE 24. (Page 100.)

Plays of the time, notably Ben Jonson's "Bartholomew Fair," show in what contempt and ridicule the first Puritans were held. Shakespeare's Malvolio, as Maria says, is "sometimes a kind of Puritan." The attitude of the obtrusive kind of Puritanism to the world, and of the world to that kind of Puritanism, is expressed once and forever in what Hazlitt terms Sir Toby's " unanswerable answer" to Malvolio, " Dost thou think, because thou art virtuous, there shall be no more cakes and ale?" Though fellow sufferers of governmental severity, the Catholics and Puritans were no less naturally antipathetic to each other. Ben Jonson, satirist of the Puritans, was, in his time, alternately Catholic and Anglican. But if the government, in support of the established church, was outwardly severe against the Puritans, they had much covert protection at court, some of the chief lords and ministers inclining their way. As to the quality of voice affected by these early Puritans in their devotions, recall the clown's speech in the "Winter's Tale:" "Three-man songmen all, and very good ones; but they are most of them means and bases; but one Puritan amongst them, and he sings psalms to hornpipes."

Note 25. (Page 131.)

The Babington conspiracy gave the occasion for removing that constant menace to England's future peace, — Mary Stuart. The skill with which Sir Francis Walsingham possessed himself, one by one, of the secrets of the conspirators, and nursed the plot forward until he had complete evidence of every participant's guilt, and of Mary's complicity, is fascinating to study. Mary of course, as an unwilling prisoner, had a perfect moral right to plot for herself; but she knew what she risked in doing so, and she and her adherents ran against their fatal rock in Walsingham. This man's journal is characteristic of himself: merely the briefest entries, of this messenger's arrival from France, or that one's departure for the Low Countries, or of a letter from X, or an order transmitted to B. What news the messengers brought, what the letters told, or the orders were, is not confided to the paper. In vigilance and craft, he was the Elizabethan predecessor of Richelieu and Fouché; yet a quiet, virtuous man, who loved his wife, died poor, and leaned toward Puritanism. His spy system has excited the righteous horror of certain historians who would never have ceased to admire it, had it been exercised for, not against, their heroine, Mary Stuart. His own direct instruments served him better than he was served by the rank and file of the law's servants, as this letter to him, from Lord Burleigh, August 10, 1586, shows: "As I came from London homeward in my coach, I saw at every town's end, a number of ten or twelve, standing with long staves, and until I came to Enfield I thought no other of them but that they had staid for the avoiding of the rain, or to drink at some alehouses, for so they did stand under pentices at alehouses; but at Enfield, finding a dozen in a plump, when there was no rain, I bethought myself that they were appointed as watchmen for the apprehending of such as are missing; and thereupon I called some of them to me apart, and asked them wherefore they stood there, and one of them answered, to take three young men; and, demanding how they should know the persons, one answered with the words, 'Marry, my lord, by intelligence of their favor.' 'What mean you by that?' 'Marry,' said they, 'one of the parties hath a hooked nose.' 'And have you,' quoth I, 'no other mark?' 'No,' said they. And then I asked who appointed them, and they answered one Banks, a head constable, whom I willed to be sent to me. Surely, sir, whosoever had the charge from you hath used the matter negligently; for these watchmen stand so openly in plumps as no suspected person will come near them, and if they be no better instructed but to find three persons by one of them having a hooked nose, they may miss thereof. And this

I thought good to advertise you, that the justices who had the charge, as I think, may use the matter more circumspectly." Harrison (writing 1577-87) complains of the laxity of these lesser arms of the law, saying: "That when hue and cry have been made even to the faces of some constables, they have said, 'God restore your loss! I have other business at this time.'"

NOTE 26. (Page 229.)

"But now of late years," writes Stow (1598), "the use of coaches, brought out of Germany, is taken up, and made so common, as there is neither distinction of time nor difference of persons observed; for the world runs on wheels with many whose parents were glad to go on foot." As to their rate of travel, Mr. Goadby instances that Mary, Queen of Scots, was from early morning to late evening of a January day, in going from Bolton Castle to Ripon, sixteen miles. Charles Dudley Warner (in "The People for Whom Shakespeare Wrote") says that, in 1640, Queen Henrietta was four days on the way from Dover to London, the best road in England (distance, 71 miles); and quotes the Venetian ambassador, whose journey to Oxford and back (in all, 150 miles, as he travelled) consumed six days, his coach often sticking in the mud, and once breaking down. Queen Mary had established a kind of postal service. Elizabeth had a postmaster-general in 1581. After the Armada, a horse-post was ordered established in every town, a foot-post (to live near the church) in every parish. But letter-writers usually sent their own messengers, or relied on the slow carriers' wagons.

NOTE 27. (Page 255.)

In this reign, many were the cases wherein people took vengeance into their own hands, in true feudal fashion, whether from the heat of their impulses, or in view of that "bad execution of the laws" and "neglect of police," for which Hume found it not easy to account. Miss Aikin gives an instance, arising from a long-standing feud between two proud families. Orme, a servant of Sir John Holles, killed in a duel the master of horse to the Earl of Shrewsbury. "The earl prosecuted Orme, and sought to take away his life; but Sir John Holles caused him to be conveyed away to Ireland, and afterward obtained his pardon of the queen. For his conduct in this business, he was himself challenged by Gervase Markham, champion and gallant to the Countess of Shrewsbury; but Holles refused the duel, because the demand of Markham, that it should take place in a park belonging to the earl, his enemy, gave him ground to apprehend treachery. Anxious, however, to wipe away the aspersions cast upon his courage, he sought a reëncounter which might wear the appearance of accident; and soon after he met Markham on the road, when the parties immediately dismounted and attacked each other with their rapiers; Markham fell, severely wounded; and the Earl of Shrewsbury lost no time in raising his servants and tenantry to the number of 120, in order to apprehend Holles, in case Markham's hurt should prove fatal. On the other side Lord Sheffield, the kinsman of Holles, joined him with sixty men; and he and his company remained at Houghton till the wounded man was out of danger. We do not find the queen and council interfering to put a stop to this private war." Markham, who wrote the poem on the last fight of "The Revenge," is a minor but prolific figure in Elizabethan literature.

NOTE 28. (Page 266.)

Moll Cutpurse, whose real name was Mary Frith, a shoemaker's daughter, born probably in 1584, is described by her biographer as in her girlhood a "very tomrig or rumpscuttle" who "delighted and sported only in boy's plays and costume." She was put to domestic service, but her calling lay not in tending children. She donned man's attire and found true outlet for her talents as a "bully, pick-purse, fortune-teller, receiver, and forger." She is the heroine of Middleton and Dekker's breezy comedy, "The Roaring Girl" (1611), and of a work thus entered on the Stationers' Register in August, 1610: "A Booke called the Madde Prancks of Merry Mall of the Bankside, with her walkes in Man's Apparel, and to what purpose. Written by John Day." Her career is set forth in the very interesting "Lives of Twelve Bad Women," recently published in a beautiful edition.

NOTE 29. (Page 314.)

The use of firearms was slow work in the earlier centuries. Concerning the wheel-lock, invented in 1515, at

Nuremburg, Greener says: "When ready for firing, the wheel was wound up, the flash-pan lid pushed back, and the pyrites held in the cock allowed to come in contact with the wheel. By pressure on the trigger a stop was drawn back out of the wheel, and the latter, turning round its pivot at considerable speed, produced sparks by the friction against the pyrites, and thus ignited the priming." "We find the greater portion of the pistols of the sixteenth and seventeenth centuries fitted with wheel-locks." Wheel-locks being expensive, the old match-locks, as a rule, were still fitted to the longer firearms, such as the arquebus, of which Greener says: "The slow match is kept burning in a holder on the top of the barrel; the flash-pan and touch-hole are at the side. The serpentine is hung upon a pivot passing through the stock, and continued past the pivot, forming a lever for the hand. To discharge the piece, the match in the serpentine is first brought into contact with the burning match on the barrel until ignited; then by raising the lever and moving it to one side, the serpentine is brought into the priming in the touch-hole, and the gun discharged, — though it is highly probable that the first arquebuses did not carry the fire in a holder on the barrel, but only the match in the serpentine." "All the early firearms were so slow to load, that, as late as the battle of Kuisyingen in 1636, the slowest soldiers managed to fire seven shots only during eight hours."

NOTE 30. (Page 374.)

In London the playhouses were allowed to be open

in Lent on all days but sermon days, — Wednesday and Friday. In 1601, Lent began February 25th; Easter Sunday was April 12th. The historical year — conforming to our present calendar — is here meant. The civil year then began March 25th.